FAMILY VIOLENCE AND POLICE RESPONSE

Advances in Criminology
Series Editor: David Nelken

Titles in the Series

Family Violence and Police Response

Learning From Research, Policy and Practice in European Countries

Edited by

WILMA SMEENK and MARIJKE MALSCH
Netherlands Institute for the Study of Crime and Law Enforcement
(NSCR), The Netherlands

ASHGATE

Published by
Ashgate Publishing Limited
Gower House
Croft Road
Aldershot
Hampshire GU11 3HR
England

Ashgate Publishing Company
Suite 420
101 Cherry Street
Burlington, VT 05401-4405
USA

Ashgate website: http://www.ashgate.com

British Library Cataloguing in Publication Data
Family violence and police response : learning from
    research, policy and practice in European countries. -
    (Advances in criminology)
    1. Family violence - Europe - Prevention - Cross-cultural
    studies 2. Wife abuse - Europe - Prevention - Cross-cultural
    studies 3. Women - Crimes against - Europe - Prevention -
    Cross-cultural studies 4. Family violence - Law and
    legislation - Europe - Cross-cultural studies 5. Police -
    Europe - Cross-cultural studies
    I. Smeenk, Wilma II. Malsch, M. (Marijke)
    364.1'555

Library of Congress Cataloging-in-Publication Data
Family violence and police response : learning from research, policy and practice in
European countries / edited by Wilma Smeenk and Marijke Malsch.
        p. cm. – (Advances in criminology)
    Includes bibliographical references and index.
    ISBN 0-7546-2506-0
    1. Family violence–Europe. 2. Victims of crimes–Europe–Attitudes. 3. Police–
Europe–Attitudes. 4. Police-community relations–Europe. I. Smeenk, Wilma Hendrika.
II. Malsch, M. (Marijke) III. Series.

    HV6626.23.E85F36 2005
    362.82'92'094–dc22

                                                                2005005674

ISBN 0 7546 2506 0
ISBN 978 0 7546 2506 3

Reprinted 2006

Printed and bound in Great Britain by MPG Books Ltd, Bodmin, Cornwall

• • • • • • •

Contents

List of Contributors

Anna Baldry (Italy) is lecturer in social psychology at the Second University of Naples, researcher at the National Statistical Institute, and holds a Marie Curie Fellowship at the Free University of Amsterdam, the Netherlands. She is the coordinator of the European project Daphne on the risk assessment of spousal assault throughout Italy, Sweden, The Netherlands, Greece, Poland and Portugal. She conducted (comparative) research into domestic violence and the relation between (witnessing of) family violence and children's problem behaviour (school bullying). Research interests include domestic violence, sexual violence, family violence and bullying in school. She has a PhD in social psychology, University of Rome 'La Sapienza' and a PhD in Criminology, Institute of Criminology, Cambridge.

Sevaste Chatzifotiou (Greece) is assistant professor at the Department of Social Work, in the School of Health and Social Welfare, at the Technological Educational Institute (TEI) of Crete, Greece. She has been researching on issues of domestic violence against women for the last decade and she has conducted pioneering qualitative research on marital violence against women in Greece. She is coordinator and/or co-partner in a number of research programmes on marital violence in Greece and abroad, including research partnerships with Austria, Spain, Sweden, Finland, and UK. Also, she is the Greek representative of the international violence against women survey (IVAWS). Research interests include marital violence against women, family support and social networks, help-seeking behaviour, police and marital violence, social work theory and practice and in feminist research. She obtained a first degree in Social Work (Greece), an MA in Social and Community Work Studies (Bradford University, UK), an MA in Social Research Methods (The University of Manchester, UK), and a PhD in Social Policy and Social Work on 'Help-Seeking Behaviour of Abused Women in Greece' (The University of Manchester, UK).

Stéphanie Condon (France) is researcher in the fields of migration studies and violence research at the Institut National d'Etudes Démographiques

(INED) in Paris, France. She was member of the multidisciplinary research team led by Maryse Jaspard who conducted the first national survey about violence against women in France (ENVEFF, 2000). Research topics: gender and migration; immigration to France; Caribbean migration to France and Britain; violence against women. Her first degree was in Modern Languages and Geography, her PhD in historical population geography (Queen Mary and Westfield College, London).

Russell Dobash (United States) is Professor of Criminology in the School of Law at the University of Manchester. He has published widely in the area of violence against women and has co-authored and edited several books including the award winning *Violence Against Wives* and *Women, Violence and Social Change*. For over two decades he has been conducting research on violence against women and with colleagues he has recently completed a three-year investigation of murder in Britain.

Rebecca Emerson Dobash (United Kingdom) is Professor of Social Research in the School of Law at the University of Manchester. She has been conducting research on violence against women for over two decades and is an internationally recognised expert in the area. She is the co-author and editor of several books including the award winning *Violence Against Wives* and *Women, Violence and Social Change*. Recent research includes an evaluation of programmes for violent men and a three-year investigation of murder in Britain.

Eduardo Fe-Rodriguez (Spain) is lecturer in econometrics at the School of Social Sciences at the University of Manchester (UK). Research topics include theoretical econometrics, non-parametric methods.

Liz Kelly (United Kingdom) is Professor of Sexualised Violence and Director of *Child and Woman Abuse Studies Unit* (CWASU) of London Metropolitan University. CWASU has completed over 50 research projects across a range of forms of violence against women and child abuse. Areas of expertise are: domestic violence; rape and sexual assault; trafficking and sexual exploitation; sexual abuse of children. Research ranges across pure research on prevalence, the impacts of abuse, attrition in reported rape cases and children's perspectives on domestic violence through evaluation of voluntary and statutory interventions to policy relevant research reviews. CWASU also provide training and consultancy in the UK and internationally, and are Special Advisors to the British Council on Violence Against Women.

Peter Lindström (Sweden) is associate professor in criminology and deputy director of the police programme at the Växjö University, Sweden. Research topics include criminal policy, crime statistics, research evaluation, police research.

Marijke Malsch (The Netherlands) studied social sciences and law at the Universiteit van Amsterdam. In 1989, she received her PhD on a dissertation entitled *Lawyers' predictions of judicial decisions: A study on calibration of experts*. In 1999, she edited with Hans Nijboer *Complex cases: Perspectives on the Netherlands criminal justice system*. Since 1993, she has been a senior researcher at the Netherlands Institute for the Study of Crime and Law Enforcement (NSCR) in Leiden, the Netherlands. Current research focuses on family violence, stalking legislation, legitimacy of the criminal justice system, experts in the criminal justice system, and the principle of open justice. Since 1997, she has also worked as a part-time judge at the District Court of Haarlem.

Juanjo Medina-Ariza (Spain) is lecturer in criminology at the School of Law, University of Manchester (UK). Research topics include interpersonal violence, social exclusion and crime, and comparative criminal justice. He is currently engaged in a ESRC-funded ethnographic study of street gangs in England.

Sami Nevala (Finland) is research Officer at European Institute for Crime Prevention and Control, affiliated with the United Nations (HEUNI). He is project manager of the International Violence Against Women Survey (IVAWS). Research topics and areas of interest include violence against women, victim surveys, crime statistics.

Natalia Ollus (Finland) works as Associate Expert at the United Nations Office on Drugs and Crime (UNODC), Regional Office for Southern Africa in Pretoria, South Africa. At the time of writing the chapter, Ms. Ollus was acting as Senior Programme Officer at the European Institute for Crime Prevention and Control (HEUNI), situated in Helsinki, where she acted as project manager of the International Violence Against Women Survey (IVAWS). At UNODC she is currently managing the implementation of the

IVAWS in Mozambique. She is also managing two regional projects in the area of trafficking in human beings, as well as being involved in several crime and drug prevention initiatives in the Southern African region. Research topics and areas of interest and expertise include violence against women (including immigrant women); comparative research; police reaction to domestic violence (including training); trafficking in women; smuggling of migrants; HIV/AIDS, gender and violence against women; juveniles and substance abuse prevention. Natalia Ollus holds a Master's degree (Soc. Sc.) from the University of Helsinki.

Corinna Seith (Switzerland) is affiliated with the Department of Education of the University of Zurich. She is project director of several studies on violence against women and children and a lecturer at the University of Zurich and Marburg (Germany). She completed a PhD research on police, social service and shelter responses to domestic violence. She is involved in an EU funded project on violence prevention programmes for women and girls in Europe (with Liz Kelly). A current research project is on 'Children and Domestic Violence' (www.nfp52.ch). Research topics include institutional responses to domestic violence, violence against women and social change, children and domestic violence, prevention of sexual violence, gender theory, sociology of organisations, gender segregation in education and in the labour market.

Wilma Smeenk (The Netherlands) is senior researcher at the Netherlands Institute for the Study of Crime and Law Enforcement (NSCR). She studied sociology at the University of Nijmegen and received her doctor's degree on a dissertation about family formation and partner choice. At the NSCR, she combines a strong interest in theory development and epistemology with quantitative and qualitative research in schools and families. Research topics of interest are family violence, cross cultural research, developmental criminology, violence against women, inter-generational transmission of violence.

Foreword

Since the 1970s, research on the policing of domestic violence has consistently demonstrated the ambiguities of law and police practice around violence. Writing in the mid 1980s, I attributed this ambiguity largely to the failure of the state – with the police acting as its agents – to understand the nature of gender and its relationship to the state's power relations. Over these past 15 years, the state in some European countries has grown more sophisticated in its use of law to address some of these ambiguities. Those countries that have responded to feminist campaigns have kept the spotlight on how the police treat the issue of domestic violence as part of fight for equality. Feminist action, social policy, and research have grown through its global conversations about 'what works' to reduce the harm of intimate violence and facilitated challenges to traditions that served to insulate institutions from making the changes necessary to take positive action against intimate violence. No country has yet found the perfect solution.

When contemporary international experiences of policing are gathered together, as in this volume, the social, cultural and political nuances found in different jurisdictions enable us to re-visit the lens domestic violence holds on gender, power and intimacy in diverse contexts. In particular, the difficulties these diversities pose to any state system of justice continue to deliver inconsistent and unequal justice. The chapters in this volume are the next instalment of the European dialogue about how to better the policing of intimate violence. We know that only a proportion of violence is reported to the police. We know our distinct definitions and legal categories of violence affect whether and how such events come to public attention. We know victims' choices around whether to disclose violence to public officials wraps around social respectability, institutional legacies and local resources.

Yet an international debate persists around how to balance prescribed, legal procedures and the autonomous decisions of front line police. As researchers continue to document inconsistent responses to 'same fact' events, there are some broad consistencies to bettering police responses. Recent meta analysis of the UK's Home Office Crime Reduction Programme (CRP) Violence against Woman Initiative found that a guilty plea was twice as likely to be entered when the victim was accompanied by an advocate. Advocacy helped because it enabled victims to engage with a criminal justice process while at the same time dealing with the emotional upheaval of 'managing' and 'exiting' an intimate relationship. Further, the CRP demonstrated that photographic evidence enhances the likelihood of an arrest and a subsequent conviction as well as increasing the likelihood that victims will not withdraw their support from a criminal case. Problems in taking action against perpetrators (bringing criminal charges and convicting) and in resolving child contact issues were found to create real barriers for women and children in being able to 'move on' in their lives. Intimate violence will always challenge justice.

The use of the police by victims is a key tool in intervention, but has different impact and outcomes. There is a wide range of criminal law charges under which 'domestic violence' might be noted and brought to police attention. Exploring the use of the police for events that cause very serious injury might help us 'unpick' what works better. Thinking about seriousness of criminal events, linked to the way women assess their safety, might help us discover the way in which events trigger disruption in the 'life history' of intimate violence.

We continue to be left with a number of unanswered questions in our musings. How does using the police 'work' holistically for victims in the disruption of domestic violence? Is there a difference in the kinds of police responses for less serious domestic violence or more serious? The debate about the police response to intimate violence though shows that no understanding of policing would be complete without knowledge of how police manage the complaints about abuse within intimate relationships. This volume helps keep this conversation dynamic.

Betsy Stanko
The Metropolitan Police, London

Chapter 1

Introduction

Wilma Smeenk and Marijke Malsch

Introduction

Researchers and policy makers across Europe are increasingly interested in studying family violence and the various interventions against this type of crime. Many recent publications demonstrate this increased level of interest. Research and its results have been fragmented, however, in the sense that European researchers have not brought together the results of their inquiries and examined them in light of the specific institutional context of their countries (Hagemann-White, 2001; Löbmann, Greve, Wetzels and Bosold, 2003). Intervention studies have been conducted but often cannot control for the specific nature of the institutional context reflected in penal code, police, prosecution, and judiciary (Kelly, Römkens and Stanko, 2001).

The relative lack of comparative cross-national research is all the more conspicuous as the degree to which family violence comes to the attention of the legal system, more specifically the police, may be influenced by a country's legal and institutional context. The so-called 'dark number' in family violence is an agreed-upon obstacle for researchers, policy makers and organisations working in the field. Being less visible than street crime, the degree to which family violence becomes known to the police is dependent on citizens' requests for police intervention. Victims' reporting behaviour is considered to be sensitive to the degree that society and police consider family violence as a crime, an assumption reflected in both general awareness-raising campaigns and police training programmes. Furthermore, organisational and institutional aspects, such as the police's task performance and attitudes, may facilitate or inhibit the entry of such cases into the legal system (Jordan, 2004).

The research literature on evaluation of police interventions and programmes mainly reflects American and British experiences, leaving room for ambiguity as to how interventions and programmes will work out in countries with different legal cultures and institutions (Kelly et al., 2001). Comparative research has focused not so much on the response to family violence but rather on the prevalence of family violence (Johnson, 2001; Ollus and Nevala – this volume). As a consequence, little investigation has taken a comparative stance to examine the interplay between the response to family violence and the local and national context. For example, the legal definition of family violence in a country conditions the response of the police to crime incidents and this, in turn, may affect the decision of victims to ask for police assistance. Studying and comparing experiences and approaches in various countries allows for a more comprehensive view of legal responses to family violence, and what may be intended or unintended consequences of a particular approach.

To undertake such comparison was the goal of a three-day workshop on the topic, held in October 2002 (Smeenk and Malsch, 2002, 2004). A generous subsidy by the European Science Foundation (ESF) enabled this workshop, titled Family Violence and Police Reaction in the EU. The workshop was organised by the Netherlands Institute for the Study of Crime and Law Enforcement (NSCR) in Leiden, the Netherlands. The combination of workshop participants from several European countries, with backgrounds in social science and legal studies, qualitative as well as quantitative in research orientation, ensured an interdisciplinary approach to this complex problem that is also reflected in this volume.

Police responses to family violence received special attention in the workshop, linking the criminal justice response with victim experiences of family violence. Nevertheless, the existence and importance of other intervention agencies was not neglected. Discussing police interventions in each country also disseminated valuable information about the law enforcement organisations involved, as well as institutions outside the legal system, thereby giving a more complete picture of how countries deal with the problem of family violence. Comparison at a European level also enabled the study of variations in legal definitions and penal codes, which influence the police response to reported incidents of family violence.

Flowing from the workshop, this volume investigates similarities and differences in the response to family violence in European countries. It also examines how the criminal justice systems of the various countries treat family violence cases. More specifically, we address interactions between general attitudes towards family violence, task performance by the police, and new developments in the applicable law. This brought together insights from research, policy and practice, and as such, the answers will have implications for each of these fields.

Key Elements in the Criminal Justice Response to Family Violence

The volume addresses issues that are considered key elements in the criminal justice response to family violence, from a comparative perspective. A first element concerns societal and legal definitions of family violence, employed in research, policy, and legal practice. In a society that defines family violence as a private rather than public problem, the police may be uninterested or unwilling to interfere, discouraging victims from reporting the violence. Also, applying a broad or narrow legal definition affects the way that family violence is registered and dealt with in the legal system. On the other hand, definitions that researchers use may affect public opinion and policy by shaping the public view of the nature and extent of this problem. In many European countries, surveys of the prevalence of family violence have contributed substantially to the public debate and awareness of this problem (Hagemann-White, 2001). Relevant questions are: What constitutes a case? Are we talking about incidents or patterns? A number of chapters in this volume demonstrate that definitional issues permeate the response to family violence in profound ways.

A second key element is how legislation covers family violence and how this affects the work of the police and the other law enforcement agencies. Do special provisions exist, or are general provisions supposed to apply to this type of family violence? Is the close relationship between offender and victim considered an aggravating condition, and do judges follow the legislator's intent in their judgments? Does the legal definition cover psychological violence and, if so, what evidence is presented to the court?

Third, specific attention is paid to how police (organisations) deal with reported incidents of family violence. Studies have documented the tendency of the police to belittle the problem of family violence. As first organisation in the law enforcement chain, the police perform a crucial role. As a consequence, policies to combat family violence have focused on the police adopting a more punitive attitude. Organisational challenges following on from these demands may include higher requests on registration, or the drafting of protocols that specify how to act when a case of family violence comes to the attention of the police. When police training is desired, a choice needs to be made between specialisation (appointing and training special persons or units), or a general approach (providing training for all police officers). In bringing about changes, the police organisational structure and culture may be a factor leading to the registration and prosecution of fewer cases than intended by legislators or policy makers. Here, the notion of police discretion deserves special attention.

Finally, the relative importance of the criminal justice response to family violence versus other interventions was considered a key element. This raises the point of what victims expect or want when they ask for third-party intervention, not only from the police but also from informal support networks or support organisations. It also raises issues of coordination and information exchange by the organisations involved in the response to family violence.

Research Definitions in the Study of Family Violence

One of the problematic aspects of research in the area of family violence is the lack of consensus on what encompasses family violence and how it should be measured. Different research traditions have developed different views on what behaviours should be studied, what the causes of family violence are, and what are the best ways to deal with it (Walby and Myhill, 2001). Such differences also pervade the policy and practice of those tasked with responding to family violence: the police, women's shelters, doctors, judges, social workers. As a result, readers on this topic may come across a number of definitions, for example: family violence, violence against women, intimate partner violence, domestic violence, domestic abuse (see chapter by Ollus and Nevala – this volume). Here, it is relevant to note that an emphasis on women as victims of violence draws attention to structural gender inequality and power imbalances in families and wider society as contributing factors to the origination and continuation of this type of violence.

As editors of this volume we abandoned the idea that all authors should use the same definition, as that would not do justice to the various approaches in the field. Instead, we have asked authors to make clear which definition they are using and, when applicable, what definitions are used in their country in policy documents, police practice and the legal domain. In the editorial chapters, we use 'family violence' as a general term that may include insights from different research traditions and disciplines. While 'domestic violence' is potentially equally broad in scope, we prefer family violence because it stresses the notion of family relationships and children as victims of violence, also in light of the transmission of violence between generations. We do so in the realisation that literature reviews have used the term in association with a particular research tradition ('family violence surveys' as distinct from 'violence against women surveys'; see chapter by Ollus and Nevala – this volume). As legal definitions often do not contain gender-specific formulations or do not specifically refer to certain groups of victims (women, children), however, and we explicitly meant to pay attention to all relevant legal definitions, we decided to continue to use the term 'family violence'.

Outline of this Volume

Various chapters in the volume address the key elements introduced above by either taking an explicitly comparative perspective, or by focusing on a specific country. Three comparative chapters address the definition and measurement of family violence in research, recent European developments in legislation, and a comparison of family violence legislation to legislation on a related phenomenon, stalking. Seven country chapters discuss research findings on family violence and/or the criminal justice response to it in Spain, France, Italy, Sweden, Greece, Switzerland and the United Kingdom.

The first chapter, by Ollus and Nevala (Finland), discusses problems in the assessment of the prevalence of (sexual) violence, and ways in which various survey traditions have tackled these difficulties. The chapter deals with issues of defining and measuring violence against women in a comparative perspective and discusses the development of a measurement tool for comparative research.

The following chapter, by Medina-Ariza and Fe-Rodriguez (Spain), argues that a more detailed picture of the magnitude of different forms of violence is needed, for theory and research as well as for public policy and practice purposes. An application of cluster analysis to Spanish data shows that a more differentiated view is preferable to the usual measures that dichotomise the population into violent and non-violent couples in rather simplistic ways.

A French contribution is written by Condon, who draws upon experience with the first French nation-wide survey, which asked about victim experiences of intimate partner violence. Information gathered in this survey enables levels of violence among migrant women to be examined. The chapter discusses the strengths and limitations of surveys as a way of investigating cultural differences in the prevalence of family violence.

The chapter by Kelly (United Kingdom) is explicitly comparative and focuses on recent developments in domestic violence legislation. It describes specific domestic violence legislation that was drafted in the 1990s in many countries, including legislation in other parts of the world. Special attention is given to innovative elements in some of these reforms, such as newly drafted powers to remove offenders from their homes, the inclusion of 'psychological abuse' in the legal definition of family violence, and laws that specify that criminal assault on a partner should be an aggravating factor in sentencing.

Moving on to a concrete example of innovative legislation, the chapter by Lindström (Sweden) reports on the implementation of the Swedish law called 'Gross violation of a woman's integrity'. This law makes punishable a repeated pattern of violation of a woman's integrity. The author discusses outcomes of evaluation research of this new offence as well as findings on the use of restraining orders as a response to family violence.

The chapter by Baldry (Italy) examines provisions in Italian law. The author demonstrates that all types of violence constituting what is called 'domestic violence' in Italy, including psychological, physical and sexual violence, are present in the Italian criminal code. Moreover, a specific reference to the wider notion of family violence exists within the code, in the article called 'Maltreatment within the family'. Also, a new law enabled protective and restraining orders to be issued especially in cases of domestic violence. The chapter discusses these legal provisions and elaborates on obstacles related to their application when domestic violence cases are reported and tried in court.

For Greece, Chatzifotiou provides a discussion of European research findings as a reference point for an exploration of the characteristics of the Greek setting that are relevant to the response to family violence. The chapter illustrates the barriers that victims encounter in getting help or having the offender prosecuted. A narrative case history of a victim of partner violence is included. Barriers lie in the police's unwillingness to record these incidents and a generally negative attitude to women reporting violence by their marital partners. The chapter addresses police officers' attitudes as well as that of the general public in Greece.

For Switzerland, Seith discusses the balance between legal and non-legal responses to family violence. The chapter reports an institutional analysis of domestic violence cases on the basis of case files of the police, social services and a shelter, as well as a number of interviews with professionals and women. Pros and cons of pro-active police intervention are discussed, with special attention paid to a victim's sense of autonomy, which may be seriously affected in situations of family violence.

The contribution by Dobash and Dobash (United Kingdom) addresses the balance between legal and non-legal approaches through a discussion of men's programmes. It considers the theoretical background related to these programmes and why criminal justice is important in this respect. The chapter locates these programmes in the context of criminal justice responses to violent men, such as, for example, arrest. The main body of the chapter is devoted to a discussion of an evaluation of two British programmes and the relationship between controlling and intimidating behaviours on the one hand, and violence on the other.

The comparative chapter by Malsch and Smeenk (The Netherlands) discusses legislation choices and outcomes that present themselves when societies takes family violence and violence against women more seriously. These choices are illustrated by comparing legislation on family violence, as discussed in the various chapters, to recent developments in legislation on stalking, where the repetitiveness of behaviours and the relationship between offender and victim pose comparable dilemmas to police, prosecution and the legislator.

The concluding chapter integrates the findings from research and signals trends in the criminal justice response to family violence in the various European countries. Special attention is given to the finding that family violence repeatedly occurs over an extended period of time, and what this entails for police and the prosecution, but also for research into this type of violence. As such, the chapter provides a look forward to future developments and issues in research, policy and practice in the legal response to family violence.

References

Hagemann-White, C. (2001). European Research on the Prevalence of Violence Against Women. *Violence Against Women, 7* (Special issue: European perspectives on violence against women), 732-759.

Johnson, H. (2001). Enhancing knowledge on violence against women. In N. Ollus and S. Nevala (Eds.), *Women in the Criminal Justice System: International Examples and National Responses* (pp. 198-213): HEUNI.

Jordan, C. E. (2004). Intimate partner violence and the justice system. An examination of the interface. *Journal of Interpersonal Violence, 19*(12), 1412-1434.

Kelly, L. Römkens, R. and Stanko, B. (2001). Guest editors' introduction. *Violence Against Women, 7* (Special issue: European perspectives on violence against women), 727-731.

Löbmann, R., Greve, W., Wetzels, P. and Bosold, C. (2003). Violence against women: conditions, consequences, and coping. *Psychology, Crime and Law, 9*(4), 309-331.

Smeenk, W. and Malsch, M. (2002). Scientific Report Exploratory Workshop 'Family violence and police reaction in the EU'. NSCR.
Available: http://www.esf.org/generic/1346/0169SReport.pdf.

Smeenk, W. and Malsch, M. (2004). Family violence and police reaction in the EU. *International Journal of Comparative Criminology, 2,* 262-269.

Walby, S. and Myhill, A. (2001). New Survey Methodologies In Researching Violence Against Women. *British Journal of Criminology, 41,* 502-522.

Chapter 2

Challenges of Surveying Violence Against Women: Development of Research Methods[1]

Natalia Ollus and Sami Nevala

Introduction

Violence that occurs within the family can involve several different perpetrators and victims. The violence may be perpetrated by men or women, by children or by adults. However, violence within the family is rarely occasional or a single, isolated event. It seems rather to be a means for one member to impose power, or exercise power and control over the others (see e.g. Lahti, 2001). According to a cross-cultural study, the most common form of violence within the family seems to be physical violence perpetrated by men against their female partners (Levinson, 1989).

Violence is thus closely related to power imbalances. Violence can be triggered by, for instance, religion, race, wealth imbalances or gender. So violence can be gendered, that is, be related to gender and differ depending on gender. Violence seems to affect men and women in different ways. It seems that world-wide, the most common perpetrators of violence targeted against women are the women's husbands or male intimate partners (The World's Women, 2000).

Violence against women is characterised by the fact that most of the violent incidents occur in or in the vicinity of the woman's home. Sexual assault or rape in a relationship seems to be not an isolated, single event, but rather one of a series of events, often taking place within a relationship

---

1 Parts of this chapter were presented at the X International Symposium on Victimology held in August 2000 in Montreal, Canada.

characterised by violence (Alvazzi del Frate, 1998, 70-71). It seems that men, on the other hand, are more often victimised in the public sphere by other males, who usually bear no family relationship.

Violence against women thus seems to differ from violence against men.[2] However, this view is often disputed and the type of research that gave rise to such statements is often called into question. Is it really so that women experience more domestic violence than men? Survey research has, since the late 1970s, been utilised to explore the types of violence that people experience and the settings in which violence occurs. Domestic violence has been the object of several studies, as has violence against women.

Studying violence in the intimate setting is a contested and ideological issue. This also affects the research setting. Research on domestic violence and violence against women has always been ideologically coloured. Stanko argues that this was necessary in order to break the silence and the taboos surrounding the violence (Stanko, 1997).

Violence and masculinity are related – and violence is one way of producing and reproducing the difference between men and women. Many men base their justification for using violence on a bodily discourse about men's social ownership over women (e.g. Hearn, 1998). Walklate (2001) argues that when women say 'no', some men simply fail or refuse to hear it since our cultural expectations do not really encourage them to acknowledge women's voices. Similarly, due to their fear of being blamed for their own victimisation, women do not necessarily want to define themselves as victims of sexual violence, especially not of rape. The younger a woman is and the better she knows the perpetrator, the less likely she is to define forced sex as rape (Koss and Cleveland, 1997).

Women's understanding of their experiences of violence is often linked to feelings of shame and fear. The experiences can be devastating for the victims and many choose not to reveal their ordeal to anyone. On the other hand, many other women go to great lengths to explain away and justify the violence perpetrated by their male partners, e.g. through notions of jealousy, alcoholism, unemployment or stressful work (Husso, 2003, see also Piispa, 2002 for a discussion on the complexities of identifying violence). Defining and seeing oneself as a victim can be difficult and even offensive to a woman. Especially in the early stages of violence in a

---

2   This chapter mainly deals with violence taking place in heterosexual intimate relationships. This chapter does not specifically deal with child abuse or violence in homosexual relationships.

relationship, women tend to join their abusive men in belittling the violence and its consequences (ibid). Hence, because of the specific characteristics of violence against women, this type of violence is not easily detected or researched. As researchers interested in quantifying these subjective and difficult experiences, we are confronted with several issues and problems.

In this chapter we will examine how survey research has been utilised to study family violence and especially male violence against women. We will also consider how surveys of violence against women have, up to now, tried to solve some of the ethical and methodological problems related to studying violence against women. Some solutions will be suggested, and the International Violence Against Women Survey will be presented as a tool to extend the available methods. Although surveys are not the only research method, we argue that surveys can, when administered well, contribute greatly to our understanding and knowledge of violence against women.

Measuring Violence in the Private Sphere

Although police statistics offer a valuable source of information on the extent of crime in society, they do not give a full portrayal of the actual level of crime. Police statistics do not show the real level of crime in society, nor can they be used as a single measure of police performance. Police statistics depend on whether victims of crime actually do report their experiences to the police, whether the police think that a crime has actually taken place, whether the police record the reported cases accordingly and, of course, what is considered or defined as a crime in the legislation. So police statistics reflect levels of control in society, trust in the police, the population's belief in the rule of law and their belief in their responsibility to report to the police (e.g. 'reporting is the right thing to do').

Police statistics and other official statistics on crime in society are characterised by three main problems: the hidden figure of crime, discretion and the legal definition of crime. The recording of gendered violence is characterised by all three problems. Women do not necessarily report their experiences to the police, as was noted above, and even if they do, the police do not necessarily record the crimes/incidents reported to them. Furthermore, the legislation defines and produces notions of crime. In many instances, the legislation has been gender-neutral or gender-blind, thus failing to define certain forms of women's experiences as violence. Historically, acts of violence against women, such as battery or rape, were not seen as criminal acts in many jurisdictions. Male power and violence over women within the family were seen as justified and right. Many of the central chapters of our criminal codes were created at this time (Nousiainen and Pylkkänen, 2001). The definitions and concepts of the criminal law therefore did not cover these acts of violence against women, which at that time were generally not seen as crimes at all. Law enforcement was not developed to deal with these types of violence either. Violent crimes in the public sphere have tended to be more heavily sanctioned. Violent crimes in the private sphere, most notably in the home, were largely omitted from official recognition until very recently (see Nousiainen and Pylkkänen, 2001).

The limitation of police statistics was generally recognised in the 1970s. New methods of collecting additional and parallel data emerged. Population-based surveys were developed to collect further information on the experiences of crime among the general public. These surveys were eventually also used to collect information specifically on women's experiences of violence.

The Development of Surveys on Violence Against Women

Walby and Myhill (2001) analyse the evolution of survey research of violence against women. They identify four different types of surveys: the generic national crime surveys; the revised crime surveys with special attention to violence against women; the dedicated domestic violence surveys; and the specific violence against women surveys. As a fifth category we would add surveys focusing on sexual violence. We will look at each type of survey and outline how it has contributed to our current understanding of researching violence against women.

Generic National Crime Surveys

The first general crime victim survey dates back to the late 1960s when, during the crisis of the US criminal justice system, US president Lyndon B. Johnson set up a working group to assess the extent of crime in society and the population's fear of crime (Heiskanen, 2002). The results from the first population survey of the general public's experiences of crime were published in 1967. The method was introduced elsewhere and gained popularity during the 1970s as a measure to assess the level of crime in society (Cantor and Lynch, 2000).

The general crime victim surveys have provided important material for the development of criminological research. The surveys aim to assess the individual's experience of crime, how the experience of crime affects the individual, what the individual thinks are the causes of crime, the risks of becoming a victim, and safety in society generally (Niemi, 1985). General crime victim surveys have thus been accepted as a means of measuring the extent of victimisation in society for certain forms of crime. As a further development, the International Crime Victim Survey (ICVS) has collected data on eleven types of crime, every three years from 1989, in a number of countries around the world (for the results of the ICVS see e.g. Mayhew and van Dijk, 1997; Alvazzi del Frate, 1998; Zvekic, 1998; van Kesteren, Mayhew and Nieuwbeerta, 2000). The ICVS has given another dimension to the estimation of crime in society: comparison between different countries over time.

However, for various reasons surveys cannot provide information on homicide, economic crime and victimless crimes. Neither can surveys generally provide information on crimes against persons who are not able to participate in a survey, such as small children.

It is largely agreed that the general crime surveys do not accurately capture women's experiences of gendered violence (see e.g. Johnson, 1996). Because the general victimisation surveys were designed to measure several forms of criminal victimisation, they have tended to overlook many features specific to violence against women. Firstly, the general crime surveys usually use one or two, usually rather broad and general screening questions to capture women's experiences of violence. Women's experiences of gendered violence have, in these studies, often been rendered as just one part of the broader theme of the surveys. The questions targeting women's experiences of violence tend to be gender-neutral in nature. There is no specific focus on violence by, for example, intimate male partners. Such broad questions do not necessarily correspond to the woman's subjective experience and understanding of the violence she has experienced. Secondly, victims of intimate relationship violence do not necessarily perceive their victimisation as a crime (or sometimes even as violence at all). They might therefore not report it in a crime victim survey (among items on other, more easily identifiable offences such as burglary or theft, which are usually perpetrated by someone outside the immediate family). Thirdly, general crime surveys often tend to overlook the sensitivity issues involved in researching women's experiences of violence. They do not always focus enough on interviewer selection, training and safety mechanisms so as to encourage disclosure and to assist the respondent if she feels distressed or traumatised when disclosing painful memories of violence. As an example, in the first national crime victim survey in the USA, all household members were interviewed together. Very little attention was paid to the fact that in cases of domestic violence, the victim is unlikely to disclose her experiences if the perpetrator is present during the interview. Rates of rape, for instance, were consequently very low (see Fisher and Cullen, 2000).

So sexual victimisation, in particular, may remain underreported in general victim surveys, due to its intimate character and the often painful memories it triggers.

Revised Crime Surveys

The revised crime surveys, such as the British crime survey, have attempted to improve the estimation of women's (especially sexual) victimisation. The U.S. National Crime Victimization Survey (NCVS) was redesigned in 1992 to better capture domestic violence and violence against women (see Fischer and Cullen, 2000 for the developments of the NCVS). The British Crime Survey (BCS) was also remodelled in 1994 through the inclusion of a self-completion component. In 1996, the BCS included a detailed module on spousal violence. Percy and Mayhew (1997) show that women's reporting of incidents of sexual victimisation in the British Crime Survey increased when they were able to use a computer to fill in the part of the questionnaire that dealt with sexual victimisation.[3] The computer-based self-completion component of the survey produce more that ten times the number of incidents (Percy and Mayhew, 1997).

The revised crime surveys pay special attention to violence against women. However, women's experiences are still only part of the broader aim of the study, and are therefore recorded among other topics. The nature of domestic violence against women makes women's experiences of violence a specific and different kind of experience of crime. Most people would clearly define burglary, car theft and robbery as crimes. Despite the fact that these crimes also cause traumatic experiences among victims, the

---

3   Otherwise the British Crime Survey uses face-to-face interviewing.

threshold to disclose these crimes is lower than for more intimate forms of crime. Furthermore, because these acts are generally defined as crimes, particularly women who have experienced less severe intimate violence may not define their experiences as a form of crime, and may therefore not disclose them in a context where the questions focus on crimes.

Dedicated Domestic Violence Surveys

Parallel to the development of the general crime surveys, a development of dedicated domestic violence surveys took place. These surveys, most notably the US National Family Violence Surveys of 1975 and 1985, focused on domestic violence mainly in terms of interaction in the relationship. They looked at everyday conflicts within marriage, seeing women and men as both victims and perpetrators. Based on this research, it has been stated that women in fact use more violence than men in marriage, and that more men than women are injured through this kind of violence (see e.g. Gelles, 1997; Straus, Gelles and Steinmetz, 1980).

The US National Family Violence Surveys used the so-called Conflict Tactics Scale (CTS) to measure different acts used in resolving disputes or conflicts within the relationship. Respondents were asked to think of any situation within the relationship where the person had engaged in or been subject to any means of conflict resolution. The (revised) scale consists of 19 items that the respondent may have engaged in, ranging from argumentation to physical violence. The first three items cover forms of rational discussion, or reasoning, such as 'discussed an issue calmly'. The next seven items cover forms of verbal aggression, including 'threw or smashed or hit or kicked something'. The final nine items cover 'minor' and 'severe' forms of physical violence, including 'slapped him/her/you' and 'beat him/her/you up'. One of the main findings of the US National Family Violence Surveys was that more wives used forms of severe violence towards their husbands than vice versa (Straus, Gelles and Steinmetz, 1980).

The CTS has been criticised for presenting violence in the relationship as symmetrical, and women and men as having equal motivations and contexts in which they use violence. The CTS includes only a narrow range of discrete acts, hence ignoring the processual nature of violence. Furthermore, it does not distinguish the gendered characteristics of domestic violence, i.e. the context, intention and motivation of violence. The CTS does not connect injury with the acts that caused the injury. Nor does the CTS at all include sexual violence as a form of interpersonal violence. It does not include male forms of controlling behaviour. Instead, physical and verbal violence are rendered equal, while important forms of emotional violence, such as threats of violence, are left out (see Dobash and Dobash, 1992 for a discussion on the CTS; see also Saunders, 1988).

According to Straus' first study, women are more likely to kick or hit their husbands with objects (Straus, 1980). Straus argues that these forms of violence are less dependent on physical strength or body size than the forms of violence that men typically engage in. The structure of the CTS, however, defines these acts as more serious than the types of violence that men are more likely to engage in, such as pushing, grabbing, or hitting. The results do not, however, say anything about the consequences of the violence, such as injuries, although Straus notes that men's greater physical strength will make it more likely for a woman to be seriously injured when beaten up by her husband than vice versa (ibid.). Although we agree that women are violent too, we believe that there are certain additional issues that should be outlined to understand why women seem to be more violent than men.

The criticism raised above outlines some of the possible explanations, focusing mainly on the structure of the CTS and its lack of contextualisation. Straus himself notes that the survey findings do not give any indication of women's violence as a response to violence initiated by men, e.g. female violence as self-defence. Furthermore, Straus raises as another possible explanation men's underreporting of acts of violence perpetrated by themselves. According to Straus, men do not perhaps perceive their own violence as noteworthy enough to report in a survey, whereas women are more likely to report violence perpetrated by themselves (since American society generally regards violence as unfeminine, out of the ordinary and thus noteworthy). It may be that women are more likely than men to report the violence they perpetrate because women are not supposed to be violent, but when they are, they are more likely to both remember the incident and disclose it in surveys. Men, on the other hand, are assumed to have more experiences of violent behaviour and thus do not necessarily see each incident as noteworthy enough to report. We would add here that some men fail to report their use of violence not just because they see violence as being an aspect of (normal) masculinity, but also because they belittle the extent and effect of their action, and perhaps do not define it as violence at all. The understanding of violence in an intimate relationship is thus linked to broader cultural and social factors. Violence is a social construct, and men and women construct it differently. So the meaning attached to violence (as perpetrator or victim) may differ between men and women. Despite the finding that women seem to be more violent than men, and engage in violence more often than men, Straus himself argues that attention should not be diverted from women as the principal victims of partnership violence (Straus, 1980). The focus should therefore not merely be on the act of violence itself, but on the intentionality and (potential) consequences. The same action can have vastly different consequences depending on whether a man or a woman carries it out, not only in terms of injuries, but also in terms of emotional trauma and long-lasting effects. Despite its flaws and a rather positivistic approach to the study of violence, many of the current surveys on violence against women owe part of their methodology to the CTS.

Specific Violence Against Women Surveys

The Canadian national violence against women survey, carried out by Statistics Canada in 1993, was the first specialised violence against women survey. This survey combined the methodology of quantitative social science research with (feminist) knowledge of the characteristics and contexts of violence against women. In designing the Canadian study, particular attention was paid to the ethical considerations of surveying violence against women, the methodology and the clarity of definitions of violence. As discussed above, it is recognised that scales allow more opportunities for the respondent to disclose experiences of violence than using one or two screeners (Walby and Myhill 2001). Screeners tend to leave out those respondents who do not identify with the general screener. The Canadian national violence against women survey, rather than using one single screening question, split up experiences of violence into specific acts so as to enable disclosure also for those incidents that the respondents themselves would not necessarily define or admit as violence. The questions were worded so as to make them both specific and sensitive. The Canadian survey also paid special attention to the training of interviewers and the sensitivity of interviewing. The survey accordingly captured almost twice as many incidents as reported in the general social survey, and almost 40 times as many cases of sexual assault than the official police statistics (Johnson 1996).

The Canadian survey was followed by similar surveys in the USA (1995-96), Australia (1996), New Zealand (1996), Finland (1997), Lithuania

(1998) and Sweden (2000). All of these surveys to some extent utilised the Canadian questionnaire and its definitions of violence. Besides simply producing data on violence against women, most of these surveys have been used to describe violence against women as a valid and real social problem.

In Finland, the national survey on violence against women contributed to the understanding and unveiling of violence against women as an acute social problem. The release of the survey data caused extensive discussions in the media as well as in the political arena about the extent of violence perpetrated by men against women in a seemingly gender-equal country. The survey quantified the problem and paved the way for both increased social efforts to prevent and counteract gendered violence, and research programmes into gender-based violence.

Sexual Violence Surveys

In addition to the surveys focusing on domestic violence and violence against women, several surveys focusing solely on sexual violence have been carried out, many of them in the United States (e.g. Koss 1985; recently a large study was carried out in Ireland, see McGee et al., 2002). In the National Survey of Inter-Gender Relationships, Koss et al., (1987) utilised a 10-item Sexual Experiences Survey scale to study sexual aggression and victimisation among more than 6,000 American female and male college students. Separate wordings were used for men and women. Female respondents were asked about any experiences of male sexual aggression, while men were asked about instances of perpetrating sexual violence against any woman. The scale covers sexual contact, attempted intercourse, intercourse and oral/anal penetration by verbal coercion, by misuse of authority, by threat/force, and under the influence of alcohol and drugs. The study showed that 54% of female respondents revealed having experienced some form of sexual victimisation[4] while 25% of male respondents revealed having perpetrated some form of sexual aggression. Koss et al. (1987) argue that it is possible that 'some men fail to perceive accurately the degree of force and coerciveness that was involved in a particular sexual encounter or to interpret correctly a woman's nonconsent

---

4   The victimisation rate is 10-15 times higher than rates based on data from the parallel generic crime survey.

and resistance' thus explaining some of the discrepancies between what women and men reported in the survey.

The scales used in sexual violence surveys have contributed to the development of specific violence against women surveys. However, despite using language with care and breaking down sexual acts into behaviourally specific definitions rather than summary terms, it is likely that many acts of sexual violence still remain unreported – for the same reasons that women do not disclose them to the authorities or others.

Comparison of Prevalence in Dedicated Violence Against Women Surveys

It is tempting to carry out comparisons between the results of the different surveys on violence against women. Through comparison, the research findings can be validated to some extent. Comparison is also needed in order to discover the specific, national characteristics of both the prevalence and phenomenon of violence against women. Comparative research aims to find similarities and differences, presenting a set of possible explanations for the variation between countries. The plausibility of the causes and characteristics of violence against women can be evaluated by testing the plausibility in another national or cultural setting. Additionally, comparison offers possibilities for assessing the national policies, measures and operations of the existing system (Howard et al., 2000). This enables examination of national strategies on, e.g., preventing violence against women or victim assistance programmes. Comparative research may thus expand our knowledge and understanding of our own society.

Although the dedicated violence against women surveys all address the same issues and the structures of the questionnaires are closely related, it is difficult to compare the findings, even when examining items that seem less problematic to measure than, say, sexual victimisation in intimate relationships. For example, with regard to violence perpetrated by a male stranger, 23% of all women in Canada have experienced violence (including sexual and physical assault) by a stranger since the age of 16 (Johnson, 1996, 93). In Australia, 15.5% of all women have experienced physical violence by a stranger since the age of 15, and 22.3% have experienced sexual violence since the age of 15 (McLennan, 1996, 23). The Finnish survey reports that 24.4% of all women have experienced at least one act of male physical or sexual violence or threats by a stranger or acquaintance other than their partner since their 15th birthday (Heiskanen and Piispa, 1998, 3). According to the US survey, 14% of the women who had been raped and/or physically assaulted since the age of 18 had been victimised by a stranger (Tjaden and Thoennes, 1998).[5] The Women's Safety Survey of New Zealand focused solely on former and current perpetrators and excluded violence committed by strangers (Morris, 1996).

The rates of violence perpetrated by strangers are strikingly similar in Canada, Australia and Finland. However, it is risky to state that the level of violence is equal in these three countries. Behind the figures presented lie small differences in survey design, making the comparisons unreliable. To compare lifetime victimisation by strangers, one must confront a problem with an overlap of different perpetrator groups as well as definitions of incidents. Without access to the raw data files and relying on the written reports only, it is difficult to determine how to compare the different surveys or whether they can be compared at all. It is important to know how the questions were constructed and how they were posed in order to assess the differences and similarities between the surveys, and identify whether the results can be compared. For example, the Finnish survey report groups all incidents, including both sexual and physical violence and threats, perpetrated by strangers or acquaintances, other than the current or previous partner. The Australian survey report, on the other hand, deals separately with physical and sexual violence perpetrated by strangers only. Thus, the acts of violence included in the different questions may differ. Also, the end points of the respondents' age distribution included in the survey vary. The respondents in the Finnish survey are between 18 and 74 years old, whereas the other surveys include women of 18 years old and over. Although the intention is to compare the same form of violence against women, the discrepancies in definitions and in question formulation hinder an accurate comparison.

Comparison between surveys may also be dubious due to differences in cultural and social factors, the method of data collection (telephone or face-to-face interviews or a postal survey), and sampling. It is evident that the national violence against women surveys were developed for national purposes and national needs. The potential for international comparison was not a priority when designing the surveys.

---

5   However, the source does not specify whether or not women's victimisation by
    strangers includes also female perpetrators.

Many of the problems of comparison mentioned above can be solved by a co-operative, international effort. The International Violence Against Women Survey is a tool for measuring violence against women internationally. The survey can be used in all parts of the world. This obviously poses special challenges to the survey design, which will be raised later in this chapter.

Development of the International Violence Against Women Survey (IVAWS)

The International Violence Against Women Survey (IVAWS) started in 1997 with the development of a draft questionnaire and methodology. In late 1999, an International Project Team was formed between the European Institute for Crime Prevention and Control, affiliated with the United Nations (HEUNI), the United Nations Interregional Crime and Justice Research Institute (UNICRI) and Statistics Canada.[6] A coordination meeting was held in Helsinki in January 2001 to plan the first stage of the preparations for the pilot stage of the IVAWS project. The questionnaire was subsequently revised and the methodology manual drafted. In March 2001, the first meeting for national coordinators was organised in Vancouver, Canada. The questionnaire and project structure were discussed, and the questionnaire then underwent a thorough revision before the pilot version was finalised in October 2001.

Preparations for pilot studies commenced in early November 2001, with Canada carrying out a 100 respondent pilot study at the end of the year. Other countries followed with pilot studies during 2002. These included Argentina, Costa Rica, Denmark, Italy, Kazakhstan, Poland, Australia, Indonesia, the Philippines, Serbia, Switzerland and Ukraine.[7] During mid-2002 the questionnaire also underwent some revisions. The second expert meeting of national coordinators was held in October 2002 in Turin, Italy. The meeting discussed the pilot experiences and reworked the questionnaire accordingly. In early December 2002 the questionnaire was ready for the fully fledged surveys. The questionnaire has already been translated into Czech, Danish, French, German, Greek, Italian, Polish, Portuguese and Spanish. Besides the questionnaire and a pre-programmed

---

6   The International Project Team currently consists of representatives from HEUNI, the United Nations Office on Drugs and Crime, and Statistics Canada.
7   Estonia carried out a pre-pilot study in May 2000.

data capture program, the survey methodology package includes a Manual with detailed guidelines on how to implement the survey. The Manual contains an extensive section on interviewer selection and training.[8]

By the end of 2003, data collection was completed in Australia, Costa Rica, Czech Republic and Switzerland. Further countries, including Denmark, Greece, Italy, Mozambique, the Philippines and Poland are set to follow suit in the beginning of 2004. Data collection is expected to be finalised by the end of 2004.

The questionnaire can be roughly divided into three parts: experienced violence, consequences of violence and background information. The victimisation screeners are composed of twelve questions, each category beginning with a question on lifetime victimisation, and continuing with a more detailed breakdown of prevalence and incidence by perpetrator. The most recent incidents of partner violence and non-partner violence are then explored in closer detail, with separate dedicated sections for both types. Case details include such matters as possible injuries, need for medical care, reporting (or not reporting) to the police, and the respondent's views on how her voice was heard.

The IVAWS can provide new insight into the extent of violence against women worldwide. Firstly, the questionnaire and the methodology manual form a survey package that can be used to conduct the survey in different countries. This might encourage certain countries, where violence against women is not a priority issue, to implement a survey. In countries where there is little or no information on the extent of men's violence against women, the IVAWS can serve as a basis for national action and debate on the issue. And in countries where research has already studied the prevalence of violence against women, the IVAWS is interesting because of its international perspective: what are the differences and similarities between various countries with regard to women's experiences of violence, willingness to report the incidents, support structures, etc.? In addition to statistical data, the IVAWS thus provides information on national circumstances and characteristics with regard to violence against women. This type of information gathering may only offer limited value as such, but the importance of the results lies in their potential for launching a firmly grounded public debate – in the media, in academia and in the

---

8   The IVAWS Manual is partly based on the Manual of the International Crime Victim Survey. The IVAWS Manual was drafted by Natalia Ollus, Holly Johnson, Anna Alvazzi del Frate and Sami Nevala. This chapter reflects some of the sections of that manual.

political sphere – about the causes, consequences and aftercare of violence against women in society.

Although national studies on violence against women have been conducted in many countries, the IVAWS and the national surveys should not be considered as mutually exclusive; both have their specific foci of interest. The IVAWS, consisting of a repeatable survey design, facilitates comparability despite potential discrepancies in applying the questionnaire in different national settings. The International Violence Against Women Survey therefore fills a gap in finding international as well as national remedies to violence against women.

In the process of developing the IVAWS, the international team tried to accommodate the concern, criticism and suggestions raised in terms of surveying violence against women. The IVAWS falls into the category of specific violence against women surveys – with the additional comparative dimension. Some of the challenges of researching violence against women have been met in the IVAWS project.

The Challenges of Survey Research on Violence Against Women

As outlined above, there are several challenges in surveying violence against women. We have here divided the issues into two broader categories: methodological challenges and ethical challenges. The methodological challenges include challenges in the definitions used and issues around data collection, including response rates, sampling and the choice of telephone versus face-to-face interviews. The ethical issues include interviewer selection and training; safety and confidentiality matters; handling of emotional trauma; and issues of ownership and community involvement in the survey.

Definitions

As discussed above, the definition of violence is the cornerstone of a survey on violence against women. Of all the items covered in the violence against women surveys, the definition of sexual violence is by far the most controversial and problematic. The criticism against questions concerning sexual violence is extensive (e.g. Travis et al., 1995; Percy and Mayhew, 1997; Walby, 1999; Walby and Myhill, 2001). It is, unarguably, difficult to produce a precise definition of sexual violence, which would categorise the different forms of sexual violence in a comprehensive yet systematic way, making the acts easily disclosable but also recognisable. Most surveys utilise a definition of sexual acts that is derived from the definitions of sexual violence in the jurisdiction. In both the National Crime Victimisation Survey and the National Violence Against Women Survey of the US, the questions screening victimisation are 'designed to leave little doubt in the respondent's mind as to what is being measured' (Tjaden and Thoennes, 2000, 5). The IVAWS, on the other hand, is intended for wide international use. This means that the survey must accommodate a variety of jurisdictions and a variety of definitions of sexual violence. The IVAWS utilises a similar approach to the Canadian survey of 1993, going from the most serious form of sexual violence (forced sexual intercourse, by threatening, holding down, or hurting in some way) to attempts, sexual touching, and finally sexual acts with a third party. Sexual acts with a third party was included as a specific category of sexual violence at the request of some of the participating countries. The question aims to give some indication of experiences of prostitution as well as of sexual coercion.

The questions were designed to provide for more nuanced lists of categories of sexual assault but, given the survey format, still do not quite fully accommodate the degrees of force and pressure involved in, for instance, rape in marriage, as called for by Walby and Myhill (2001). One of the problems of the IVAWS and the dedicated violence against women surveys is that in order for the questions on violence not to become too long, some forms of physical violence have been grouped together. Some of the screening questions actually combine less serious forms of violence with more serious forms of violence, so the categories do not necessarily correspond to acts of violence as outlined by the penal code.

Data Collection

Response rates, sampling, methodology
Violence against women is a sensitive topic. The sensitivity of the topic is one factor that contributes to respondents' willingness to participate. The survey may trigger traumatic memories of past events and the respondent may refuse to participate, or may wish to terminate the interview. Other reasons for non-response include lack of time, lack of privacy to respond (especially related to respondents' own perception of safety), and lack of interest in participating in surveys.

In order to minimise initial refusals, the IVAWS is introduced as a survey not on violence, but on personal safety. Efforts are taken to ensure that the interview can be conducted in private. If the respondent is unavailable, measures are taken to reschedule or relocate the interview. In order to prepare themselves for different scenarios during fieldwork, interviewers and researchers need to familiarise themselves with the community and the different social and cultural issues in the areas where they are interviewing (e.g. intergenerational households, high unemployment, dowry, customary marriages, polygamous marriages, etc.).

In the experience of the IVAWS, it seems that women are generally willing to participate and that the topic of the survey is perceived to be important. Many respondents feel that through participating they contribute towards a greater good, and that their experiences may help other women in similar situations. Several women have also stated that the interview has been their first opportunity ever to talk about their experiences of violence. It is thus important to treasure the trust that the respondents show towards the interviewers.

For women with several experiences of victimisation the interviews tend to take a long time (45 minutes to over an hour). Interviewers therefore need to be equipped to encourage completion of the questionnaire. However, interviewers or respondents should not be pressurised too much if respondents refuse to participate in the survey.

The main challenge in terms of sampling is to capture those who presumably experience the highest levels of victimisation, such as the homeless and those staying in institutions, hostels and refuges (most notably those staying in refuges for battered women). Walby and Myhill (2001) propose to include additional samples to the main sampling frame to cover these often marginalised populations. The Sexual Abuse and Violence in Ireland study included, besides the representative main sample of 3,000 randomly selected male and female respondents, also a sample of 100 homeless women. The study also approached so-called travellers, women in prostitution, people with learning disabilities, prisoners, and patients in psychiatric settings. These subgroups were not approached directly, but were covered through discussions with key informants at organisations and institutions working with the groups. The aim of studying the subgroups was to highlight possible differences in risk, challenges in disclosing sexual violence and problems in seeking help (McGee et al., 2002).

The mode of inquiry that is chosen should 'reflect an intimate understanding of the cultural context in which the research takes place' (McGee et al., 2002). However, other aspects that affect the choice of methodology are funding and practicalities, such as access to respondents. Ever since victim surveys were introduced, there has been discussion on the superiority of face-to-face interviews over telephone interviews and vice versa. Telephone interviews are generally more anonymous than face-to-face interviews and may therefore enhance disclosure (Morris 1996). On the other hand, surveys conducted by telephone may suffer from sample bias due to limited coverage and the ethnic, socio-economic, and other characteristics connected with telephone ownership, or, on the other hand, with the increasing prevalence of mobile phones.[9]

Face-to-face interviews may help the respondent deal with different and difficult questions, support the respondent if they become distressed, and encourage reluctant respondents to reply (Heiskanen, 1999). The IVAWS will utilise both telephone and face-to-face methods. In countries with an adequate telephone coverage, and a history of telephone interviewing, computer-assisted telephone interviews (CATI) are carried out. However, in developing countries, and countries with inadequate telephone coverage, face-to-face interviews are preferred.

Interviewer selection and training

As shown above, special consideration must be given to interviewer selection and training to ensure that respondents in a range of countries feel comfortable enough to disclose their victimisation, and that interviewers are capable of handling the trust vested in them by the respondents. The most important aspect is selection of interviewers. The IVAWS uses only female interviewers. The use of female interviewers only is a special feature of the dedicated violence against women surveys.[10] Interviewers should ideally also be paired with the respondent so that their

---

9   If mobile phone numbers are included in the sample and random dialling is used, persons with both a mobile phone and a landline have greater probability to be included in the sample. However, in many countries mobile phone numbers are not included in random dialling samples, and therefore persons with only a mobile phone are excluded. In many countries, persons with a mobile phone as their only phone tend to be younger than the average population. Because this group of persons also experiences the highest victimisation risk, it is a problem if they are excluded from the sample.

10 The gender of the interviewer (and possible interpreters) is even more crucial when it comes to interviewing immigrant women, or women from certain ethnic/language minorities.

relationship in terms of age, ethnic belonging and religion does not clash in a way that is harmful for the interview.

The interviewers should have some previous experience of survey interviewing but, most importantly, they should possess some knowledge of and comfort in discussing issues related to violence against women. They should also be non-judgmental, non-biased and empathetic towards victims of violence against women. It is also crucial to highlight that interviewers should not consider themselves to be counsellors. While interviewers should have some knowledge of the topic of violence against women, they should not themselves possess any unprocessed traumatic experiences of male violence.[11]

Interviewer training is critical for the implementation of the survey, especially for acquiring accurate and reliable data, for increasing disclosure, and for minimising non-response or terminations. The training module of the IVAWS gives the interviewers tools for understanding the dynamics and mechanisms of violence against women. The training also equips the women with knowledge of how to ensure safety for respondents and interviewers, how to respond to emotional trauma that may surface through responding to the survey, for both respondents and interviewers, and how to ensure honest disclosures of violence.

Safety and confidentiality

Interviewing women about their victimisation involves many methodological considerations. One of the most important is to ensure that the interview situation is confidential. In order to gather reliable and accurate data, it is of foremost importance that the interviewers are familiar with the issues related to violence against women. Additionally, they need to know how to respond in different situations that might come up during the interview process. Well-prepared and trained interviewers obviously have a positive effect on the interview situation.

Interviewers do not know whether the respondent has experienced violence or not. Furthermore, they cannot know whether the respondent is living with her abuser. The interviewers must therefore be equipped to deal with situations where the abuser, or some other family member, enters

---

11 Personal experiences of male violence is not a hindrance to being enrolled as an interviewer and in many instances personal experiences contribute to a greater understanding of the issue at hand. However, the interviewer should have processed her own experiences so that she feels comfortable in encountering women with similar experiences.

the scene of interview. In such situations the interviewers may need to use a set of dummy questions on some less threatening topic, or skip to some less threatening section of the questionnaire. Privacy during interviews is crucial, and interviews may have to be relocated or rescheduled in order to ensure privacy. Although privacy can be difficult to achieve during interviews, interviewers must be constantly aware of the interview setting and prepare for the possibility that the interview could be overheard by someone.

Emotional trauma

It is well-known that the disclosure of experiences of violence may cause respondents distress and emotional trauma. This might be the first time that she reveals her experiences to anybody. The interviewer needs to be able to show empathy towards the respondent, and also to treasure and respect her trust. The interviewer thus has a responsibility to ensure that the respondent gets access to some form of assistance, if distressed after the interview. However, the interviewer is not a therapist. Her main task is to gather information and to encourage the respondent to reply to as many questions as possible. Interviewers therefore give respondents information on where to go and whom to contact if they feel they need to discuss their experiences of violence with professional counsellors. In this way interviewers can help respondents cope with the trauma, without compromising their own role as an interviewer.

The empathetic attitude of the interviewer towards the respondent helps create a confidential and comfortable interview setting. However, the interviewer herself might become exposed to trauma through the respondents' accounts of their experiences of violence. In the fourth generation violence against women surveys, interviewers have had an opportunity to share their experiences of distressing interviews with professional counsellors. IVAWS interviewers are also provided with possibilities for debriefing and counselling, both individually and in a group.

Quantitative Versus Qualitative Research

A common concern is that quantitative research, such as surveys, cannot truly capture the trauma, fear, anger and pain caused by violence. Many feminist researchers argue that quantitative surveys are unable to accurately capture the subjective experiences of the victim/survivor, and that statistical research is therefore unable to fully reflect women's experiences of abuse. Survey research is thus often seen as an inherently masculine, positivist social science (see e.g. Fonow and Cook, 1991).

An alternative route is the combination of qualitative and quantitative methods. The South African national violence against women study (Rasool et al., 2002) combined aspects of both methods. The study utilised a questionnaire that included a range of open-ended questions, so as to better capture the respondents' experiences.[12] Furthermore, the researchers did not want to risk the confidentiality or safety of respondents and therefore chose to use a non-random sample. The 1,000 women respondents were captured through snowballing, which was made possible through the utilisation of the interviewers' networks. The interviewers were mainly counsellors, psychologists and social workers working within the violence against women sector. The sample was then weighted to represent the diverse South African population. The study also utilised focus group interviews and case studies to further validate the survey results. In our opinion, this type of combination of methodologies is important. Quantitative studies increase our understanding of the extent of the problem of violence against women. Qualitative studies, on the other hand, are crucial for our understanding of the context, nature and consequences of the problem. Without the in-depth knowledge produced through qualitative studies we could not engage in measuring the extent quantitatively – because we would simply not know what to ask and how to ask it.

Conclusion

One may ask oneself what right we as researchers have to tear open women's traumatic experiences of violence. To this we would like to respond that although a survey does not necessarily have any immediate value for the respondent, it may, in some cases, be an opportunity for the respondent to air her experiences and perhaps talk about them for the first time with someone. However, one should not forget that the main aim of this type of research is of course to increase our understanding of violence and its consequences. In the best of cases, the interview may help the

---

12 However, as Rasool et al. (2002) point out, the quantification of the open-ended responses by the 1,000 respondents meant 'losing the complexity and the intense trauma that characterises violence against women'.

respondent to process any experience of violence she may have. But one should not overemphasise this, either. It is only the respondent herself who knows best what is best for her: that is, to talk about the violence, or not to talk about it.

Another question is how we as researchers can grasp women's subjective and traumatic experiences and feelings. This is, of course, difficult. As discussed above, a survey may not be the best possible method for truly capturing the horrors of violence. The questionnaire format and its pre-coded response categories may not, for instance, capture the strong sentiments caused by some seemingly minor incident that happened a long time ago. However, surveys can capture the most common forms of women's experiences and, most importantly, can do so over time, thus showing whether change related to legislation, education, awareness campaigns or new services has taken place. Despite the criticism, surveys are needed precisely also for the 'hard facts' that they provide. It is these hard facts that are (unfortunately, as some would agree) needed to influence policy-making.

Furthermore, one may ask oneself how well surveys have managed so far to grasp the subjective experiences of the respondents. Few researchers have admitted that they have failed in their research endeavour. The most crucial and also difficult aspect of research is still perhaps how to bring about social change in preventing and responding to violence against women. The prevention of violence would be the best way to tackle the problem, both from an individual perspective and from the perspective of society. Surveys can reveal some of the trends in when and where and how violence takes place, as well as how often and where women seek assistance. This information is useful in designing preventive measures. However, the problems of violence seem largely to be universal (violence remains hidden, victims do not want to define themselves as victims, etc). What research can do, and should do, is show that violence against women *is* a real problem and that victims do require assistance, although they may not initially admit to that. As Lahti (2001) points out 'the reluctance to be helped is not necessarily a permanent state of affairs. After some weeks, months or years, the same woman might have different thoughts in her mind; she is ready to leave her partner. At that moment, she needs legal and social support'.

References

Alvazzi del Frate, A. (1998). *Victims of Crime in the Developing World.* UNICRI, Publication No. 57. Rome: UNICRI.

Cantor, D. and Lynch, J.P. (2000). Self-Report Surveys as Measures of Crime and Criminal Victimisation, pp. 85-138 in *Criminal Justice 2000,* Vol. 4. US National Institute of Justice, 2000.
Available at http://www.ojp.usdoj.gov/nij/criminal_justice2000/vol4_2000.html

Dobash, R. Emerson and Dobash, R. P. (1992). *Women, violence and social change.* Routledge: London and New York.

Fisher, B. S. and F. T. Cullen (2000). Measuring the Sexual Victimization of Women: Evolution, Current Controversies, and Future Research. Pp. 317-390 in *Criminal Justice 2000,* Volume 4. Washington D.C.: National Institute of Justice.

Fonow, M. and Cook, A. (eds) (1991). Beyond Methodology: Feminist Scholarship as lived research. Indiana University Press.

Gelles, R. J. (1997). *Intimate Violence in Families.* Third Edition. SAGE: Thousand Oaks.

Hearn, J. (1998). *The Violences of Men. How Men Talk About and How Agencies Respond to Men's Violence to Women.* London: SAGE.

Heiskanen, M. (1999). How to study sensitive topics. Paper presented at EU Expert Meeting on Violence Against Women. Jyväskylä, Finland, 8-10 November 1999.

Heiskanen, M. (2002). *Väkivalta, pelko, turvattomuus. Surveytutkimusten näkökulmia suomalaisten turvallisuuteen.* [Violence, fear, insecurity. The point of view of survey research on the security of Finnish people] Tilastokeskus, tutkimuksia 236 [Statistics Finland].

Heiskanen, M. and M. Piispa (1998). *Usko, toivo, hakkaus: Kyselytutkimus miesten naisille tekemästä väkivallasta.* Tilastokeskus, Oikeus 1998:12, Tasa-arvoasiain neuvottelukunta. Edita: Helsinki.

Howard, G. J., G. Newman and W. A. Pridemore (2000). Measurement and Analysis of Crime and Justice, pp. 139-211 in *Criminal Justice 2000,* Volume 4. Washington D.C.: National Institute of Justice.

Husso, M. (2003). *Parisuhdeväkivalta. Lyötyjen aika ja tila* [Relationship violence. The time and space of the battered]. Tampere: Vastapaino.

Johnson, H. (1996). Dangerous domains. Violence against women in Canada. Toronto: Nelson Canada.

Johnson, H. (2000). Enhancing knowledge on violence against women. Paper presented at the Workshop on Women in the Criminal Justice System, Tenth United Nations Congress on the Prevention of Crime and the Treatment of Offenders. Vienna 10-17 April 2000.

Koss, M. (1985). The hidden rape victim: Personality, attitudinal, and situational characteristics. *Psychology of Women Quarterly,* No. 9, 193-212.

Koss, M. and Cleveland, H. H. (1997). Stepping on Toes. Social Roots of Date Rape Lead to Intractability and Politization. In Schwartz, Martin D. (ed.) *Researching*

Sexual Violence Against Women. Methodological and Personal Perspectives. SAGE: Thousand Oaks.

Koss, M., Gidycz, C. and Wisniewski, N. (1987). The Scope of Rape: Incidence and Prevalance of Sexual Aggression and Victimization in a National Sample of Higher Education Students. *Journal of Consulting and Clinical Psychology*, Vol. 55, No.2, 162-170.

Lahti, M. (2001). Domesticated Violence. The power of the ordinary in everyday Finland, *Research Series in Anthropology*. Helsinki: University of Helsinki.

Levinson, D. (1989). Family *violence in cross-cultural perspective. Frontiers of anthropology, Volume 1.* SAGE Publications: Newbury Park.

Mann, C. R. (1996). *When Women Kill.* State University of New York Press: Albany.

Mayhew, P. and J. J. M. van Dijk (1997). *Criminal Victimisation in Eleven Industrialised Countries. Key findings from the 1996 International Crime Victims Survey.* Onderzoek en beleid 162. Research and Documentation Centre, Ministry of Justice of the Netherlands.

McGee, H., Garavan, R., de Barra, M., Byrne, J. and Conroy, R. (2002). The SAVI Report. Sexual Abuse and Violence in Ireland. A National Study of Irish Experiences, Beliefs and Attitudes Concerning Sexual Violence. The Liffey Press in association with the Dublin Rape Crisis Centre: Dublin.

McLennan, W. (1996). *Women's Safety Australia 1996.* Australian Bureau of Statistics.

Morris, A. (1996). *Women's Safety Survey 1996.* Wellington: Victimisation Survey Committee.

Niemi, H. (1985). *Uhritutkimuksen käyttökelpoisuus Oikeuspoliittisen tutkimuslaitoksen julkaisuja* 72/1985 [The usefulness of victim surveys. Publications of the National Research Institute of Legal Policy].

Nousiainen, K. and Pylkkänen, A. (2001). *Sukupuoli ja oikeuden yhdevertaisuus Forum Iuris* [Gender and the equality of law]. Helsinki: Helsingin yliopiston oikeustieteellisen tiedekunnan julkaisuja [Publications of the Faculty of Law, University of Helsinki].

Percy, A. and P. Mayhew (1997). Estimating Sexual Victimisation in a National Crime Survey: A New Approach, pp. 125-150 in *Studies on Crime and Crime Prevention*, Vol. 6 No. 2. Swedish National Council For Crime Prevention. Stockholm: Scandinavian University Press.

Piispa, M. (2002). Complexity of Patterns of Violence Against Women in Heterosexual Partnerships. *Violence Against Women*, July 2002, Vol. 8, Issue 7, 873-900.

Rasool, S., Vermaak, K., Pharoah, R., Louw and A. Stavrou, Aki (2002). *Violence Against Women: A National Survey.* Pretoria: Institute for Security Studies.

Saunders, D. G. (1988). Wife Abuse, Husband Abuse or Mutual Combat? A Feminist Perspective on the Empirical Findings. In Yllö, Kersti and Bograd, Michele (eds.) *Feminist Perspectives on Wife Abuse.* SAGE: Newbury Park.

Stanko, E. A. (1997). 'I Second That Emotion'. Reflections on Feminism, Emotionality, and Research on Sexual Violence. In Schwartz, Martin D. (ed.)

Researching Sexual Violence Against Women. Methodological and Personal Perspectives. SAGE: Thousand Oaks.

Straus, M., Gelles, R. and Steinmetz, S. (1980). *Behind Closed Doors: Violence in the American Family.* Sage Publications: Newbury Park.

The World's Women 2000 (2000). United Nations. Social Statistics and Indicators Series K, No. 16. New York.

Tjaden, P. and N. Thoennes (1998). Prevalence, Incidence, and Consequences of Violence Against Women: Findings from the National Violence Against Women Survey. In Research in Brief, November 1998. U.S. Department of Justice, Office of Justice Programs.

Tjaden, P. and N. Thoennes (2000). Extent, Nature, and Consequences of Intimate Partner Violence. Findings From the National Violence Against Women Survey. National Institute of Justice and Centers for Disease Control and Prevention.

Travis, G., Brown, D., Egger, S., Hogg, R., O'Toole, B. and J. Stubbs (1995). The International Crime Surveys: Some Methodological Concerns pp. 346-361 in *Current Issues in Criminal Justice*, 6.

van Kesteren, J., Mayhew, P. and Nieuwbeerta, P. (2000). *Criminal Victimisation in Seventeen Industrialised Countries. Key findings from the 2000 International Crime Victims Survey.* Wetenschappelijk Onderzoek- en Documentatiecentrum: The Hague.

Walby, S. (1999). Comparing Methodologies Used to Study Violence Against Women. Paper presented at Council of Europe seminar 'Men and Violence Against Women'. Strasbourg 7-8 October 1999.

Walby, S. and Myhill, A. (2001). New Survey Methodologies in Researching Violence Against Women. *British Journal of Criminology*, Vol. 41, 502-522.

Walklate, S. (2001). *Gender, Crime and Criminal Justice.* Willan Publishing: Cullompton.

Zvekic, U. (1998). Criminal Victimisation in Countries in Transition. United Nations Interregional Crime and Justice Research Institute (UNICRI), publication No. 61. Rome.

Chapter 3

Critical Issues Related to the Measurement of Intimate Partner Violence: A Clustering Analysis of Psychometric Scores

Juanjo Medina-Ariza and Eduardo Fe-Rodriguez

Introduction

Debates about the measurement of intimate partner violence are very controversial, as are many of the debates about research findings and policy solutions related to this social problem. Although researchers have been using surveys and questionnaires to measure this phenomenon since the early 1970s, the debate as to the best way to measure intimate partner violence still continues.

Many instruments have been developed to measure intimate partner violence. The literature has identified two different measurement traditions: domestic violence surveys and violence against women surveys (Walby and Myhill, 2001; Dobash and Dobash, 2004). Although the picture is perhaps more complex, this bi-polar model certainly constitutes a good starting point. Domestic violence surveys emphasise the link between intimate partner violence and the conflicts that emerge from cohabitation and family dynamics. Researchers in this tradition see intimate partner violence as a form of the broader problem of family conflict. These researchers have often used the Conflict Tactics Scales (CTS) as their main research tool. This instrument relies on the measurement of discrete acts, such as a 'slap' or a 'punch'. Violence against women surveys, on the other hand, emphasise the link between intimate partner violence and women's subordination and control in today's society. Researchers in this tradition see intimate partner violence as a specific manifestation of the broader problem of male violence against women. These researchers have tried to develop instruments that, although influenced by the CTS, can overcome some of its limitations. The emphasis is placed on the broader context of the abuse. Findings from these two research traditions and interpretations of the resulting findings have often been at odds, even if considerable common ground also exists.

This classification of research traditions suggests that the debates about measurement, as technical as they can be at times, have serious implications for theory and policy, and that the debates are often underlined by ideological differences in the interpretation of what the real problem is (e.g., family conflict versus female victimisation and control). The advocates of the CTS, for example, argue that intimate partner violence perpetrated by females is 'a serious social problem' (Straus, 1993). They have used findings from surveys taking this approach to challenge the view that intimate partner violence is a matter of primarily male violence and the reproduction of gender disparities (Straus, 1999; Felson, 2002). This position has gathered new strength in the last few years. A recent meta-analysis of this research has come to such a conclusion (Archer, 2000). Archer (2000) finds that women are slightly more likely than men to use more acts of physical aggression and to use such acts more frequently. This interpretation of the problem has obvious policy implications. Moffit and her colleagues (2001) recently suggested the need to promote research into abuse by women in the context of intimate partner relationships and to further explore the possible use of conjoint therapy as a solution to this problem.

On the other hand, critics of the CTS-based research have suggested that this instrument provides an account of marital violence that is neither reliable nor valid. They argue that most physical violence by women in the context of intimate partner relationships is defensive (Dobash et al., 1992). From this perspective, the serious social problem is male violence against women, and all solutions to the problem of intimate partner violence should assume this premise.

Johnson (1995) has argued that the apparently contradictory findings from these two literatures could reflect the fact that the different traditions of measurement are capturing different aspects of intimate partner violence. He suggests that some families suffer from occasional outbursts of violence, by either husbands or wives, which he calls common couple violence. Other families are characterised by systematic male violence, which he calls patriarchal terrorism. Is this the case? To what degree can our current instruments capture this heterogeneity of forms and levels of abuse? These questions have not received enough research attention.

Macmillan and Gartner (1999) made the first serious attempt to address the second question. Using data from the Canadian Violence Against Women Survey, these authors relied on latent structure analysis to classify their respondents according to empirically established patterns of abuse. They identified a four-class model. Group I was composed of women who had not experienced any form of abuse. This group represented 84% of the sample. Group II comprised women with a moderately high (.55) probability of being pushed, shoved or slapped, and a moderately low (.19) probability of being threatened. This group represented 11% of the sample. The authors suggest that this group's experiences are probably similar to what Johnson calls 'common couple violence'. Group III included women who experienced higher probabilities of violence and a wider range of violent acts. They are almost certain (.97) to have been pushed, shoved and slapped, very likely to have been threatened, and moderately likely to have had something thrown at them or to have been kicked or hit. Their probabilities of more serious forms of violence (e.g., beating, choking or forced sex) remained relatively low. Macmillan and Gartner label this group 'non-systematic abuse', although their measures do not collect information on frequency of the behaviours. This group represented 3% of the sample. Finally, respondents in the fourth and smallest group have the highest probabilities of each type of violence, including more serious forms of abuse. The authors contend that the 'substantial prevalence of multifaceted and life-threatening violence suggests that these women have been subjected to the "patriarchal terrorism" Johnson (1995) describes' (Macmillan and Gartner, 1999: 952). This group represented about 1% of the sample. This research suggests that partner abuse can vary from very extreme forms to less severe ones. Equally important, Macmillan and Gartner's (1999) research shows that a risk factor analysis for these four groups of abused women indicates relevant differences in terms of the impact of a variety of risk factors across these different degrees of violence.

Are the studies relying on the CTS providing a picture that is as sophisticated as the one suggested by Johnson and backed by the Canadian research? From a face validity point of view, the answer to the question should start with an examination of the scoring rules of the CTS. The newest version of the CTS, the CTS2, is composed of a number of scales and subscales. There are five major scales: negotiation, psychological abuse, physical abuse, sexual abuse, and injury. Each of these scales is represented by several items in the instrument, each of which describes an act or a variety of acts. If a respondent answers 'yes' to any of the items that compose the five abuse scales, he/she will be classified as a victim of abuse, regardless of the frequency of that behaviour, its motivation, its consequences, its intentionality, or its coexistence with other abusive acts that are measured by the CTS. The abusive scales are also divided into two subscales, a less severe and a more severe subscale of sexual, physical, psychological abuse and injury. Again, it is enough to answer positively to any of the items on the subscales to be classified accordingly. Basically, answering 'yes' to any of the items on any of the subscales make a woman a victim of severe physical abuse or minor sexual abuse, and so on. As has been adequately noted, this approach 'may not fully capture the nature and complexity of violent incidents' (Gondolf and Beeman, 2003). To compensate for this, Straus has suggested more sophisticated ways of scoring the CTS (e.g. weighting). But these alternative methods are rarely used and, in any case, present their own limitations.

The basic scoring method suggested by Straus has two fundamental problems. First, this method does not use all the information that researchers' questionnaires collect. The scoring method ignores the degree to which a respondent suffers more than one of the acts included in the scale. The standard method of scoring is unaffected by the number of different types of behaviours that a respondent suffers. This is relevant in terms of identifying severity of the abuse. For example, suffering one of the items in the psychological abuse scale is not the same as suffering all of them in conjunction with other forms of physical and sexual abuse. For that reason, some researchers are using variety scales instead of the more traditional scales of the CTS. Basically, variety scales sum the number of 'Yes' responses to abusive items (Moffit et al., 2001). However, these scales present their own problems. They cannot be easily used to present rates of violence. In addition, they give equal weight to all acts regardless of their seriousness.

In addition, although the CTS response options take into account the frequency of the behaviours (they are not dichotomous questions), most researchers rarely use this information. Some argue, with good reason, that frequency reports are slightly more unreliable: '"Has X happened" is a more accurate response format than "How many times has X happened?", especially among respondents whose violent acts have lost their salience because they happen frequently' (Moffit et al., 2001: p. 15). However, the fact remains that having suffered a slap only once is a different matter from suffering repeated incidents in which one has been slapped. Equally, it is true that the use of frequency reports produces more skewed distributions than the use of an alternative such as variety scales (Moffit et al., 2001). Nevertheless, although reducing variability may be a desirable property of variety scales for some purposes, this is not the case if we want to produce appropriate estimates of violence in the population.

Moreover, the traditional CTS scoring methods try to establish clear types of violence, based on the degree of severity of the specific behaviour and the modality of the abuse (sexual, psychological, physical). Most research shows, however, that these clear types do not exist. Some have described the Straus approach as: 'a slap is a slap is a slap.' And it does seem easy to lose sight of the heterogeneity of situations that can come under the label intimate partner violence when one classifies respondents as victims or non-victims in such a black-and-white fashion. The limitations of the common CTS scoring rules cause the CTS to simplify and distort the nature of the events it attempts to measure.

This chapter suggests that it is important not to lose sight of the complexity of the phenomenon of abuse. We aim to expand the research initiated by Macmillan and Gartner (1999), by examining what different forms of patterns of violence we can find using data from a nationally representative survey, conducted in Spain, which relied on the CTS2. In using the CTS2, we can classify respondents according to the degree to which they suffer different forms of abusive behaviour, as Macmillan and Garner did. We can also take into account the frequency with which these behaviours occur.

This chapter is necessarily technical and the general reader may find some of the discussion difficult to follow. Those untrained in quantitative techniques might want to skip most of the findings section, until the paragraph where we describe the composition of the three patterns of abuse that we identify in our data (see section 'Patterns of abusive behaviours').

Methods

Data and Measures

The data were obtained from the 1999 National Survey on Safety, Families and the Health of Spanish Women (for details, see Medina-Ariza and Barberet, 2003). This nationally representative, face-to-face survey (N=2,015) tried to combine the best elements from the domestic violence and violence against women approaches. The survey used several tools to assess the prevalence of intimate partner violence in urban Spain, but the data analysed in this chapter will rely primarily on those collected using the Spanish version of the CTS-2. All the analysis presented here refers to this dataset.

The data matrix collates the answers of 2,015 women who were asked about their exposure to different kinds of abuse. There are 31 variables (the conflict tactic scales that do not tap into abuse were excluded from the analysis and a couple of abusive items had to be excluded because of missing data), representing a number of situations (see Table 3.4 for a list of the items). Each of these variables allows seven scores (ordered by increasing periodicity), representing 'frequency of occurrence' of a given variable. The minimum score is 0 (no occurrence) and the maximum score is 6 (an act or range of acts repeated more than 20 times). In-between these two extremes, the CTS offers the following response options: the incident happened 2 times, it happened 3 to 5 times, it happened 5 to 10 times, or it happened more than 10 but less than 20 times.

Analytical Approach

Our primary goal is to use the CTS2 information collected to group the respondents in ways that better differentiate patterns of abuse and, thus, reflect in a more appropriate way the epidemiology of intimate partner violence in the general population. Macmillan and Gartner (1999) used a latent structure analysis approach primarily because the Canadian Violence Against Women Survey framed the response options to the questions about abusive acts as dichotomous, with valid responses 'yes' or 'no'. That approach only allowed these authors to estimate to what degree different abusive acts coexisted, when trying to establish their classification of patterns of abuse. The CTS2, on the other hand, seeks to estimate not only whether the acts take place or not, but also how frequently they take place.

Therefore, the amount of information collected is, in terms of the measurement scale, richer. Some have also argued that the CTS2 approach is also conducive to revelations of more abuse, particularly of a minor type. Because of the different nature of the measurement scale, we can use analytical techniques that take into account not only the coexistence of different acts of abuse, but also their frequency. This places us in the realm of clustering techniques.

The aim of clustering techniques is to group objects based on the commonality of characteristics they possess. Cluster analysis classifies objects (e.g., respondents) so that each object is very similar to others in the cluster with respect to some predetermined selection criterion. The resulting clusters should, if appropriate, exhibit high internal (within-cluster) homogeneity and high external (between-cluster) heterogeneity. The clustering is based on the set of variables that the researchers determine a priori. In our case, the cluster 'variates' are the scores for each of the abusive items in the CTS2, as described in Table 3.4. Cluster analysis is similar to factor analysis, but differs in that cluster analysis groups respondents, whereas factor analysis is primarily concerned with grouping variables.

We should be careful, however, when examining our results. Cluster analysis has important limitations. Hair et al (1998: 474) summarise these as follows:

> Cluster analysis can be characterised as descriptive, atheoretical and noninferential. Cluster analysis has no statistical basis upon which to draw statistical inferences from a sample to a population, and it is used primarily as an exploratory technique. The solutions are not unique, as the cluster membership for any number of solutions is dependent upon many elements of the procedure, and many different solutions can be obtained by varying one or more elements. Moreover, cluster analysis will always create clusters, regardless of the 'true' existence of any structure in the data. Finally, the cluster solution is totally dependent upon the variables used as the basis for the similarity measure.

It is perhaps too forced to think of clear types of patterns of abuse. Clustering techniques are, by definition, going to find different types. But the method may help us to examine with new eyes the degree to which the traditional CTS scoring methods produce an accurate representation of intimate partner violence.

Findings

K-Means analysis

As explained in the endnotes, we applied the K-means algorithm to our sample, giving as input 2 and 3 clusters. Solutions with more clusters were clearly inappropriate, as revealed by analysis not shown here.[1] Other clustering techniques, different from the K-means method, provided similar results. Table 3.1 presents the within-cluster sum of squares and the cluster sizes for a two-cluster and a three-cluster solution. The three-cluster solution shown in Table 3.1 adds a smaller group of 10 cases where, as we shall see later, a particularly high level of abuse was experienced.

Table 3.1 Within-cluster sum of squares and cluster size: K-means cluster solutions for a two-cluster and three-cluster solution (N=884)

Two cluster solution
Within-cluster sum of squares:
[1] 10587.80   7766.99
Cluster sizes:
[1] 783 101
Three cluster solution
Within-cluster sum of squares:
[1] 6139.069   1030.000   9084.565
Cluster sizes:
[1] 125 10 749

Source: 1999 National Survey on Safety, Families, and the Health of Spanish Women.

---

1   From this family of techniques, we present the results from using the *K-means* method. Alternative methods were employed (hierarchical, fuzzy, etc.), but the K-means seem to offer the best solutions. The K-means procedure takes as input the number of clusters that the sample is to be split into. This number of clusters could be based on some theory or preliminary analysis. Once this number is available, the K-means algorithm computes a 'centroid' for each group, that is, a vector in R^k (where k is the number of variables) equivalent to the unidimensional mean. Observations are then assigned to clusters by a Least Squares method. That is, the algorithm minimises the dispersion in the classification with respect to the centroids.

One of the problems of relying on cluster analysis is that one cannot employ straightforward objective selection procedures to decide how many clusters should be formed. Practical judgement, common sense, and theoretical foundations all play an important role in this process. Based on these types of considerations, the three-cluster solution seems more appropriate, since it better replicates previous research conducted by Macmillan and Gartner (1999) and makes more conceptual sense, once, as we do below, the characteristics of the members of each group are observed. We proceed now to describe these groups.

Developing an Understanding of the Clustering

We used principal component analysis to gain further insight into the nature of these clusters. Principal component analysis is a technique that allows researchers to reduce the number of observed variables to a smaller number of artificial variables (called principal components) that account for most of the variance in the observed variables. It is a useful technique when we have data in a number of variables and believe that there is some redundancy in those variables. By redundancy we mean that some of the variables are correlated with one another, possibly because they measure the same construct. Our analysis looks for possible dominance of one component over the others. If this were the case, the main variables involved in this component will be responsible for most of the variability in the sample. Any statistical method based on minimising the dispersion in the sample will be highly led by those variables. Consequently, this reasoning should apply to the K-means method, due to its 'dispersion' driven nature. In other words, we are simply trying to determine if a limited set of variables seems to be particularly relevant to understand the grouping in three clusters.

The screenplot in Figure 3.1 plots the eigenvalues against their indices $i=1, 2,...$ The height of each bar gives an idea of each component's relevance. Observe that the first ten components account for 84.5% of the total variance. If one applies Kaiser's criterion for relevance of components, only the first seven components are to be considered.[2] Two interesting

2   This is done by (1) squaring the standard deviation component of the principal components object to obtain the vector of eigenvalues, (2) taking the mean of the vector of eigenvalues, and (3) excluding those components with eigenvalues less than the mean. The mean, calculated in this way, equals 0.877. Only the first

features are inferred from the screeplot. Firstly, there is a dramatic break between component 1 and 2. This shows the relative importance of component number 1. Secondly, for components 2 onwards, the marginal contribution of each new component to the overall variance is fairly low. Thus, component 2 accounts for an increase of 11.2%, component 3 increases an additional 10.2%, and so on. These remaining components seem to contribute discretely to the variance, without a clear dominant factor existing among them. Therefore, we have clear evidence pointing to the key role played by component 1 when explaining the overall variability in the sample.

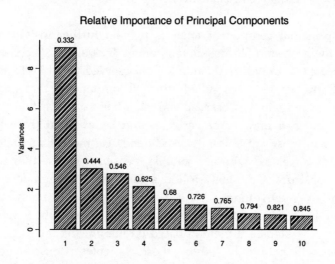

Figure 3.1   Eigen values of components from Principal Component Analysis (N=844)

Figure 3.2 is an *importance-of-components* plot. It gives information about what variables form each of the successive principal components. For the first component, variables CTSLY3, CTSLY18, CTSLY13, CTSLY34, CTSLY25, and CTSLY9 (see Table 3.4 for detailed interpretation of these labels) are the most important.

seven components exceed the mean, and therefore, only these seem to be statistically significant.

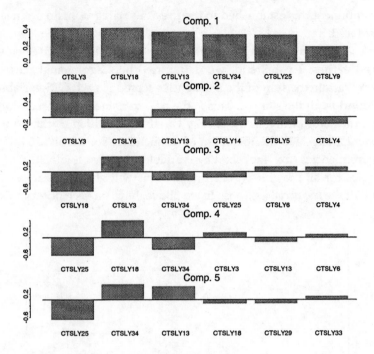

Figure 3.2   Importance-of-components-plot

The first row of results in this figure shows that these variables load more heavily in the first component. These variables all represent verbal forms of abuse, such as 'My partner shouted at me' or 'My partner did something to annoy me', with the exception of item CTSLY9, which refers to an item classified by Straus as minor physical abuse (e.g., pushing). This last item, as the first row of Figure 3.2 shows, is the lowest and therefore makes the smallest contribution of the six variables to the component. In sum, we can say that these six variables are largely responsible for the classification in 3 clusters in our sample, and we shall refer to them as the *key variables*.[3] The

---

3   For triangulation purposes, we employed a multinomial regression based on a Poisson distribution in order to find further evidence about the effect that each of the 31 variables has over observations' membership. The purpose was similar to the principal component analysis. For the likelihood function we allowed a discrepancy smaller than 0.00001. The variables CTSLY3 to CTSLY38 entered linearly in the regression equation. The details of the output can be provided on request. Given the sample size, the asymptotic values of the t-distribution were set as the benchmark to discriminate insignificant variables. It was clear from

other components, as established in the previous paragraph, do not need to be considered.

We use these last findings to examine the structure of the three clusters discussed earlier. To this end, we define two new aggregated variables. First we compute the sum of the frequencies scored in each CTS variable by each individual in the sample. This is the new variable *Suma*. Secondly, we calculate the contribution of the six key variables identified by the principal component analysis to the total sum of frequencies. So, we divide the sum of the frequencies for the six key variables by the total sum of the frequencies for all the abusive CTS items. This will give us an idea of the weight that the *key variables*, those listed above, have on each observation.[4]

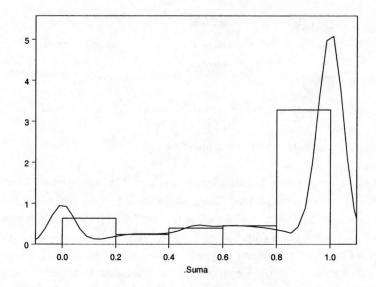

Figure 3.3a   Relative contribution of key variables to total frequency of abuse: Histogram and kernel estimator of cluster 1 (n=749)

---

the output that only CTSLY3, CTSLY18, CTSLY13, CTSLY34, CTSLY25, and CTSLY9 were significant variables. Not surprisingly, these six coincide with the six variables identified by means of principal component analysis.

4   A Kernel Density Estimator is then used to obtain the smooth of the relative weight of the six variables for each of the three groups identified in the cluster analysis. We use a Gaussian Kernel, and in order to select the bandwidth we use Biased Cross Validation.

Figure 3.3a represents the histogram and kernel estimator of the largest cluster (n=749). The X-axis represents the percentage of the total sum of frequencies due to the six key variables, whereas the Y-axis represents the percentage of women. As we move to the right in the X-axis, the relative contribution of the key variables in explaining the total frequency of abuse increases. The graph clearly shows that most of the women in this cluster tend to have, indeed, a high relative contribution of these variables in the overall frequency of abuse. One can see that women in this cluster are characterised by forms of abuse almost exclusively defined by the six variables defined as 'key' for the classification. The peak at 100% reaches 45% of the frequency, which means that the key variables explain all the abuse suffered by nearly 45% of the women in the sample. In other words, this group of women suffer almost exclusively verbal or minor forms of abuse.

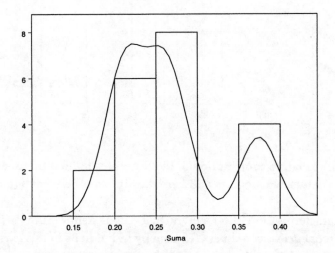

Figure 3.3b   Relative contribution of key variables to total frequency of abuse: Histogram and kernel estimator of cluster 2 (n=10)

The second cluster presented in Figure 3.3b is the smallest (n=10), and the women included in it experience a wide range of types of abuse with a high frequency. From the smooth, we see how the same key variables, mostly capturing the less severe forms of abuse, here only explain around 20%-30% of the women's abuse.

The last cluster in the classification is a more problematic one. The weight of the key variables is spread across the observations in the cluster. Although the six key variables play a significant role, this is not as major as in the first cluster. The percentage of women for whom the contribution of the six key variables to the total sum is somewhere between 50% and 70% is not dissimilar to the percentage of women for whom the contribution of the six key variables is somewhere between 70% and 90% (the last two columns to the right in the histogram in Figure 3.3c).

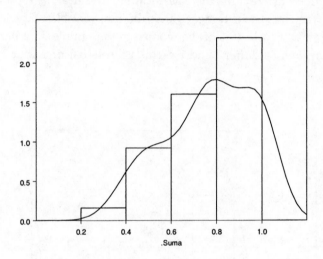

Figure 3.3c   Relative contribution of key variables to total frequency of abuse: Histogram and kernel estimator of cluster 3 (n=125)

We can characterise this cluster a bit further. Let us define 'Sum' as the sum of all the frequencies scored per CTS item by individuals in this cluster. Let 'Count' be a variety scale, measuring the number of variables that have been scored positively, in other words, the items of abuse the women experience. Finally, let 'Density' be the ratio of 'Sum' over 'Count', so that 'Density' is the average frequency of abuse. Women in this group score relatively high in Density, as would do women in the smallest cluster. However, whereas in the smallest cluster the high density is the product of high values of Count (variety of abusive behaviours) and high values of Sum (frequency of abusive behaviours), this high Density for cluster 3 is due to small values of Count together with small values of Sum.

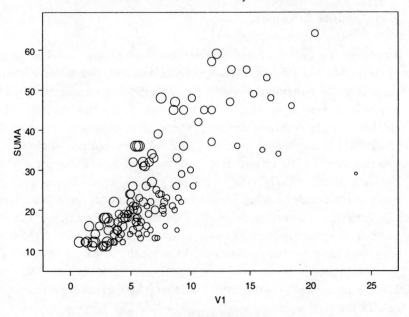

Figure 3.4   Bubble plot of variety and frequency of abusive behaviours for cluster 3 (N=125). V1=COUNT

To illustrate, Figure 3.4 presents a bubble plot where each circle represents one observation with centre at *COUNT=x* and *SUMA=y* for women in cluster 3 (N=125). The diameter of each circle corresponds to the value of Density, so the larger the diameter, the higher the density.[5] The bubble plot shows how women in this cluster score relatively low Count and relatively low Sum, with the exception of a few observations that could be considered as outliers for this group (mainly, those at the right of 15 counts). This could suggest some kind of specialisation in the forms of abuse characterising this cluster. The more extreme Counts suggest that there is a group of women who face a narrow range of forms of abuse, which are, however, repeated frequently.

---

5   We have added to each observation of COUNT a negligible random number, in order to avoid the overlapping of observations in the figure. This is a rather frequent technique when researchers have to plot graphs with discrete variables such as COUNT.

Patterns of Abusive Behaviours

In summary, the three clusters can be described as follows. The largest group, with 749 individuals, is composed of women who suffer a limited range of abusive behaviour, mostly psychological in nature, with a low frequency and repetition. The violence in this group may correspond to what Johnson calls 'common couple violence'. The second group, with 125 respondents, has women who exhibit a more severe pattern of abuse, not just psychological, with a more diverse range of abusive behaviours and a higher frequency. Finally, the smallest group, with 10 respondents, probably corresponds to what Johnson calls 'patriarchal terrorism'. These women suffer from a very wide range of abusive behaviour in the CTS and the pattern of repetition indicates very serious violence. If we add to these three clusters the group of women who do not suffer any form of abuse, the percentages in the sample would be distributed as shown in Table 3.2. Table 3.4 at page 52 shows the central tendency for each of the abusive acts in the CTS per cluster group.

Table 3.2 Different patterns of abuse based on the K-Means analysis (N=1965)

	Frequencies	*Percentages*
Categories of abuse		
No abuse	1081	53.6
Common couple abuse	749	37.2
Serious abuse	125	6.2
Patriarchal terrorism	10	0.5

Contrasting Groupings Based on Traditional CTS Scoring Rules and Those Based on Clustering Techniques

We now consider the prevalence of different types of abuse, as outlined by the traditional scoring rules of the CTS, among the three groups of abused respondents identified through the clustering techniques.

Table 3.3 clearly illustrates that our 'common couple violence' group comprises women who for the most part do suffer forms of psychological abuse and, to a considerably lesser extent, minor forms of other types of abuse. At the other extreme, the group that we defined as 'patriarchal terrorism' suffer all types of abuse defined by the CTS. Notably, all the women in this group consider themselves to be victims of abuse, as a self-perception subjective measure of abuse suggests.[6] Between these two groups lies an intermediate group, which we have called 'serious abuse'. All the women in this group suffered psychological abuse as defined by the CTS. In addition, a significant proportion of this psychological abuse is considered severe by CTS scoring rules. Another distinguishing feature of this group is that the psychological abuse often seems to be accompanied by forms of physical or sexual abuse.

Table 3.3 Types of abuse by cluster group

	Common couple violence	Serious abuse	Patriarchal terrorism
CTS psychological	89.5%	100.0%	100%
CTS psychological severe	23.0%	87.0%	100%
CTS physical	12.2%	38.8%	100%
CTS physical severe	7.3%	21.7%	100%
CTS sexual	20.8%	42.4%	100%
CTS sexual severe	8.6%	14.0%	100%
CTS injury	10.0%	19.2%	100%
CTS injury severe	3.5%	5.7%	100%
Self-definition as battered woman[7]	3.8%	30.3%	100%

6 As described in Medina-Ariza and Barberet (2003), we included a subjective measure of abuse in the self-administered component of the survey that included the CTS-2. At the end of the CTS, we asked the respondents whether 'they consider themselves to be victims of maltreatment' (approximate translation of the colloquial term employed in Spain to refer to women who suffer domestic abuse).

7 As described in Medina and Barberet (2003), we included a subjective measure of abuse in the self-administered component of the survey that included the CTS-2. At the end of the CTS, we asked the respondents whether 'they consider themselves to be victims of maltreatment' (approximate translation of the colloquial term employed in Spain to refer to women who suffer domestic abuse).

Table 3.4 Distribution of abusive acts per cluster group

	Common violence (N=749)	Serious abuse (N=125)	Patriarchal terrorism (N=10)
Partner insulted or swore (CTSLY3)	44% Never	37.3% 20 or more	40% 6-10 and 40% ≥ 20
Partner threw something that could hurt (CTSLY4)	95.1% Never	81.2% Never	50% 6-10 times
Partner twisted arm or hair (CTSLY5)	98.2% Never	88.1% Never	30% 3-5 and 30% 6-10 times
Had a sprain, bruise, or small cut (CTSLY6)	92.7% Never	85.3% Never	30% ≥ 20
Partner made her have sex without condom (CTSLY8)	95.3% Never	87.3% Never	22% 6-10 times
Partner pushed or shoved (CTSLY9)	96.4% Never	65.5% Never	30% 6-10 and 30% 11-20 times
Partner used force to make her have oral or anal sex (CTSLY10)	99.2% Never	100% Never	33.3% Never
Partner used a knife or gun (CTSLY11)	99.6% Never	100% Never	55.6% Never
Passed out from being hit on the head (CTSLY12)	98.5% Never	98.3% Never	30% Never
My partner called me fat or ugly (CTSLY13)	85.0% Never	28.7% Never	40% > 20
My partner punched me or hit me with something that could hurt (CTSLY14)	97.1% Never	87.3% Never	40% 3-5 times
My partner destroyed something belonging to me (CTSLY15)	92.0% Never	61.7% Never	40% > 20
I went to a doctor because of a fight with my partner (CTSLY16)	99.5% Never	96.6% Never	37.5% 3-5 times
My partner choked me (CTSLY17)	98.5% Never	93.2% Never	44% > 20
My partner shouted or yelled at me (CTSLY18)	57.5% Never	16.7% Never	70% > 20
My partner slammed me against a wall (CTSLY19)	98.1% Never	82.0% Never	30% 6-10 times
I needed to see a doctor because of a fight with my partner, but I didn't (CTSLY21)	98.7% Never	97.5% Never	22% 2 times
My partner beat me up (CTSLY22)	99.2% Never	93.3% Never	33% > 20
My partner grabbed me (CTSLY23)	97.7% Never	78% Never	40% 6-10 times
My partner used force to make me have sex (CTSLY24)	99.9% Never	96.7% Never	30% Never
My partner stomped out of the room during a disagreement (CTSLY25)	69.0% Never	22.9% 20 or more times	22% 11-20 times
My partner insisted on sex when I did not want to (CTSLY26)	91.4% Never	70% Never	20% categories > 3 times

My partner slapped me (CTSLY27)	98.1% Never	82.5% Never	33% 6-10 times
I had a broken bone from a fight with my partner (CTSLY28)	98.9% Never	99.2% Never	50% Never
My partner used threats to make me have oral or anal sex (CTSLY29)	93.0% Never	90.9% Never	Various with 20%
My partner scalded or burned me on purpose (CTSLY31)	97.3% Never	99.2% Never	77.8% Never
My partner insisted on having oral or anal sex (CTSLY32)	96.6% Never	92.35 Never	40% Never
My partner accused me of being a lousy lover (CTSLY33)	95.9% Never	66.1% Never	30% 3-5 times
My partner did something to annoy me (CTSLY34)	74.6% Never	25.8% 3-5 times	30%11-20 and 30% ≥ 20
My partner threatened to hit or throw something at me (CTSLY35)	97.3% Never	73.3% Never	30% 6-10 and 30% ≥ 20
I felt physical pain the day after a fight with my partner (CTSLY36)	99.6% Never	91.7% Never	30% 6-10
My partner kicked me (CTSLY37)	99.5% Never	94.2% Never	30% 3-5 and 30% 6-10
My partner used threats to make me have sex (CTSLY38)	98.4% Never	93.4% Never	30% 3-5 times

Note: two items, which were excluded from the clustering analysis because of missing data, are included in this table for descriptive purposes.

There is another way of looking at the relationship between the CTS classifications and the clustering groupings. Previously, we have been able to ascertain the prevalence of different forms of abuse across the three clusters identified. But one of the main arguments presented in this chapter is that a clustering approach, which takes into account the range and frequency of the abuse, is a more appropriate way of establishing the severity of abuse than that allowed for by the scoring rules of the CTS. The following table shows how our three clusters contribute to different types of abuse, as classified by these CTS-scoring rules.

Table 3.5 shows very clearly that although the CTS scoring methods correctly identify as serious the abuse experienced by the patriarchal terrorism group (as we saw in Table 3.3), all the groups based on the CTS scoring rules, even the groups classed as suffering serious abuse, are dominated by respondents whom the clustering methods consider to be less severely abused, once we control for the range or variety of abuse and the frequency of the abuse. For example, 57.4% of women who suffer, according to the CTS, physically severe abuse, correspond to the group that we have classed as common couple violence. The women within the common couple violence category who suffer these forms of abuse are a minority within this group (7.3% for severe physical abuse as we saw in Table 3.3), but they still dominate the CTS classification. In other words, the CTS traditional severity scoring rules do not clearly distinguish between women who suffer a wide range of serious abusive acts very frequently and those who suffer predominantly a very narrow range of minor abusive acts with a low pattern of repetition. To the degree that the pattern of repetition and the range of the abuse are fundamental dimensions of the severity of abuse, the labels employed in the CTS scales are misleading when they classify respondents as victims of severe abuse.

Table 3.5 Types of abuse by CTS-scales

	Common couple violence	Serious abuse	Patriarchal terrorism
CTS psychological	80.0%	15.1%	1.2%
CTS psychological severe	58.4%	35.9%	3.4%
CTS physical	58.2%	30.7%	6.5%
CTS physical severe	57.4%	27.7%	10.6%
CTS sexual	68.9%	22.8%	4.6%
CTS sexual severe	68.5%	18.5%	10.9%
CTS injury	66.4%	20.9%	9.1%
CTS injury severe	60.5%	16.3%	18.6%
Self-definition as battered woman	31.4%	41.9%	11.6%

It seems also clear from this analysis that a small section of the respondents, who do not suffer a wide range of abusive behaviour and do not suffer repeated abuse, do report experiences of acts that the CTS classifies as serious. It could be that some of these cases, in time, would transform into more serious patterns of abuse. It could be that these cases of more localised, less repeated, but nonetheless severe abuse exist in relationships where control is established through other, less explicit means. Further research of a longitudinal nature is needed to develop an understanding of these cases. What these cases show in any case is that neither the CTS classifying nor an alternative clustering approach can convincingly produce a clean system to order the heterogeneous experiences of these women. Labels such as 'severe' or 'minor' abuse should therefore always be used with a great deal of caution.

Conclusions

We believe it is necessary to take a more refined approach to the measurement of intimate partner violence than that suggested by the traditional scoring rules of the CTS. The analysis in this chapter shows that the use of additional criteria of severity, such as the range of abusive behaviour and its reoccurrence in time, produces different classification schemes to those produced by the CTS scoring rules. This has implications for theory and for policy. From a theoretical point of view, the risk factor analysis models that one can build may vary significantly, depending on how one defines the dependent variable. Macmillan and Gartner's (1999) research suggests that the risk factors for women who experience abuse of different severity are slightly different, with the less serious violent group becoming the most difficult to predict. A contested risk factor for domestic abuse is gender. Some researchers argue, based on studies that have relied on the CTS, that a high degree of gender symmetry on domestic abuse exists. Other researchers are highly critical of this conclusion. It could be that the appropriate consideration of the severity of the abuse implicit in the CTS scoring rules could be artificially producing the findings of gender symmetry. We are in the process of replicating our clustering approach with Straus 1985 data, to ascertain the issue of gender symmetry when this more refined approach is taken.

But this clustering approach also has implications for policy and allocation of resources. Because of the way that intimate partner violence has been constructed as a social problem in the media, people often think of the worst-case scenario when the term 'wife abuse' is employed. Politicians confronted with survey figures are often under the impression that these prevalence figures represent 'worst-case' patriarchal terrorism scenarios. However, these cases, as we have seen, are a minority of the instances of intimate partner abuse measured by surveys. This is not to say that intimate partner abuse is not a serious social problem or that those less severe forms of intimate partner abuse do not constitute a social problem requiring a serious health, social and criminal justice response. Sustained psychological abuse, on its own, can have devastating consequences for the lives of the women who suffer from it. But it is likely to be the case that the needs of women who suffer different type of abuse patterns may also be different. It is, therefore, important to develop more sophisticated measurement strategies that can adequately estimate these different needs.

Some have argued that, despite its limitations, the CTS2 is probably an adequate surveillance instrument for intimate partner aggression, which can be used with samples of the general population (Gordon, 2000). It has also been argued, however, that the CTS2 is 'probably not adequate for capturing more serious abuse and violence because they do not assess the full range and patterning of severely physically and psychologically abusive and controlling behaviour characteristic of more severely violent couples' (Gordon, 2000). Walby and Myhill (2001), in addition, have suggested that the sampling procedures employed in most intimate partner violence surveys are likely to under-represent the worst-case scenarios, given the exclusion of high-risk groups (e.g., women in shelters, homeless women, incarcerated women, etc). Our analysis clearly points in that direction since, once we take into account the frequency and co-existence of different forms of abuse, the group that we could refer to as victims of serious abuse shrinks somehow.

A word of caution is needed about the conclusiveness of our findings regarding the existence of different types of abuse. As we stated earlier, there are important limitations to cluster analysis, and for these reasons it is important to interpret our findings with caution. What our study shows, however, is that once we try to develop types that take into account two important dimensions of severity (frequency and co-occurrence of various types of abusive behaviours), the resulting classifications are different from the ones obtained by using the traditional scoring rules of the CTS. This suggests that such scoring rules do not appropriately capture the severity of abuse as measured by the co-occurrence of different forms of abuse and the frequency of the abuse. Also, our findings suggest that the prevalence figures based on the CTS or, for that matter, on victimisation measures are, at the end of the day, social constructions that depend heavily on the methods employed to obtain them. They should never be taken as exact accurate representations of the prevalence of this phenomenon, but rather as gross approximations, often open to improvement. It is our contention that measures that most appropriately reflect the severity of the abuse, the co-occurrence of different forms of abuse, its frequency and its longitudinal dynamic will provide a better approximation for policy-making purposes and for theoretical development. Certainly, more research is needed to arrive at better measures, rather than taking for granted that the existing measures are the best possible. In this sense, a potential development in measuring victimisation of violence would be the adaptation of the life-

calendar methods that some criminologists are using to better represent the dynamics of chronic offending.

References

Archer, J. (2000). Sex Differences in Aggression Between Heterosexual Partners: A Meta-Analytic Review. *Psychological Bulletin, 126*(5).

Dobash, R.P. and R. Emerson Dobash (2004). Women's violence to men in intimate relationships: Working on a puzzle. *British Journal of Criminology, 44,*3: 324-349.

Dobash, R.P., R. Emerson Dobash, Margo Wilson and Martin Daly (1992). The Myth of Sexual Simmetry in Marital Violence. *Social Problems* 39(1): 71-91.

Gondolf, E.W. and A.K. Beeman (2003). Women's Accounts of Domestic Violence Versus Tactics-Based Outcome Categories. *Violence Against Women.* 9(3): 278-301.

Gordon, M. (2000). Definitional Issues in Violence Against Women. Surveillance and Research from a Violence Research Perspective. *Violence Against Women* 6(7): 747-783.

Hair, J., R. Anderson, R. Tatham and W. Black (1998). *Multivariate Data Analysis.* 4th Ed. London: Prentice-Hall.

Johnson, M.P. (1995). Patriarchal Terrorism and Common Couple Violence: Two Forms of Violence against Women. *Journal of Marriage and the Family* 57(2): 283-294.

Macmillan, R. and R. Gartner (1999). When She Brings Home the Bacon: Labor-Force Participation and the Risk of Spousal Violence against Women. *Journal of Marriage and the Family* 61(4): 947-958.

Medina-Ariza, J.J. and R. Barberet (2003). Intimate partner violence in Spain. *Violence Against Women* 9(3): 302-322.

Moffitt, T., R. Robins, and A. Caspi (2001). A Couple's Analysis of Partner Abuse with Implications for Abuse Prevention Policy. *Criminology and Public Policy* 1(1): 5-36.

Straus, M. (1993). Physical Assault by Wives: A Major Social Problem. In Richard Gelles and Donileen Loseke (Eds.). *Current Controversies on Family Violence.* Newbury Park, CA: Sage.

Walby, S. and A. Myhill (2001). New Survey Methodologies in Researching Violence Against Women. *British Journal of Criminology* 41(3): 502-522.

Chapter 4

Violence Against Women in France and Issues of Ethnicity

Stéphanie Condon

Introduction

Feminist and women's studies have tended to leave aside cultural and social differences in women's experiences, the universality of male domination being upheld. For this and other reasons, there has a been a wide resistance to a culturalist perspective of gender relations. This has been the case in the study of violence against women, although recent local-level and national-level studies across the globe have suggested contexts in which women are more exposed to violence than others (Population Reports, 1999; Watts et al., 1999). These contexts may be as much political (armed conflict, civil war) as cultural (norms restricting women's partner choice, those imposing male authority in the home etc.). Emigration presents contexts in which women may either be protected from or more at risk of violence (Shah and Menon, 1997).

Statistical studies of violence against women in ethnic minorities in Europe are of course rare, as are national level studies enabling us to situate experiences of such groups (Hagemann-White, 2002). Accounts of violence revealed in anthropological studies or local monographs on migration are analysed in relation to the societies in which these women – or their mothers – spent their childhood and youth and to often traditional values that remain intact after migration to more modern societies. These values, and their impact on women's lives, are seen as an obstacle to social integration in the 'host society'. Thus differences in levels of fertility, in labour market participation and so on between migrant groups or ethnic minorities and the general population have been explained in terms of the maintenance or loss of such values. In the case of violence against women, few data sources have been available in order for such comparisons to be made.

Generally, in Europe and North America, it is upheld that there is little regional variation in intimate partner violence. Media reports and declarations made by some women's associations tend to suggest that in some areas of France social deprivation and social exclusion combines with gender and ethnicity to increase the risk of interpersonal violence.[1] Accounts of sexist and sexual violence experienced by young, and often adolescent women reveal a heightened vulnerability of these groups. The issue of the status of women from ethnic communities has been brought to the fore further still by renewed debate on the Islamic veil. This controversy[2] is revealing with regard to representations of the status of women in the Muslim religion, but is also revealing about the contradictions in the French political arena and in the state's institutions on how to deal with identity politics, in particular with public expression of religious identity, as well as with processes of discrimination and social and gender inequality. These debates are however largely detached from recent ones surrounding violence against women in France, which has focused on the cohabiting couple.

In France, very few studies of immigration take on board the theme of family violence suffered by migrants. Most accounts of experiences are related by women's associations giving support to victims. Apart from rare specific studies as that on the experiences of Turkish women (Petek-Salom, 1997) or young women of North African origin (Poinsot, 2001), most references to violence within the couple or the family have been made in studies of particular groups of women immigrants (for example, Nicollet, 1992). Women in couples where the partner is of the same origin are assumed to be subjected to the same patriarchal relations and traditional values as in the country of origin. Moves toward emancipation, for example, making of friends outside the family circle, joining an association,

---

1   *Ni putes ni soumises* (Neither whores nor submissive women) is the name that has been given to the movement in protest against two images of immigrant women and their descendants ; the former, by dressing as most young women of their age group and participating in social activities, the latter, stereotyped view of these women being dominated – and accepting this domination – by husbands and fathers. The former representation   is a product of local community, the latter, the outsider view.

2   Le Monde, 14th October 2003, item on front page and several articles focusing on the fifteen schoolgirls in Aubervilliers (suburb in northern Paris) who went to class dressed in veil.

taking a regular job, may be seen by the partner or other members of the family as threatening to these values and to the position of the husband in the couple and the household. Similarly, young women who migrated during childhood or who are born in France, having parents born in the same regions, are often subjected to restrictions based on such values, with frequent examples of forced marriage, forced return to the country of their parents, family violence resulting from intergenerational conflict. However, not all immigrant women in couples have partners from the same village or region. Women who migrated alone or have been divorced or widowed often have a partner born in France. Such 'intermarriage' has long been considered as an indicator of integration into the society of immigration. Yet as Michèle Tribalat has shown, there are high divorce rates in such couples (Tribalat, 1996). Situations of violence may precede these cases of divorce. A principal question we must ask is whether such immigrant women consider themselves victims of violence and if they do, whether they report the violence endured.

To explore such issues we now have the results of the French national survey on violence against women (Enveff) conducted in 2000. This survey, which reached 6970 women aged 20-59 years, included questions on account nationality of origin and country of birth of respondents and also of their parents. The Enveff sample in effect represented the principal immigrant groups in France. However, many of the most socially isolated, and possibly most vulnerable women would not have been reached by the survey. The method used, based on a telephone survey (see Appendix I), implied not only residence in an ordinary household enabling access to a fixed telephone but sufficient command of the French language. Bearing in mind this limitation, the results are very interesting and indicative of social situations in which women may suffer violence: public spaces, work, intimate partner relationships, the family circle. For the purpose of this chapter, we will focus on intimate partner relationships. Before analysing intimate partner violence reported by immigrant women or women of the second generation, we will summarise the general results of the Enveff survey.

Measurement of Self-Reported Intimate Partner Violence

The General Results of the Enveff Survey

Analysis of the data on violence reported over the twelve months[3] preceding the survey validated the approach by context (Appendices I and II). The types of violent acts and their meaning to individuals vary and are linked to social relations in each particular context (Appendices II and III). We will present first of all the overall results by context before examining in more detail intimate partner violence experienced by women in France.

Before presenting the results, it is necessary to explain how the indicators were constructed. A single instance of physical or sexual assault is sufficient to identify it as an act of violence. However, in other types of abuse, such as insults, denigration, contempt, control and other forms of emotional abuse or psychological pressure, the situation of domination results from an accumulation of events which, if taken separately, might seem quite trivial. Thus in order to establish a scale of these forms of abuse, the indicators had to combine both a measure of frequency and the nature of the events.

The most striking result appearing from Table 4.1 is that in each life context, whatever the type of violence concerned, young women in the 20-24 age group are those who claim to have been subjected to the most violence (Table 4.1). It is within intimate partner relationships that highest levels of physical violence was found to occur and also most psychological pressure, whereas sexual violence is reported more often in contexts outside the home. Public space is revealed to be a context in which verbal abuse is very frequent.

---

3   The last section of the questionnaire investigated experiences of violence during the whole of adult life (physical violence) or since childhood (sexual violence); see Jaspard M. and the Enveff research team (2003).

Table 4.1 Proportion of women reporting acts of verbal, psychological, physical or sexual violence over the preceding 12 months, by life context and age (in percentage of respondents in each age group)

Age group	20-24 yrs	25-34 yrs	35-44 yrs	45-59 yrs	Total
Type of violence					
In public areas	n = 717	n = 1934	n = 2122	n = 2197	n = 6970
Verbal abuse, threats	24.6	15.2	11.7	8.6	13.2
Physical assault	2.7	1.6	1.2	1.7	1.7
Sexual advances, assault, rape	6.4	2.6	0.9	0.5	1.9
In the workplace	n = 336	n = 1410	n = 1593	n = 1411	n = 4756
Verbal abuse, threats	11.7	10.1	8.8	6.2	8.5
Psychological pressure	20.2	18.6	15.2	15.7	16.7
of which emotional harassment	5.2	4.7	3.6	3.1	3.9
Physical assault	0.6	0.6	0.7	0.5	0.6
Sexual advances, assault, rape	4.3	2.8	1.9	0.8	2.0
Intimate partner*	n = 464	n = 1707	n = 1872	n = 1865	n = 5908
Verbal abuse, threats	6.1	4.1	4.3	3.9	4.2
Emotional blackmail	2.7	1.4	2.3	1.6	1.8
Psychological pressure	37.6	26.1	23.0	21.0	24.3
of which emotional harassment	12.1	8.3	7.7	6.7	7.9
Physical assault	3.9	2.5	2.5	2.2	2.5
Rape or other forced sexual acts	1.2	0.9	1.0	0.6	0.9

* Violence experienced by women in a couple, living with or apart from partner during previous 12 months. *Source*: National Survey on Violence Against Women in France (Enveff), 2000.

Intimate Partner Violence: General Results

The Enveff survey used a broader definition of the couple than that restricted to the domestic context. We studied women living as a couple, whether the couple has legal status or not, whether the partners cohabit or live apart. Of the 6970 interviewees in the sample, 5908 women were in such relationships. A minority of these (115) had separated during the previous year and these women have experienced a level of violence three to four times higher than all women in couples: for example, 27.3% reported psychological harassment as compared with 7.3% of women still with their partner at the time of the survey and 6.9% reported repeated physical violence as against 1.3% of the latter group (Jaspard et al., 2003, p. 61). In addition to continuation of acts of violence subsequent to the separation, these higher rates demonstrate that increasing numbers of women are managing to escape violent situations.

A global indicator of 'violent situations' was constructed (global rate) and subdivided into two 'levels' (A and B) so as to show the progression in the seriousness of situations. The 'serious' level (A) mainly corresponds to psychological violence (see Appendix III for list of items). The 'very serious' level (Level B) refers to an accumulation of acts of violence; in this case physical and sexual violence are more frequent, are repeated or associated with verbal insults and emotional harassment (2.7% of women). Whilst deconstruction of various elements of the indicator was deemed necessary to understand the different forms, it is recognised that distinguishing different types of intimate partner violence is not pertinent in analysis of mechanisms as different forms are intertwined (Brown and Jaspard, 2001).

At older ages the proportion of 'serious' violent situations declines, which seems linked more to a decline in emotional harassment. However, 'very serious' situations are encountered at all ages. Married women, and more generally those who live with their partners, report around a third fewer acts of violence than women in a partner relationship who do not share the same dwelling, 2.2% women living with their partner report 'very serious' violence as compared with 13% (Jaspard et al., 2003, p. 65). However the age factor may combine with this characteristic, as women in this group are generally younger.

The frequency of such violent situations was not found to be affected by the presence of children or by the length of the partner relationship. There is not necessarily an escalation of violence over time: situations of accumulated acts of violence may be triggered off very early and last a long time, in a cycle of violence. On the other hand, situations of emotional harassment may occur during a whole lifetime without evolving towards physical or sexual aggression.

A significant amount of variation in levels of reported violence is observed from one socio-economic group to another (Table 4.2).

Table 4.2 **Proportion of women living as a couple and in a situation of domestic violence, according to socio-occupational category of women and form of violence experienced (as percentage of women in each category)**

| | | | of which | |
Occupational and employment status of female respondent	*Number of women*	*Global rate in category*	*Serious violence (Level A)*	*Very serious violence (Level B)*
Farmers, craftswomen, trades women, small business owners	131	7.7	6.6	1.1
Senior management, higher intellectual professions	425	8.7	6.1	2.6
Middle management, middle-level professions	1189	8.3	6.8	1.5
Clerical, sales or service staff	1726	8.3	6.3	2.0
Industrial or other manual workers	311	7.9	4.6	3.3
Unemployed	489	11.9	9.0	2.9
Students	176	11.1	9.8	1.3
Other women not in employment	1346	9.4	6.3	3.1
Total number with intimate partner	5793	9.0	6.7	2.3

Unemployed women and students report the highest overall level of violence (over 11%). However, there are twice as many unemployed women as there are students reporting a 'very serious' situation of violence (2.9% compared with 1.3%), a proportion similar to women in the blue collar workers group (approximately 3%), and, perhaps unexpectedly, also to women in the managerial and senior executive social group (2.6%). Sensitivity to acts of violence differs from one socio-economic group to another, being apparently higher amongst more qualified social groups.

However, whilst this phenomenon is certainly perceptible in the 'serious' level in which emotional harassment is a relatively important component, it has hardly any impact in situations of accumulated acts of violence. This result confirms that serious domestic violence concerns all social categories.

Although such violence does not increase as one moves 'down' the social scale, high occupational instability and withdrawal from the labour market seem to foster the emergence of situations of accumulated violence (Table 4.2). Job instability among men has an even greater impact on violence within the partner relationship (Jaspard et al., 2003, pp. 70-74). This occurs very frequently among the unemployed who do not receive unemployment benefit (16%, of which 8% are 'very serious' violent situations) or others who do not work, no doubt linked to their reaction towards exclusion from the labour market. For either of the partners, having experienced just one period of unemployment increases relatively little the development of situations of violence within the partner relationship. On the other hand having experienced several periods of unemployment doubles the overall proportion of violent situations and triples that of 'very serious' violence. Although the perpetration of violence within intimate partner relationships seems not to be related to the woman's level of education, when the partner has a lower level of education this seems to increase the woman's exposure to the risk of violence (Brown and Jaspard, 2001).

Investigation into a Possible Ethnic Dimension in Intimate Partner Violence

During analysis of the Enveff survey, an effort was made to broaden the scope beyond the major groups resulting from the post-colonial labour migrations and to attempt to take into account experiences of other migrant women. 'Migration' was hypothesised to play a role in the risk of experiencing violent acts. Whilst building of categories is necessary to proceed with statistical analysis, the intention is not of course to create fixed boundaries between groups. On the contrary, constant attention was given in the initial publication to highlighting social and economic diversity within each subgroup, diversity resulting from different periods of immigration, age and family status on migration, education, social background, area of residence, household circumstances (Jaspard et al., 2003, pp. 181-187). In each of the life contexts studied in the survey, work, public space, couple, family, these characteristics play a more or less important role in the risk of experiencing violence. Given the relatively small numbers representing some migrant populations, it was necessary to regroup subpopulations in order to conduct statistical analysis. Factor analysis was used to statistically validate groups of migrant women.

Immigrant Women and Intimate Partner Violence

The majority of foreign-born immigrant women were living with their partner at the time of the survey.[4] The survey found that foreign-born immigrant women more frequently reported situations of intimate partner violence than other women (Table 4.3).

Table 4.3 Proportions of immigrant women in couples reporting intimate partner violence over the previous twelve months

Reported IPV	Country and nationality of origin						
	North Africa	Other Africa*	Italy, Spain, Portugal	Other Europe or North America	Other countries	Overseas territories	Rest of sample
Overall rate	12.8	(36.2)	10.5	16.9	12.8	7.2	8.7
Serious violence (A)	11.6	(27.4)	8.8	14.4	4.5	1.7	6.4
Very serious violence (B)	1.2	(8.9)	1.8	2.5	8.3	5.5	2.3
Total number	81	22	125	74	36	39	5416

* The very small numbers of Sub-Saharan African concerned do not allow measurement of statistical significance of the results, so percentages are presented in brackets. However, contrary to the first publication of the results (Jaspard et al., 2003), these women are detached from the North African group in order to indicate the nonetheless high rates of reporting (grouping together produced an overall rate of 19.3 for all women from the African continent).

---

4 Similar to non-immigrant women, only one-fifth of women of European or North Africa did not live under the same roof, and only 15% of women from Italy or the Iberian peninsula, whereas 42% of women from the Caribbean or other overseas territories lived apart from their partner and 30% of women from Africa or the rest of the world. This was one of the aspects of differentiation amongst immigrant women living in a couple (Jaspard et al., 2003, p. 200).

Women from the Other Europe/North America group and from Sub-Saharan Africa more often experience 'serious' partner relationship violence (Level A) and, along with women from North Africa, they report twice as much emotional harassment than other women. Although small numbers were interviewed, the group including women mainly from South America and Asia (category 'other countries') experienced significantly higher rates of 'very serious' violence (Level B). Whilst these results are linked to the demographic characteristics of these groups, notably age and marital or family status, they also depend on other criteria such as social isolation, economic hardship and conflict between different sets of cultural norms and values.

Various phenomena influence social perceptions of male and female roles within couples, and more generally the social representations of women. Aspects of the upbringing and education of women and men, such as the society in which they grew up, religion and so on, shape these representations. For example, religion often structures gender relations, setting a moral code by which men and women are expected to live. Two questions in the survey explored the religious aspects of women's lives. For the majority of women who said that they were brought up in a religion, this concerned the Catholic or Protestant religions (three-fifths) but only 40% of these said that religion currently plays an important part in their lives. The remainder brought up in another religion – mainly Muslim – said that generally religion was important: 86% of Muslim women, 72% of Jewish women. Social differences did not diminish this distribution, indicating the stronger influence of these religions as a spiritual or cultural dimension of their daily lives. It is among foreign immigrant women that the highest proportions of women who give importance to religion are to be found, this proportion being 83% among women from North Africa and for two thirds of women from other African countries or the French overseas territories. Although numbers are too small to conduct statistical analysis on this aspect, a strong relationship is indicated between situations of 'very serious' violence and a high importance of religion in the everyday lives of these immigrant women, and this whatever the religion considered. For the whole sample, including non-immigrants, 5% of women for whom religion was very important reported 'serious' violence as compared with 2% of those for whom it had little or no importance (Jaspard et al., 2003, p. 76). This said, it must be reminded that the survey does not provide information on the religious upbringing or beliefs of the partner.

An important result to note is that, whatever the indicator is considered, situations of violence are as frequent among mixed couples as among those of the same origin. Representations of the 'immigrant family' suppose that the majority of women have partners of the same origin. This is far from general in some migrations or in more recent flows. Many women from Spain and Portugal migrated alone, as have numerous women from other European countries, South America and Africa, and formed a couple with a partner born in France (or from another country), as have women who migrated during childhood. As mentioned earlier, the results of the 1992 immigration survey (Tribalat, 1996) revealed higher divorce rates amongst mixed couples. However, numbers in the survey were too small to pursue the investigation further and this theme needs to be addressed in an in depth study.

Intimate Partner Violence Reported by Women of North African Parentage

We now turn our attention to women born in France whose parents were born in North Africa. These women constitute the largest group of 'second generation' with immigrant parents in France and numbers in the survey allowed analysis of their experience of violence.

Whilst most immigrant women in intimate partner relationships live under the same roof as their partner – and are mostly married – a fair proportion of younger women of the 'second generation' still live with their parents, or otherwise live alone. Women living with their parents spend time with their partners mostly outside a home environment; those living alone however may live some of the time with their partner. For women who are 'second generation' immigrants, with parents from North Africa, the global indicator of partner relationship violence is doubled, this high rate is mainly due to situations of 'very serious' violence (see Table 4.4). No difference was found between women who had partners of the same origin as themselves and the other women in this group. Over half these women continued education beyond the age of 18, a considerable proportion are full-time students (11%), one quarter are unemployed, each of these characteristics placing them in the groups reporting the most violence. Although numbers are too small to measure the statistical significance of the results, reporting of 'very serious' intimate partner violence was very often by women still living with their parents and by those who are unemployed, whereas 'serious' violence is reported mostly by women living with their partners and by women in employment. Looking again at the influence of religion, about two-thirds (68%) of all North African origin women were brought up in a religion (55% as Muslims). However, most (82%) of the North African origin women having an intimate partner relationship and brought up in the Muslim religion say that religion plays an important or very important role in their everyday life. In the case of this group, analyses of the relationship between attitudes to religion and having experienced intimate partner violence did not give any conclusive results.

Table 4.4   Women of North African parentage* born in France reporting intimate partner violence (%)

		Reported violence		
	Global rate	Serious	Very serious	Total women
20-34 years	12.6	6.2	6.4	54
All ages	17.1	6.5	10.7	77
Whole sample	9.0	6.7	2.3	5793

* Women born in France with both parents born in North Africa (who were of Moroccan, Algerian or Tunisian nationality at birth).

Reporting of Violent Experiences to the Police or Other Persons

In general, women report when the violent act is of a physical nature in public spaces or at work: nine-tenths of women interviewed said that they had spoken to someone about the incident soon afterwards (Jaspard et al., 2003, chapter 11). Having done so increases the likelihood of an official report to the police. However, with regard to intimate partner violence, only about half the women (55%) had spoken of it to someone. There is some evidence of reporting of 'serious' violence but official complaints are rarely made. It is mainly women who report 'very serious' violence who engaged legal proceedings. Of course, numbers of immigrant women interviewed who had experienced intimate partner violence are relatively small, but investigation into the extent of talking about or officially reporting incidents revealed that women from North Africa, from Southern European (Latin) countries and women from the North African second generation spoke to someone about experiences but very rarely went to the police.

A number of factors specific to women from immigrant groups may explain the low rate of reporting to the police. Fear of consequences when partner and his relatives learn of her having laid a complaint, fear of extradition of their partner or a more general fear or suspicion towards the police force owing to experiences prior to migration in the country of origin. Another reason for not denouncing a male partner can be the result of not wanting to further justify racist behaviour by the police to men from one's own ethnic group, as Amina Mama described for the case of Afro-Caribbean men in Britain (Mama, 1993). Women may also feel that they will not be taken seriously, even less seriously than other women in France given the attitude of many institutions to immigrants. They may anticipate such institutional racism, as well as an individual racist attitude of the person at the reception desk in the police station. From the point of view of the police force, attitudes may be ambivalent. Representations exist of cultures in which family relations are violent and cultures in which the status of women is particularly low. Reactions to reports may then range from ignoring the incident on the grounds that the police officer considers it a private affair, private within the ethnic group as well as the woman's family, to a xenophobic or racist reaction leading to a desire to prosecute the immigrant man accused of violence. Research exploring this issue in detail is necessary.

Discussion

Intimate partner violence experienced by immigrant women and their daughters in France is the result of processes and mechanisms common in the general population, as well as a number of other factors. Migrant women are more exposed to the risk of certain forms of violence as a result of migration: distance from close family, often difficult material living conditions in France, vulnerability linked to citizenship status. In addition, conflicting attitudes within the family on the preservation of norms and values from the society of origin and the desire of women to negotiate change lead to tensions and sometimes violence. Attitudes to religion are linked to higher than average rates of violence reported by these women as well as by women from the second generation.

The fact that women from ethnic minorities reported experiences of violence to the survey indicates that they recognise certain acts, words and physical contact as abnormal, an affront to their dignity, a threat to their autonomy. They thus reported violence as least as often as the rest of the women interviewed. Furthermore, many women in this population relate to the positive image of the young women of North African parentage who demand recognition of their rights as individuals and stake their claim to a place in French society whilst at the same time defending their North African roots. Their agendas include the issue of violence against women. These collective demands have been joined more recently by those of women of Turkish or West African parentage. Locally based migrant women's associations too have become more visible. In such a social context, women are likely to want to denounce violent situations and not hide them. Detailed studies within specific groups are necessary to investigate experiences and examine which women are more at risk. Such studies would also be able to cover types of women not reached by the Enveff survey: recent migrants, women who do not speak French and so on.

As shown for the whole of the population, some social contexts prove fertile ground for stress and violence; for example unemployment of either partner or, for women, leaving the labour market leads to relationship adjustments in which partners who culturally are accustomed to a position of authority feel threatened. Women in such situations appear more vulnerable, despite actively trying to maintain a position of independence.

The general results for all women in France show that such experiences of violence are reported as much by women not living with their partner as those cohabiting. They also show that women who have recently left their partners are those who have experienced most violence; revealing a process by which women are managing to escape situations of intimate partner violence. Younger women appear to be more vulnerable to acts of violence. At the same time, this surely reflects their resistance of domination, acceptance of confrontations with their partner in order to maintain their autonomy and also their readiness to report violence.

Appendix I Background to the Enquête National Sur Les Violences Envers Les Femmes en France (Enveff)

1. The need for a survey on violence against women in France

The Beijing platform drawn up in September 1995, at the Fourth International Conference on women, encouraged governments to take action to prevent and eliminate violence against women. This action was to include the gathering of reliable data enabling the provision of statistics relating to the prevalence of the various forms of violence against women and to encourage research into the causes, nature, severity and consequences of such violent acts as well an evaluation of the efficiency of preventative measures taken by public authorities.

Quantitative surveys had already taken place in some countries, some on a local scale (for example in London: Hanmer and Saunders, 1984), some national (the first, by Statistique Canada, 1993). The issue of violence specifically directed to women had been approached in various ways: as an element of family violence in USA (Straus and Gelles, 1986), as experienced by women in cohabiting couples in Switzerland (Gillioz et al., 1997) and Netherlands (Römkens, 1992), or in all contexts in Finland (Heiskanen and Piispa, 1998). Towards the end of the decade, the number of surveys around the world multiplied (Population Reports, 1999).

France was still without any means of measuring the scale and nature of the phenomenon within the general population. Existing statistics concerned only acts of violence reported by women to the police or other services (S.D.F, 1990). Violence experienced by women contacting crisis centres, refuges, crisis lines was well understood, since studies on their activities, numbers and characteristics of women had been conducted (Cesur-Gers, 1998; Collectif féministe contre le viol, 1996-97; Cromer, 1995). However, a range of other types of violence experienced by other groups of women remained unknown. In such a context, and given the status of statistics – notably national-level statistics – in modern society, surveys concerning the general population become indispensable in order to fully measure the scale of violence individuals are subjected to. Especially since debate reveals the existence of a great many preconceived ideas on the issue. The production of reliable data, obtained from a representative sample of the female population residing in France aimed to supply information useful to the different institutional partners (political, social, the media, etc.) and society at large.

Thus, having found that the pilot survey (November 1998) had been successful in reaching most social groups, a representative survey on a national scale was considered feasible. The data produced by the Enveff survey (2000) will add to existing knowledge of the phenomenon and not compete with previous studies and enable decision-making leading to integrated action.

2. Methodological issues

Preceding surveys had been based on a variety of protocols and tended to emphasise particular contexts in which violence could occur or specified certain types of violence. Some methodologies are more appropriate than others for studying violence against women. Perusal of the research reports and questionnaires of the Canadian, Finnish and Swiss surveys, as well as those of French crime and security surveys, was particularly useful in the early stage of our research.

The objectives of the survey were to:
- Identify different types of interpersonal violence against women of 20-59 years in all spheres of life, whoever the perpetrator;
- Measure the prevalence of violence against women in the course of the previous 12 months, as well as during their whole life;
- Define the temporal aspects of violence, that is to define whether it is isolated or limited, continuous or repeated, in order to identify situations of harassment and cycles of violence as well as to analyse cumulative mechanisms;
- Analyse the context of violence, using social and demographic characteristics, the living conditions and lifestyle of women and, wherever possible, the characteristics of the family and social circles, as well as the characteristics of the perpetrator of the violent act;
- Examine fear of violence through the use of public space;
- Trace the biographies of women in order to observe the relationship between the family schooling and occupational histories and the emergence of violence;
- Study types of reactions to violence, what kind of help women seek from family and friends and from official or voluntary organisations;
- Identify the consequences of violence of physical and mental health, on family and social life and on the use of public and private space.

Since we sought to explore the diversity of contexts in which violence occurs, we compiled a questionnaire with separate sections dealing with experiences in different spheres of life (see Appendix II for structure of the questionnaire). It was hoped that by such an approach we would obtain a clearer picture of the position of intimate partner violence in relation to other types of violence experienced by women. Six sections refer to violence experienced during the twelve months preceding the interview in different situations: in public places, at work or at school/university, in intimate partner relationships, with a former partner, within the family or circle of contacts. Each module records the occurrence of events or acts[5] described in a more or less identical fashion according to the context; the investigation also concerned the circumstances, as well as the reactions on the part of the women and the help they sought from friends and family or institutions, for the most serious event in the respondent's opinion.

The final section of the questionnaire concerns acts of physical or sexual violence: physical violence experienced since the age of 18 and sexual violence at any moment in the respondent's lifetime. The age, the perpetrators, the circumstances, and legal actions are recorded. In the case of repeated acts, the first and the last act were taken into account.

Our definition of violence was that violence originates within a power struggle or a situation of domination of one person by another or others and is distinct from situations of conflict, a more normal aspect of a relationship between two persons of fairly equal status. The research design highlights the fact that violence may be carried out by men or women, that it manifests itself in a multitude of ways and is present in all social contexts but in varying forms. In addition, violent acts are seen to be all the more traumatising when they are out of step with norms and cultural rules in the social group to which the victim belongs, and this fact

---

5   Acts measured are the following:
      - Physical acts of violence: slaps, blows with a blunt instrument, threats made with a weapon, attempts to strangle or kill, other brutal physical acts, locking up or preventing from going out, abandoning on the roadside (from a car), preventing from entering the home.
      - Sexual violence: rape, unwanted sexual acts, unwanted petting, forced sexual acts with other people; at work, sexual harassment, imposing pornographic images.
      - Spiteful acts using an object: throwing, tearing, destroying an object, something made by the other person (a prepared dish, a piece of artwork...).
      - Obscene and threatening phone calls, with or without sexual connotations.
      - Verbal violence: insults, abusive remarks.

contributes to subjective definitions of violence. Thus whilst drawing up the questionnaire, we adhered to a number of precepts:

We have avoided inferring any hierarchy of violence amongst the different types – physical, sexual and psychological – or contexts of violence (see Appendix III for types of violence described in questions).

We do not use the word 'violence' in the questionnaire itself, referring rather to gestures, acts, words, incidents without qualifying them as violent.

The gender of the perpetrator of the violent act is not implicit in the questions (no use of 'him', 'his' etc).

The data was collected using the CATI method (computer-assisted telephone interviewing) was used to interview 6970 women. The survey institute worked in close collaboration with the research team, a member of which was present every day throughout the data gathering period. The training of women interviewers lasted three days, including a half day of awareness building provided by members of women's rights associations. Contact with the general population was optimised through the acquisition of an ex-directory list of numbers, the possibility of several calls to each number and of offering an appointment to carry out the interview at a more convenient time.

3. Qualitative results of the survey

Before going on to look at the statistical results of the survey, three important points must be made with regard to the reliability of the data and to what the survey revealed about the scale of silence surrounding violence against women and the extent to which victims hide the violence.

The survey was well accepted, despite the length of the questionnaire and the intimate nature of many of the questions. We attribute this to the neutral, anonymous interview situation as well as to a greater awareness of violence against women (rape, domestic violence, sexual harassment) in the general population and a desire amongst women to eradicate such violence.

Over half the women having experienced violence spoke about it for the first time, (particularly so in the case of sexual violence) and thus we feel that the survey helped interviewees describe violence experienced. Some women were stimulated into reassessing situations they had endured and thus mentioned violent acts that they might not immediately have thought of. The existence of violence against women was never denied by interviewees. They apparently wished to describe all types of violence experienced, including acts committed by other women.

A low level of reporting of violence was confirmed, whether to official authorities or to intermediate persons such as doctors. Only a small minority of women having experienced violence had reported a violent act, usually in the case of physical violence.

Appendix II   Structure of the Enveff Questionnaire

I   Social and demographic characteristics

- Sexual behaviour, history and fertility history;
- Physical and mental health status.

II   Measurement of violence experienced during the previous twelve months (in general, number of acts, characteristics of perpetrator

- work, or place of study for full-time students;
- public space;
- semi-public space (e.g. visit to doctor, private tuition);
- couple;
- previous couple;
- relationships within the family and close friends.

More detailed questions are asked on the act considered most serious by the interviewee, i.e. the duration and location of the violence, reaction of the victim, the presence of witnesses, whether or not help was sought.

III Measurement of violence experienced prior to the last twelve months

- physical violence since the age of 18 years;
- sexual violence since childhood.

The questionnaire closes with a couple of questions relating to specific types of violence of a sexist nature. The interviewee then is given the opportunity to comment. A telephone number for information on violence against women is provided.

Appendix III   Types of Violence Described in the Enveff Questionnaire

Physical violence

- Throwing an object at someone, grabbing hold of, pushing someone;
- Hitting, punching and other physical brutality;
- Attempting to strangle or kill;
- Death threats;
- Threatening with a knife or firearm;
- Preventing someone from leaving a room, family home, building, or abandoning someone on the roadside (from a vehicle);
- Preventing someone from entering the home, a room, etc.

Sexual violence

- Forced sex;
- Forced sexual behaviour;
- Unwanted physical, sexual contact;
- Leering, sexual advances;
- Exhibitionism;
- Forced showing of pornographic material, obscene comments.

Psychological violence

- Preventing someone from talking to or seeing family and friends;
- Speaking ill of family or friends;
- Criticising, ridiculing what a person does, her work;
- Criticising someone's appearance, her way of dress;
- Ignoring someone, refusing to talk to her;
- Blocking access to money (domestic context), to information (at work);
- Threats, intimidation, emotional blackmail;
- Shouting, insulting or humiliating remarks, giving of orders, coarse remarks;
- Damaging, breaking or throwing of objects belonging to a person;
- Malicious telephone calls, with sexual connotations or otherwise.

Appendix IV   Questionnaire Items Exploring Emotional Abuse or Psychological Pressure in the Respondent's Relationship with her Partner

During the last 12 months, did your spouse or partner:
　　never/rarely/sometimes/often/regularly

-    prevent you from meeting or talking to friends or family members?
-    prevent you from talking to other men?
-    criticise, ridicule what you were doing?
-    make unpleasant remarks concerning your physical appearance?
-    impose certain clothes, hairstyles, or public behaviour?
-    did not take your opinion into account, expressed contempt or tried to tell you what to think? a/ at home b/ in public?
-    insist on knowing where and with whom you had been?
-    refuse to speak to you, refused point-blank to discuss anything?
-    refuse access to household funds for daily expenses?

References

Brown, E. and Jaspard, M. (2001). Violences conjugales, premières résultats de l'enquête Enveff: violences dans tous les milieux. *Ecole des Parents*, (2): 36-38.

Cesur-Gers (1998). *Les violences conjugales en France : des démarches, des recours, des parcours*. Paris: IHESI (Institut des hautes études sur la sécurité intérieure).

Collectif féministe contre le viol, 1996-97. Statistiques générales, 1996-1997. Viols Femmes Informations, 56p.

Cromer, S. (1995). *Le harcèlement sexuel en France: la levée d'un tabou, 1985-1990*. Paris: La Documentation Française, 228p.

Gaspard, F. (1996). Pourquoi avons-nous tant tardé? *Cahiers du Mage* (3), 115-118.

Gillioz, L., De Puy, J. and Ducret, V. (1997). *Domination et violence envers la femme dans le couple*. Lausanne: Editions Payot Lausanne, 269p.

Hagemann-White, C. (2001). European research on the prevalence of violence against women. *Violence against Women*, 7 (7): 732-759.

Hanmer, J. and Saunders, S. (1984). *Well-founded fear: a community study of violence to women*. London: Hutchinson.

Heiskanen, M. and Piispa, M. (1998). Faith, hope and battering. A survey of men's violence in Finland. Helsinki, Statistics Finland, 64p.

Jaspard, M. and the Enveff team (2001). Nommer et compter les violences envers les femmes : une première enquête nationale en France. *Population et Sociétés*, n°364, Paris, INED. (Publication available in French and in English on the internet http.//www.ined.fr.)

Jaspard, M., Brown, E., Condon, S., Fougeyrollas-Schwebel, D., Houel, A., Lhomond, B., Maillochon, F., Saurel-Cubizolles, M.J. and Schiltz, M.A. (2003). *Les violences envers les femmes en France : une enquête nationale*, Paris: La Documentation Française, 370p.

Mama, A. (1993). Woman abuse in London's Black communities. In W. James and C. Harris (eds). *Inside Babylon. The Caribbean diaspora in Britain*. London: Verso, pp. 97-134.

Nicollet, A. (1992). *Femmes d'Afrique noire en France. La vie partagée*. Paris: CIEMI/L'Harmattan.

Petek-Salom (1998). Situations de violence rencontrées par les femmes et les jeunes filles turques en France. In ELELE, Honneur et violence: fatalité ou conjoncture pour les femmes turques. Actes du colloque à l'UNESCO (12.12.97), ELELE/FAS/Service des Droits des Femmes (unpublished).

Poinsot M. (2001). Les violences familiales sur les jeunes filles d'origine étrangère et de culture musulmane. *Hommes et Migrations*, n°1232: 99-104.

Population Reports (1999). Ending violence against women. *Population Reports, vol XXVII* (4) December.

Römkens, R. (1992). *Gewoon geweld? Omvang, aard, gevolgen en achtergronden van geweld tegen vrouwen in heteroseksuele relaties* [Ordinary violence? Prevalence, nature, consequences and backgrounds of violence against women in heterosexual relationships]. Amsterdam: Swets and Zeitlinger.

Shah, N.M. and Menon, I. (1997). Violence against women workers: issues, data and partial solutions. *Asian and Pacific Migration Journal*, (1): 5-30.

Simon, P. (2003). L'impasse de l'analyse statistique dans une France sans 'races'. *Hommes et Migrations*, n°1245: 42-53.

Statistique Canada (1993). L'enquête sur la violence envers les femmes: faits saillants. *Le Quotidien*, n°11-001F, 10p.

Straus, M.A. and Gelles R.J. (1986). Societal change and change in family violence from 1975 to 1985 as revealed by two national surveys. *Journal of Marriage and the Family*, vol. 48: 465-479.

Tribalat, M. (1996). *De l'immigration à l'assimilation. Enquête sur les populations d'origine étrangère en France*. Paris: La Découverte/INED.

Watts, C., Heise, L., Ellsberg, M. and Garcia-Moreno (1999). Multi-country study on women's health and domestic violence against women. World Health Organisation.

Chapter 5

Moving in the Same or Different Directions? Reflections on Recent Developments in Domestic Violence Legislation in Europe

Liz Kelly

Introduction

Over the last three decades law reform and law enforcement has been a key element in efforts to address domestic violence, to transform it from private family concern outside the ambit of the state to a public matter in which the rights of individuals to personal safety are paramount. This is the outcome of a historic process, initiated by women's groups and feminist scholars in the 1970s which determined to challenge the historic discrimination in how domestic violence was responded to by police, prosecutors and courts (Dobash and Dobash, 1979; Zorza, 1995). The call to respond to domestic violence as a crime was both substantive and symbolic. Two decades later, at the level of rhetoric at least, a profound shift has gathered momentum across the globe, aided by the UN Human Rights Conference in Vienna in 1993, which pulled violence against women in the family within its terms of reference. Alongside the move to de-privatise domestic violence has been a parallel campaign to have it treated as a crime, through changes in both statute law and procedural implementation.

The forms that legal changes have taken are diverse globally, although a number of common threads are evident. Whilst legal and procedural reforms were slower to develop on mainland Europe, there has been significant movement in the last decade and different trajectories can be traced, only in part accounted for by the presence of both adversarial and investigative legal systems. This chapter explores some of the more recent legal reforms across Europe, within a broader perspective that asks what kind of crime domestic violence is, and what women are seeking when they call upon legal systems for intervention and support. These wider issues provide a context within which to ask not only whether European countries are travelling in the same direction, but also how far recent reforms mesh with the needs and concerns of those they are meant to benefit.

A Brief Overview

Before setting this frame for the chapter, however, a brief overview of the nature and range of new statute law that has been enacted in the last decade is presented (anyone needing a more complete overview should consult an audit of current legislation of violence against women published by the Council of Europe, 2001). It is not my intention to review the reforms as such, rather to highlight elements that have been innovative, and the progress they represent from previous law. With this perspective in mind the broad changes that can be discerned include the following:

-   The creation of specific 'domestic violence' criminal offences or changing the status of assaults in the home, to for example, make it a state offence or specify that such assaults when in the home are more serious than assaults between strangers (Belgium, Cyprus, France, Spain, Sweden, Switzerland).
-   Improving protection through civil law orders that restrict perpetrators' behaviour and access to the family home. In some countries these provisions were introduced for the first time (Finland, Spain), in others how they worked was tightened and/or they were extended to previously excluded groups, such as those who were not married or living together (Ireland, England and Wales).
-   The extension of police powers to remove perpetrators, to ensure protection and linking this to intervention and advocacy by civilians (Austria, Germany, Switzerland).
-   The development of domestic violence courts (UK).
-   Linking civil and criminal processes – protection and prosecution (Cyprus).
-   Recognition in law of children witnessing domestic violence as a form of psychological abuse: this may be part of any criminal proceedings

and/or inform the practice of social workers/child protection bodies (Cyprus).

- What I term 'integrated law' – reforms that not only create changes in penal and civil law provisions to directly intervene in individual cases, but which specify and mandate state responsibilities in terms of funding support services, monitoring and prevention (Austria, Cyprus, Denmark, Finland, Sweden).

As yet, however, no European country has enacted legislation similar to that in New Zealand, which recognises domestic violence as a specific context for child contact/access, and which presumes contact should not take place with a violent parent unless it can be shown to be safe for the children and the non-abusing parent.

'Domestic Violence is a Crime'

This phrase has been used as a chant in many women's demonstrations in the late twentieth century. That it needed to be chanted at all demonstrates that when physical and sexual assaults took place in the family they were not considered criminal assaults. Research in a number of countries reveals that police viewed 'domestic disputes/disturbances as outside the criminal law best dealt with by delicate negotiation, calming down and mediation' (see Dobash and Dobash, 1979 for Scotland, Kelly, 1999 for England, Kelleher and O'Connor, 1999 for Ireland and Seith, 2003 for Switzerland). The tolerance of violence towards wives has been documented historically, and is best illustrated in the twentieth century by the marital rape exemption in most sexual offences law that remained the case in many European countries until the 1980s/90s.[1] Even where the crime was one of murder, it was often treated differently. In some European countries murder of a sexual partner was a 'crime of passion' and subject to less serious penalties, in others the defence of 'provocation', which reduced the crime to one of manslaughter, was all too often allowed on the grounds that the female partner had 'nagged' or had an affair (Edwards, 1996). The gendered way in which crime was defined, understood and on occasions excused became a key focus in the emergent field of feminist jurisprudence

---

1 The major exception here was the Soviet Union, and many communist countries, which criminalised rape in marriage much earlier in the century.

(Edwards, 1996; Weisberg, 1996), and domestic violence one of the paradigmatic exemplars.

Moving this form of violence against women from the margin into the mainstream of criminal law – in theory and practice – was most strongly promoted in the English speaking countries (Dobash and Dobash, 1992). The most explicit moves here took place in North America, with mandatory arrest policies in the USA, in no drop prosecution policies and domestic violence courts in Canada (Hague et al., 2001). Variations of such policies have emerged in the UK, but not on the same scale and, until this point, usually as local demonstration projects (Kelly, 1999; Taylor Browne, 2001). In all these jurisdictions civil law protection orders had been applied to domestic violence since the 1970s, although their reach and effectiveness[2] was subjected to substantial critique, not least because breaches of orders were seldom prosecuted, and where they were the sanctions were paltry (Barron, 1990; Hague and Malos,1998; Kelleher and O'Connor, 1999).

The argument for criminalisation was that assaults inside the home should be treated in the same way as crime outside it, and thus the tolerance and non-intervention by police and other criminal justice agencies needed re-examination. Establishing this philosophical principle required establishing that this was a form of discrimination between crimes that apart from their location were in all other respects equivalent. The reality, however, is rather more complex – domestic violence is not a crime like any other, in a number of significant respects it is substantially different. Historically constructions of assault law have presumed one or more of the following: that the parties are strangers; that both parties are male; that the event is taking place in public; that this is a one-off event. None of these presumptions hold for domestic violence, which takes place in the context of an intimate relationship (even if no longer ongoing), most commonly involves a male aggressor and female victim, and any specific incident takes place within an existing pattern of coercive control. Thus, the context, the patterns of behaviour and the meaning of the events differ substantially from those assault laws were intended to cover, and for this reason it may be difficult to encompass.

As critically the definition of domestic violence preferred by researchers and practitioners alike includes a wide range of behaviours – often named as physical, sexual, psychological and financial – not all of

---

2   Some versions limited availability to married parties who were in the process of divorce.

which were, or even are today, within the ambit of the criminal law. More recently stalking and harassment laws have addressed some of the behaviours that were not previously prosecutable, but few European countries, in contrast to Latin America, include psychological abuse in their criminal law. In this sense, the slogan 'domestic violence is a crime' is inaccurate. The differences between domestic violence and other violent crimes are also apparent in the underlying wishes and motivations of victims of domestic violence when they turn to law, as the next section illustrates.

What Women Want

Kathleen Ferraro (1993) referred to 'irreconcilable differences' when analysing the variation in the motives and resources of women, police and courts in the US state of Arizona. Her ethnographic data do reveal that many women seek short-term instrumental goals from intervention – such as an immediate cessation of the violence, and for their partner to be 'taught a lesson'. The police and courts, on the other hand, are more interested in whether the evidence 'proves' a crime has been committed. There is, therefore, an open question as to whether the legal system as a whole – and here I include civil and criminal law – could be more responsive to the needs and aspirations of abused women. To assess the extent to which this is, or could be, the case we need to explore these needs and aspirations in a little more detail.

In a rather unusual process a public consultation with survivors and the domestic violence sector took place in the UK following publication of *Safety and Justice* (Home Office, 2003) which contained proposals for legal reform. The formal consultation was organised by the Women's National Commission, and involved women throughout England and Wales. All the direct quotes below are taken from the report *Unlocking the Secret* which documented women's responses (WNC, 2003).

Overall the women strongly supported pro-active interventions, including by the police, and had an expectation that government and agencies ought to be able to deliver protection and safety. In terms of specific proposals there was consensus that protection orders should not cost anything[3] and should last at least a year. There was also extremely strong support for policy and practice which enabled women and children to stay safely in their own homes (see also Kelly and Humphreys, 2001; Mullender et al., 2001).

> The whole idea of women having to leave is repellent. Why not put men in a different place while it is all sorted out?
>
> You should never release a man without a cooling off period – it needs to be at least seven days – in that time you need the crime prevention people to come over, assess what you need to make your home safe from him and get it done before he gets out.
>
> Injunctions last for a few months. If he doesn't breach it, courts won't renew them. Do they think men are stupid? My ex said 'I can wait.' And he did – waited till the injunction ran out, then came round to get me.

The consultation also revealed poor and differential implementation of existing legislation. It was difficult for women to believe in the law's ability to protect them when they were not able to access rights to protections when giving evidence, or have a separate waiting room to that of their assailant and his family.

> They said to me, you can't have the screens[4] today – they're in another court!
>
> In court, the bloke interviewing me was very intimidating. It is very difficult to give evidence. People don't seem to understand that. Half way through I was told he had sacked his solicitor and was going to cross-examine me himself... They all thought it was very funny that the man was psychiatrically ill and going to cross-examine me.

---

3   Current practice in England and Wales is that anyone financially reliant on public assistance qualifies for full legal aid, but anyone in paid work who earns above the minimum wage is expected to pay some or all of the legal fees. For a lawyer to obtain a basic order, which may only last for three months, can cost between 1900 and 3200 euros.

4   Under the Youth Justice and Criminal Evidence Act 1999, vulnerable and intimidated witnesses can apply to give their evidence behind screens, so that they do not have to directly face their attacker in the court room.

Poor case preparation by police and prosecutors could lead to criminal cases being dropped, charges lowered or evidence supporting the brutality of the assaults being missing. These technical errors, combined with the fact that many lawyers and judges still appeared to view domestic violence as 'not serious' crime, meant that many women felt let down at this stage.

> They can withdraw charges without telling you. They can reduce the charges without telling you. They should have to tell you, and explain why they have done it. They are patronising – they think you won't understand.

> The CPS[5] is absolutely useless. They do not speak to you. My husband was arrested and charged. The first time I met the CPS was ten minutes before I went into the court. In court, there was just one piece of paper, as the basis of my case. My husband's lawyer had a huge file, and they threw everything at me.

> My ex came round to kill me. He had come four weeks before, and scratched my mother with a knife. Against the advice of the police, the magistrate let him out after one night. He came back to kill me but killed my mother instead, because she stood in the way, trying to protect me. He is now in prison. I felt like it was me up in the court for murdering my mother.... I had a letter from the Criminal Injuries Compensation Board to say that because I hadn't left him at the start of the violence, I was partly to blame for him killing my mother. I wish I could sue the magistrate that let my ex out.

> If you are brave enough to prosecute you should not be let down. It took me 25 years before I took him to court. He strangled me unconscious; I have back, neck and throat injuries. He got fined £15 and bound over for a year.

> It needs to be at least the same as for assaults on people in the street. It is worse in my eyes. This should be a factor in sentencing. The chance of a stranger attacking again is very remote. In the home, you have to see your attacker every day. *They know where you live.* [original emphasis]

---

5   Crown Prosecution Service, which in England and Wales is the name for the state prosecutors.

Clearly whilst a number of these women continued with criminal prosecutions, the outcomes neither reflected the seriousness and ongoing nature of the abuse, nor acted as a form of protection from further violence. Some women eloquently illustrated the ways in which gendered experiences and perspectives played out in court, but that this was not understood, let alone addressed in the legal process. The final example illustrates that on occasion these omissions and perceptions can have tragic consequences.

> They expect perpetrators to come in with tattoos and a pink Mohican but he's good looking, 6'2", in a suit he's very powerful.... My ex was very controlled and the judge said he was very impressive. I was stood there in a right state because it was the first time I'd seen him since the violence and he's smirking and giving me the eye. It all comes back. I was a wreck, hysterical. No wonder women come over badly in these situations.... They gave him custody of the kids even though he was arrested for stabbing my dad eight times in the face. He already had been arrested on a malicious wounding charge, but got off. *None of that can be said in court.* [original emphasis]. They couldn't bring charges because they couldn't find the knife. He told them a load of lies, said I was easy, a tart. The judge believed him.... I can't tell you what losing my kids did to me: my son was two. Having to live everyday knowing your children are with a man capable of the things he's capable of. Now my teenage daughter is threatening suicide because she is too scared to leave.

These women's accounts tell a different story to that reported by Ferraro – their hopes and aspirations were not at odds with the kinds of interventions that justice systems ought to be able to deliver, they sought not only immediate protection but also justice and sanctions. Despite legal reforms, considerable training and policy changes, however, they were still let down by the police and/or the legal system. It is undoubtedly the case that at the time they call the police all women are looking for immediate protection, a proportion – or maybe the same woman at a different point in time – seek more than this – they want the kinds of rulings that courts make on criminal violence between parties who were strangers at the time. There is not *one* story here – of women not wishing to take cases against current/ex partners – but a more complex set of needs and aspirations, which can change over time and where the desire for justice is supported.

Defining Domestic Violence in Research and in Law

A long-standing, and ultimately unhelpful debate within the field about the reach of the term 'domestic violence' (see Dobash and Dobash 1992 for a discussion) has been partly resolved through the introduction of the term 'intimate partner violence (IPV)'. IPV allows a clear differentiation between its remit and the broader concept of 'family violence'. It may be, however, that a further clarification would be useful, especially in relation to accurately assessing the scale of the problem. Having a definition of IPV/domestic violence that includes *any* incident of physical violence, threats or psychological abuse casts the net widely, and is partly responsible for findings of high incidence rates amongst men in prevalence studies that draw on an adult population sample, as opposed to only adult women (see Walby and Allen, 2004 for the latest example). One of the key features of domestic violence, as a crime, is that it is a *pattern* of behaviour – that there are repeated incidents which take place in a climate of fear and control. It is the repetition, the cumulative impacts and the consequences of weak/ineffective intervention that creates the process of entrapment that so much research has documented (Davies et al., 1998; Kelly, 1987; Kirkwood, 1993). Whilst there may be single assaults which warrant legal intervention, unless there is repetition they are not part of a pattern of coercive control that corrodes confidence in oneself and trust in others. It is the latter cases which are the concern of specialist services and public policy. Taking these observations as elements to reflect in a definition one possibility would be:

> Intimate partner violence is a pattern of coercive control by one, current or prior, intimate partner of the other. It includes at least one, but frequently a combination, of the following: physical violence, sexual violence, psychological/ emotional abuse, threats and intimidation, stalking and harassment.[6]

Few legal codes are able to reflect this reality in offences, since the elements that comprise domestic violence are often located within a wide range of other more general crime categories: sexual offences; physical assault; threats; criminal damage; stalking and harassment; breach of the peace and other public order offences. Few European countries have moved in the direction of many countries in Latin America, where specific

---

6   Proposed by the author at a meeting of the Women's National Commission, July 2003.

criminal offences of domestic violence encompass a range of acts, often including psychological abuse. It is rather ironic that a number of the abusive acts referred to in definitions of domestic violence, including the ones that victims report as the most debilitating, are not criminal offences. Within Europe, only Cyprus has moved decisively in this direction, and has also defined in law child witnessing as a form of psychological child abuse. The UK is currently discussing encoding a definition of domestic violence in a new law, but has reached an impasse with respect to those who seek a broad inclusive 'family violence' framing and those who prefer the IPV formulation.

Creating an inclusive definition within statute can make the slogan 'domestic violence is a crime' real, but whatever the breadth of definition, there are strong arguments for including one in the law since it can ensure that state agencies use the same definition for data collection, which in turn makes monitoring of implementation and responses over time more systematic. These are not inconsiderable issues, since many studies of police and legal responses (see Seith, this volume) have had to collect data from case files, since there are no police statistics.

Re-defining Existing Law

A core problem already noted has been the differential implementation of law when the violence takes place in the private sphere. Revising legal codes minimally, but in ways ensure assaults in the domestic sphere are brought within the ambit of existing laws has been a mechanism used by many European countries. For example, one route to criminalise rape in marriage has been simply to remove the word or phrase in rape law that excluded it. A number of European countries have enacted reforms that specify that criminal assaults between partners should be considered an aggravating factor in sentencing, for example Belgium did this in 1997, France in 1994, and Spain in 1999. This strategy both draws attention to the fact that assault law applies in private and seeks to reverse the attitudes and practices that treated it as less serious than assaults in the public sphere.

Whilst these strategies are undoubtedly the simplest route to reform, they fail to address the fact that many of the actions comprising domestic violence are either not criminal offences at all, or register at the lower levels, where prosecutions either only taken where the victim lays a charge themselves, or if pursued by the state result in a reprimand rather than a sanction. Also in a number of countries low level offences are not deemed 'arrestable' limiting the protective function police can exercise when attending a call out.

Simply pulling domestic violence into the mainstream of penal law, applying existing laws equally, fails to address what is specific about it, and thus may risk being ineffective with respect to either protection or sanction. Recent law reform in Switzerland has defined a range of violence and abuse, including repeat common assault and threats, in the context of partnership as 'state offences', taking the responsibility of prosecution away from the victim. The fear that this would remove women's right to self-determination was strongly argued by the shelters, and resulted in an ingenious, but as yet untested compromise: in cases of IPV a special rule will apply which allows the victim to withdraw from the procedure, but also to re-instate it within six months of the offence in question. The UK is currently considering making common assault an arrestable offence.

None of these strategies, however, move us on from the problem that at the lower level assaults will not be considered serious offences by magistrates or judges. It is the attempt to overcome this limitation that has led a number of countries to enact specific domestic violence laws. An intermediary position is that adopted by Sweden. Often the event that prompts a call to the police is not especially 'serious' in legal terms, and may even fall outside the penal code all together. A new law in Sweden, passed in 1999, recognises this by creating an offence of 'gross violation of a woman's integrity'.[7] This permits prosecution for what might be termed a 'course of conduct', which recognises that the whole is greater than the parts. This charge can be made separately, as well as in conjunction with charges for individual assaults (see Lindström, this volume, for more detailed discussion). Similar provisions exist in most stalking laws, since many of the actions involved in stalking are not criminal offences as such, they only become sinister when placed in the context of the situation, and the course of conduct they are part of.

The main advantages of making IPV a state/arrestable offence is that this is a relatively easy reform to undertake, and can be done with considerably more speed that more profound legal reform. Its benefits can

---

7   A similar offence enables prosecution for course of conduct in cases of repeated sexual abuse of children.

be considerably enhanced if measures that address the unique features of IPV, such as recognition of repeat victimization, are also addressed.

Enhancing the Protective Role of the Law

It is here perhaps that Europe has made one of its most innovative contributions to legal responses to IPV. The possibility of using civil injunctions as ways to protect women and children is not novel, the UK passed legislation enabling this in the late 1970s, and both it and Ireland updated their laws in the 1990s. Strong implementation, however, has been dogged by traditional attitudes in the judiciary which sought to protect men's property rights – over their homes if not their wives – and limited the provisions to those who had been married (Barron, 1991).

By the late 1990s, however, social attitudes about both gender relations and IPV had shifted and Austrian feminists crafted an innovative approach that combined the protective function of civil law, the ability to sanction abusive behaviour and the provision of quality support services. The law provides police with the power to remove the abusive party from the household for 10 days. Police are also required by law to refer both parties to an Intervention Project – and the law required that these be provided in all parts of the country. The 'Austrian Law', a version of which how exists in Germany (Violence Protection Law, 2001) and various cantons in Switzerland[8] (see Seith, this volume), moves civil protection into a new dimension, delivering something that activists and victims had long argued for – that it should be the perpetrator who has to leave.

The Austrian Protection from Violence Act came into force on May 1, 1997, and all the powers related to were located in three different laws: the Security Police Act (Sicherheitspolizeigesetz – SPG); the Enforcement Act (Exekutionsordnung – EO); and the Civil Code (Allgemeines Bürgerliches Gesetzbuch – ABGB). The provisions apply to anyone living in a 'common household for at least three months' before the incident/application. Whilst overcoming the married/heterosexual bias of many previous civil law provisions, there is still a gap with respect to those who are separated, but still harassed by the ex-partner.[9] The Security Police Act grants powers to

---

8   The most recent European legislation on protection orders is in Spain, 2003 (Samartan, 2004).

9   Recent amendments may have addressed this, it is certainly addressed in the proposed Swiss federal law, and possibly also in the German law.

the police to remove perpetrators from the home, wherever they judge that a significant risk of further or future violence exists. This order lasts for 10 days, and police are also required to check compliance with the order at least once and refer the victim and perpetrator to an Intervention Project. Breach of the order is an offence, although not a criminal one.[10] The Enforcement Act allows the Family Court to extend the order into an injunction for up to three months, and widen its remit; further extensions are possible if divorce proceedings are instituted.

When the law first came into effect there were relatively few Intervention Centres established, but under the law resources were made available to ensure that there was at least one in all Austrian Länder by 1999. All operate with a pro-active model, contacting all those referred by the police, and inviting them into various modes of structured support. Between May 1997 and December 2001, 13835 removals had been effected, and in only 10 per cent were breaches reported to the police.[11]

A limited early evaluation was undertaken (Dearing and Heller, 2000) examining 1000 police files, interviewing 25 victims, seven perpetrators and a small sample of professionals. The report documents the previous response of 'dispute resolution' – a form of mediation with similar forms common in Switzerland and Germany. Within the 1000 case files, 43 per cent of cases were dealt with under the new law, 52 per cent by mediation and 5 per cent resulted in criminal charges. Unsurprisingly nine out ten victims were female and 97 per cent of perpetrators male, and three quarters of the victims reported previous violence, although most had not reported to the police. A quarter of the interventions under the new law resulted in an injunction.

Within the small group of victims interviewed those who had experienced the new law had mixed assessments – some welcomed it, whereas others viewed removal as too harsh. Most revealing, however, were those who received mediation – all these women were dissatisfied, primarily because they saw such interventions as not just reinforcing, but also enhancing the power of the perpetrator. Use of the new law was highest in urban areas, whereas police in rural areas preferred the mediation tradition; implementation was strongest in areas where police had had prior training on domestic violence provided by the women's

---

10 This has been highlighted as one of the shortcomings of the original statute, since for the minority of perpetrators who do not respect the terms of the removal, a stronger sanction through the criminal law is needed.
11 Personal communication from Rosa Logar.

sector. The evaluation also revealed reluctance in child protection agencies to use new powers to apply for 'third party' injunctions to protect children living with domestic violence. A desire not to alienate either parent was the justification for not availing themselves of these new powers (Dearing and Heller, 2000).

More recent data shows the numbers of removals increasing until 2000, followed by a slight drop in 2001. It remains the case that mediation is used in more cases and especially in rural areas – turning IPV from private pain into public matter is a long and complex process, and legal reform but one step in a longer and difficult journey.

Assessment of the 'Austrian Law'

At the time the law was first proposed discussion from outside Austria focused on whether the civil sanction of removal was only a slightly more sophisticated form of 'decriminalisation': that whilst it might offer more of what women want in the moment they call the police (Kelly, 1999; Ferraro, 1993) – an end to the violence, and a strong message to the perpetrator – it still represents a move to treat IPV differently from violence outside the home. The fact that so few cases in the evaluation resulted in charge (5%) offers some support for this position. At the same time, however, this legal reform delivers far more of what victims want, including that they and children do not have to leave the home to be safe,[12] than any other to date. It has also provided the police with powers that enable them to act in ways that protects women and children, and the mandatory provision of intervention projects recognises that whilst domestic violence is a crime, it is not a crime like any other.

Integrated Laws

Few European countries have a legal tradition that echoes the Violence Against Women Act (VAWA) in the USA, first enacted in 1994, and renewed a number of times since. The Act covers a number of forms of violence – most importantly sexual assault, stalking and harassment and IPV – and allocates resources to areas of policy and practice that the

---

12 There will always be a proportion whose partners have no respect for the law, and for whom safety requires provision such as shelters/refuges.

government is interested in promoting. Recent examples include: enhanced evidence gathering; domestic violence courts; inter-agency coordination groups for sexual assault (SARTs); forensic nursing.[13] Projects wishing to implement these ideas locally have to apply through their state machinery. The outcomes of implementation are monitored by an office in the Department of Justice, and the lessons so far have been combined in a very useful Toolkit, available on their website (http://toolkit.ncjrs.org).

The only equivalent in Europe is the Women's Peace law in Sweden, enacted in 1999 to comply with the state responsibilities signatories to the UN Beijing Platform for Action. In addition to the violation of integrity laws discussed previously, the package addressed sexual harassment and Sweden became the first country to make the purchase of sexual services illegal. The law also committed resources to service provision and research.

Integrated laws communicate a strong message about how the state understands IPV – that it is a form of violence against women, gender violence as defined by the UN. This in turn locates law reform within wider processes of change, as encouraged by international policy at the global and European levels. The allocation of resources for service provision and research makes such decisions transparent, as do the policy steers which the VAWA in the US is able to prompt. The process of renewal of the VAWA is also much preferable to the single period investments that have been evident in government policy in Scandinavia and the UK.[14] Taking the 'long view', and a strong commitment to ongoing prevention, is yet to find its way into European public policy on gender violence.

Procedural Innovations and Specialisation

Legal reforms are rather easier to effect, than is changing the historic traditions and practices of institutions. Implementation of new legislation presents new, and in some ways, more intractable barriers to change. Again the violence against women sector has been innovative, attempting to develop entry points and strategies that undercut resistance and/or

---

13 Here nurses are trained to gather forensic evidence for criminal cases.
14 For example, the Crime Reduction Programme in the UK included two waves of investment in pilot projects on domestic violence, rape and prostitution. The investment, however, was less than a tenth of that devoted to domestic burglary. Finland invested in a five year research, policy and prevention project – STAKES – on violence against women, but decided not to renew the funding in 2002.

marshal the energy and efforts of those most committed to transformation. One key strategy that has been used is specialisation: creating groups of police officers, prosecutors, magistrates and judges who have designated responsibilities for improving responses to domestic violence.[15] This response is perhaps most highly developed in the UK and Ireland, but specialist multi-agency teams, often headed by a police officer, that have acted as beacons for wider change are also evident in Sweden and the Netherlands.

A logical outgrowth of professional specialisation is the domestic violence court, a set of officials who through training and experience deal with all domestic violence litigation. Pioneered in Canada (Hague et al., 2000) and common in areas of the USA, the model has its European pilot currently in the UK. The strongest models appear to be those where: criminal and civil elements can be heard together; all hearings with respect to a specific offender are dealt with by the same judge; and where enhanced evidence gathering, specialist prosecution, probation and victim advocacy[16] projects work together to create a seamless web of responses to victim and perpetrator. Such systems make it possible to embed sanctions within a wider network of responses that ensure protection and support for victims. Proponents of specialist courts also argue that they are a way of increasing the status of the crime, especially where judges develop expertise that straddles the criminal and civil codes, and give judgments that are widely reported. One example here is the court in Dade Country Florida, which has been externally evaluated. Not only are judges rigorously trained, but also all cases are monitored for compliance. Judges are known for placing an emphasis on the needs of children and using perpetrator programmes as an element in 'therapeutic jurisprudence'. Locally the judges are regarded as important 'change makers', delivering a strong message that IPV will not be tolerated.

One of the most interesting, but least well known internationally, examples of integrated criminal justice responses to domestic violence can be found in Canberra, Australia. Here the outcomes of the Family Violence Intervention Project (FVIP) show a choice of careful incremental change, based on a problem solving rather than confrontative way of working.

---

15 Similar strategies are currently being implemented with respect to rape in the UK.

16 Advocacy is differs in a number of critical ways from support or advice, since its primary aim is to ensure that the person being advocated for is able to exercise their rights to services and justice (Kelly and Humphreys, 2000).

Over a period of twelve months the pro-active prosecution policy resulted in a 152 per cent increase in charges and 126 per cent increase in convictions (Holder and Mayo, 2003). Rather than increased prosecution deterring women from reporting there was also an increase of almost a quarter (23%) in the number of calls to the police. A significant element in the increase in prosecutions has been enhanced evidence gathering, including use of digital cameras that enable the police to send pictures to the court overnight: the combination of strong prosecutorial policy and better evidence has increased early guilty pleas, which now stand at 61 per cent (Holder and Mayo, 2003).

Not only can a focus on procedural change address the multiple barriers and resistances to change, but creating mechanisms whereby civil and criminal proceedings can be heard together both limits the number of court appearances for victims, and is cost effective for the public purse. The creation of multi-agency interventions can also lead to joint training, which builds a shared perspective across the various elements of the criminal justice system. The evidence from Canberra demonstrates that when all these aspects are combined, the results can be dramatic.

Controversial Crossovers

As this chapter is being completed a number of untested, and controversial legal changes have been proposed by the UK government. Interestingly the two that are most controversial do not have origins in the women's sector, but are crossovers from policy on sexual offences, and seem likely to have originated with the police. One proposal is to extend the right to anonymity, currently enjoyed by victims of serious sexual offences whose cases reach court, to victims of domestic violence. The other that a 'register' of offenders, similar to the Sex Offender Register be established. The rationale for both is not explicit in *Safety and Justice* (Home Office, 2004). The anonymity provisions seem strangely out of place, since there has been no evidence that this acts as a deterrent to reporting to the police. If implemented it will create rather bizarre anomalies, whereby in cases where the parties are married it will not be possible to name the perpetrator, since this would by implication identify the victim, whereas no similar restrictions will apply to cases involving unmarried (and therefore all non heterosexual) parties. The current low level of convictions for domestic violence raise serious doubts about the value of a register of offenders, and quite how it is envisaged that this would provide any preventative value. The danger would be that professionals, especially social workers, might use registration to 'warn women off' new partners, in a way that could become coercive if linked to child protection concerns. Making such a move early in a new relationship (which may even be a marriage) when hopes are high is unlikely to be effective in most cases, and would act as a disincentive to women seeking help should they be subjected to abuse. Since the legislation is still being discussed in parliament it is impossible to state whether these will be in the eventual law, or what impact, if any, they will have on women's safety.

One suggestion that has received guarded support, however, has been to apply the practice of homicide reviews to cases where domestic violence is involved. This process seeks to gather all the material known to agencies before the fatal event, in order to discover if any preventive interventions might have been possible. The reviews are intended to draw out lessons, which might be usefully applied to future cases.

Not a Crime Like any Other

With almost three decades of legal reform, research and changed professional practice a paradox has emerged with respect to the ambition to respond to violence inside the home in the same way as it is dealt with outside the home. It has become increasingly clear that IPV is not a crime like any other, but has a number of unique elements. Jeffrey Fagan (1996) argued that within criminal violence it is unique in the concentration of continued risk and limited levers for external control since the parties are connected by emotional, legal and financial ties, are in daily contact within the private sphere where traditional criminological surveillance methods are unavailable. He also argued that the deterrent threat of law has less purchase, and cognisance needs to be paid to the strategic decisions women make using the law in an instrumental way to enhance their safety and survival, in the hope that it will prompt change in their partner. We now have research that confirms what many women have always known – that prosecution without increased protection can place some women in increased danger (Dugan et al., 2003, p. 192).

The web of connections between the parties means that ending violent relationships is a process within which the role of law is but one element. Future reforms need to be based on a more sophisticated understanding of

IPV, the ways in which it is similar and different to other forms of violence, and how both statute and procedural changes can better straddle the roles of setting standards for unacceptable behaviour and supporting victims in their struggles to create lives free of violence. This way of thinking about legal reform requires a combination of protection and sanction at the core but which, as the Austrian law demonstrates, need not focus only on repressive measures that require a criminal prosecution. At the same time when victims and/or the state do bring charges against perpetrators, statute law and its implementation should reflect the repeated nature of the abuse, not just the most recent incident. The next series of reforms, therefore, need to negotiate the ways in which IPV is both the same and different as assaults that occur in the public sphere.

References

Burton, S., Regan, L. and Kelly, L. (1998). *Supporting Women and Challenging men: Lessons from the Domestic Violence Intervention Project*. Bristol: Policy Press.

Council of Europe (2001). Legislation in the member States of the Council of Europe in the field of violence against women. Strasbourg : COE. [http://www.coe.int/T/E/Human_Rights/Equality/04._Violence_against_women]

Davies, G., Lyon, E. and Monti-Catania E. (1998). *Safety Planning with Battered Women: Complex Lives, Difficult Choices*. Thousand Oaks: Sage.

Dearing, A. and Haller, B. (2000) (Eds). *Das österreichische Gewaltschutzgesetz*. Vienna.

Dobash, R. and Dobash R., (1979). *Violence Against Wives: A Case Against the Patriarchy*. New York: Free Press.

Dobash, R. and Dobash, R. (1992). *Women, Violence and Social Change*. London: Routledge.

Dugan, L., Nagin, D., Rosenfeld R., (1999). 'Explaining the decline in intimate-partner homicide: the effects of changing domesticity, women's status and domestic violence resources'. *Homicide Studies*, 3:3, 187-214.

Dugan, L., Nagin, D., Rosenfeld R. (2003). Exposure reduction or retaliation: The effects of domestic violence resources in intimate-partner homicide. *Law and Society*, 37:1, 169-198.

Edwards, S. (1996). *Sex, Gender and the Legal Process*. London: Blackstone Press.

Fagan, J. (1996). The Criminalisation of Domestic Violence: Promises and Limits. Washington DC: National Institute of Justice.

Ferraro, K. and L. Pope (1993). Irreconcilable Differences: Police, Battered Women, and the Law, pp. 96-126 in N.Z. Hilton (Ed). *The Legal Response to Battering*. Newbury Park: Sage.

Fisher, K. and Rose, M. (1995). When 'enough is enough': battered women's decision making around court orders of protection. *Crime and Delinquency*, 41:4, 414-429.

Hague, G., Kelly, L. and Mullender, A. (2001). *Challenging Violence Against Women: The Canadian Experience*. Bristol: Policy Press.

Holder, R. and Mayo, N. (2003). What do women want? Prosecuting domestic violence in the ACT. *Current Issues in Criminal Justice*, 15:1, 5-25.

Home Office (2004). Safety and Justice: The Government's Proposals on Domestic Violence. London: Home Office.

Humphreys, C. and Holder, R. (2002). It's challenging but no rocket science. *The Domestic Abuse Quarterly*, Bristol WAFE.

Kelleher, P. and O'Connor, M. (1999). Safety and Sanctions: Domestic Violence and the Enforcement of Law in Ireland. Dublin: Women's Aid.

Kelly, L. (1987). *Surviving Sexual Violence*. Cambridge: Polity Press.

Kelly, L. (1999). Domestic Violence Matters: An Evaluation of a Development Project. Home Office Study 188. London: The Stationery Office.

Kelly, L. and Humphreys, C. (2001). Supporting women and children in their communities: outreach and advocacy approaches to domestic violence. In Taylor-Brown, J. (Ed.). *What Works in Reducing Domestic Violence? A Comprehensive Guide for Professionals.* London: Whiting and Birch.

Kirkwood, C. (1993). *Leaving Abusive Partners: From the Scars of Survival to the Wisdom for Change.* London, Sage.

Little, K. et al. (1998). Assessing justice system Responses to Violence Against Women: A Tool for Law enforcement, Prosecution and the Courts to Use in Developing Effective Responses.
Available at: www.vaw.umn.edu/documents/promise/pplaw/pplaw.html.

Maxwell, C., Garner, J. and Fagan, J. (2001). The effects of arrest on intimate partner violence: new evidence from spouse assault replication PROGRAM. National institute of Justice: Research in Brief, July.

Mullender, A. et al. (2002). *Children's Perspectives on Domestic Violence.* London: Whiting and Birch.

Sanmartin, J., Molina, A. and Garcia, Y. (2003). *Partner Violence against Women: Statistics and Legislation.* Valencia: Centro Reina Sofia para el Estudio de la Violencia.

Sen, P. (1998). Searching for routes to safety: a report on the needs of ethnic minority women dealing with domestic violence. London: Camden Equalities Unit.

Weisberg, D. (1996). *Applications of Feminist Legal Theory to Women's Lives: Sex, Violence, Work and Reproduction.* Indiana: Temple University Press.

Women's National Commission (2003). Unlocking the Secret: Women Open the Door on Domestic Violence. London: WNC.

Zorza, J. (1995). Mandatory arrest for domestic violence: why it may prove the best first step in curbing repeat abuse. *Criminal Justice,* Fall, 2-9, 51-54.

Chapter 6

Violence Against Women in the Swedish Context

Peter Lindström

Introduction

Violence against women has historically been high on the political agenda in Sweden. Over the last decade the Swedish parliament has discussed more than 300 bills on this topic and has passed a number of important pieces of legislation. The year 1982 constituted a starting point of sorts for introduction of reforming legislation. It was at this point that assault in private settings became an offence that the police were required to investigate, regardless of the victim's approval[1] (SOU 2002: 71). In 1988, restraining orders prohibiting a person from visiting, calling, or in any other way contacting the person being protected by the order were introduced into the penal code. The intention of this law was first and foremost to protect women from assaults and threatening behaviour at the hands of current or former partners. More recent pieces of legislation include the prohibition of the purchase of sexual services (1999). In 1998, a new offence of 'Gross violation of a woman's integrity' was introduced into the penal code. This offence consisted of repeated sanctionable acts committed by a man against a present or former female partner. Violence against women appears to be equally important to all political parties in

---

1   Not everyone was pleased with this reform. A well-known prosecutor wrote in a journal published by the National Council for Crime Prevention that this reform could have negative consequences for the victimised woman, especially if she was going to remain in the relationship with the man (Östberg, 1980, p. 15). Furthermore, if a woman did not wish to proceed with the legal process, she could simply deny what she had said in the police report. According to Östberg, it would be better to try to increase the willingness of victimised women to make an official report in the first place.

Sweden, regardless of their political complexion. In fact, there has been political consensus that Sweden needs both harsher sanctions for men who assault, and more shelters and support services for battered women. Overall, the political interest in violence against women may be viewed, at least among certain political parties, in the wider context of gender inequality.

Increased political pressure, not only at the national level but also from international declarations, has caused public sector agencies at the national, regional and local levels to give violence against women a higher priority, at least in the documents they produce. Local social services, for example, are to provide support for crime victims, and particularly for victims of domestic violence, including children. The police and prosecutors have been instructed to develop measures so that they can work more effectively to prevent violence against women. These measures should also result in more convictions of violent men. Finally, the national prison and probation service is currently developing programmes for men who have been sentenced for assault in the context of intimate relationships.

Research on violence against women has also expanded substantially over the last decade. In 1991, a professorship in sociology with a special focus on violence against women was established at Uppsala University. In 1997, the National Council for Crime Prevention, a research-oriented body administered under the auspices of the Swedish Ministry of Justice, was given directives to increase its work on violence against women, and introduce improvements to the official crime statistics in this area. The purpose of this chapter is to summarise some of the research on violence against women that has been conducted in Sweden over the last few years. One rather more specific objective is to describe how the criminal justice system in general, and the police in particular, deal with the new offence of 'Gross violation of a woman's integrity'. Data collected both from official crime statistics and from interviews with police and prosecutors will therefore be analysed. The chapter uses information from previous research and from an ongoing research project on violence against women being conducted by this author.[2]

One preventive measure that has been discussed extensively over the past few years is the use of restraining orders. In 2003, police and

---

2   The results partly refer to analyses that have not been previously published. Also, since data on police-recorded incidents of gross violation of a woman's integrity are continually being updated, numbers may not correspond with statistics published earlier.

prosecutors were given the opportunity to issue an instant restraining order, even if the man who was the object of the order was permanently domiciled at the same address as the woman. The National Council for Crime Prevention is currently evaluating this change in the law. The final section of the chapter presents the findings from previous research on restraining orders.

Defining and Measuring Violence Against Women

The concept of violence against women may include both physical and non-physical incidents. Offences such as assault and rape, but also threatening behaviour and sexual harassment, may all constitute part of the overall concept of violence against women. In their 1995 report, the National Commission on Violence against Women argued that incidents that are not criminalised, such as humiliating or controlling a woman's contacts with relatives and friends, should be included in the offence 'Gross violation of a woman's integrity'. The Swedish government concluded, however, that this would not be possible from a legalistic perspective. In the following, the term violence against women refers exclusively to criminalised incidents. More specifically, the focus is directed at criminal incidents committed by a man against a current or former female partner.

Two basic sources of information can be used to describe the level of violence against women in Sweden.[3] The first source, and perhaps the one employed most often, comprises incidents reported to the police. One obvious problem associated with this source of information is of course that the majority of incidents of violence against women are not reported to the police. The second source of information comprises surveys asking women whether they have been victimised and, if so, where and by whom. Victim surveys have been conducted both on a one-off basis and also more regularly, in association with measurements of Swedish living conditions (see below). Under certain circumstances, surveys may also be used to

---

3 Information on violence may also come from the health care sector. In connection with inpatient treatment, hospitals are required to collect data relating to the incident that resulted in the need for treatment. However, the classification system employed has yet to be fully developed as regards the information on violent incidents collected. No information is as yet collected on the relationship between the victim and the perpetrator, for example.

estimate the so called dark-figure, i.e. the total number of incidents in relation to the number of incidents reported to the police. This technique is not error-free, of course. Some women, for example, may be reluctant or unable to answer survey questions of this nature, perhaps out of embarrassment or because they are still living with the perpetrator (for a discussion of the problems associated with such methods, see Piispa, 2002). In combination, knowledge based on both of these sources of information should nonetheless yield a fairly adequate picture of violence against women in Sweden. Definitional issues and non-overlapping target populations mean, however, that there will always be room for ambiguity.

Prevalence and Incidents of Violence Against Women

Statistics Sweden has conducted annual surveys of the living conditions of Swedish citizens since 1978. These surveys have included a number of questions relating to crime victimisation (SCB, 2004). Overall, the proportion of women reporting that they had been victims of violence in 2002/2003 lay at 4.1 percent, which constitutes the highest level ever reported in this quarter-century-long data series.[4] A large proportion of these women had been victimised at work. The survey of 2000, which included in-depth questions on violence,[5] showed that less than one percent of the women had been victimised in their own home by a person with whom they were acquainted. The most vulnerable group found in these data comprises single mothers, whose risk of becoming the victims of threatening behaviour or violence in their own homes is seven times greater than that of other women (Estrada and Nilsson 2004).

Two recent studies have asked more specifically about violence in intimate relationships. In a large-scale survey, Lundgren and colleagues (2002) found that about seven percent of women aged 18-64 had been the victims of violence at the hands of a current male partner over the last five years. Three percent had been victimised in this way within the last twelve months. More than a quarter of all women had been victimised by a former male partner. The definition of violence employed in this study was more inclusive than that employed in the studies conducted by Statistics Sweden. A study by the Swedish National Council for Crime Prevention estimated that approximately one percent of the country's working women are

---

4 Levels of violence requiring medical treatment have decreased somewhat over the recent years, however.
5 In-depth questions on violence are included every eighth year.

exposed to violence in an intimate relationship over the course of a given year (Nilsson, 2001). The possibility of drawing general conclusions on the basis of this study are of course restricted, due to the fact that the study only included women in the workforce. The research estimated that between one-quarter and one-fifth of all incidents of violence against women that actually take place are reported to the police. Other studies have arrived at similar estimates.

With the exception of the new offence of 'Gross violation of a woman's integrity', which will be described more fully below, official Swedish crime statistics do not reveal information about the relationship between the victim and the perpetrator in cases of violence against women. Although the police often record information about the relationship between the victim and perpetrator in their crime report, this information may only be fully revealed by specially focused studies. In respect of assault, however, it is possible to identify offences that have been committed by a person acquainted with the woman. This crime category has often been interpreted as an indicator of the volume of violence against women in intimate relationships. The meaning of the term 'acquainted' is fairly vague, however. The perpetrator may be a female friend, for example, or a male work colleague.

In a detailed study of acquaintance assaults against women, it was found that about two-thirds of these offences related to a heterosexual intimate relationship, of which the majority related to an ongoing relationship (Nilsson, 2002). In 2003, almost 17,000 assaults against women were reported as having been committed by acquaintances. On the basis of the findings from Nilsson's study, about 11,000 of these offences can be expected to have been committed by a former or current male partner.

Trends Over Time

Over the last two decades, the number of police-recorded assaults against women has increased at a rate of about eight percent per year. A recurring question both in the media and among researchers is whether this increase is due to a change in reporting behaviour on the part of the victims, or if it represents a real increase. Data from the national victimisation study show an annual average rate of increase of about six percent for the same period. Among men, the same comparison shows a rate of increase of eight percent per annum in recorded violent crime but only a two percent increase in the victimisation data. Overall, the conclusion that violent crime has increased in Sweden cannot be ruled out. Interestingly, the number of cases of lethal violence in intimate relationships did not seem to increase during the 1990s, but has rather remained fairly stable (Rying, 2000). On average sixteen women are killed by a current or former male partner every year in Sweden, which gives a homicide rate of about 0.80 per 100,000 married and divorced females. For the USA, Rosenfeld (2000, p. 155) has estimated the female spousal homicide rate at 1.39 per 100,000 married and divorced females.

Repeated Victimisation

Violence against a woman by a current or former male partner does not generally occur in isolation from other forms of intimidation, such as sexual harassment and subjection to physical restrictions. Both fiction and non-fiction literature describe how loving relationships can gradually transform into hostile and violent ones as a result of jealousy, drug abuse, mental health problems, etc. The victimised woman may also redefine and neutralise the violence she is experiencing. Two terms employed in the literature to describe these processes are the 'cycle of violence' and the 'normalisation process' (Karlsson, 2002).

One Swedish study found that between 25 and 30 percent of women reporting violence by a partner to the police make a second report within 12 months (Carlstedt, 2000). On the basis of interviews and police reports, it has been found that approximately half of the victimised women had been exposed to violence on more than one occasion. It is also very common for the perpetrators of lethal violence to have previously threatened and assaulted the woman in question. Rying (2000) has shown that in spousal-related homicides, previous threats or evidence of violence can be found in between 30 and 40 percent of cases.

This understanding that violence against women is in general repeated and often tends to escalate in seriousness, became the corner-stone in the new offence of 'Gross violation of a woman's integrity', which was introduced into Swedish penal law in 1998.

Gross Violation of a Woman's Integrity

If a man engages in certain criminal acts, such as assault, threatening behaviour or coercion, sexual or other molestation, or sexual exploitation against a woman to whom he is, or has been married, or with whom he is, or has been, cohabiting, and the acts are such as may seriously damage the victim's self-confidence, he is to be sentenced for gross violation of the woman's integrity, rather than for the individual offences that each act comprises (BrB 4:4a).[6] The sanction for this offence has been set at imprisonment for no less than six months and no more than six years. The law contains a similarly phrased article that applies if a man or a woman commits such acts against a child, a relative or a same-sex partner. The article then refers to the offence as 'Gross violation of a person's integrity'.

This regulation means that repeated offences of this kind are to be considered jointly and are to result in a more stringent sentence than would be the case if each of the acts were to be considered separately (Wennberg, 2000). The preamble to the law emphasises that for a man to be convicted of gross violation of a woman's integrity, the acts committed must be specifiable. A further requirement is that these acts must have taken place within a specified period of time. There is no requirement that the woman subjected to the acts should be able to specify the date of each incident, however.

The law was enacted in July 1998 but, as early as 2000, the wording of the law was reformulated with regard to the requirement that 'the acts must have constituted part of a repeated violation'. A judgment by the Supreme Court in March 1999 had interpreted this to mean that the man had to have been convicted of similar offences against the woman at some earlier point in time. The intention behind the introduction of a new formulation, that 'each of the acts must have constituted part of a repeated violation', was to abolish the requirement that the man must have a previous conviction for a crime against the woman before he can be convicted of gross violation of a woman's integrity. The following analyses employ data beginning in the year 2000.

Police Handling of Gross Violation of a Woman's Integrity

The police recorded approximately 1,860 offences relating to gross violation of woman's integrity in 2003. As described above, offences recorded by the police as assault by an acquaintance often represent incidents of violence that were committed by a current or former partner, and that also constitute part of a repetitive pattern of victimisation. So such

---

6   Swedish Penal Code, Chapter 4.

incidents might be recorded as gross violation of a woman's integrity. Theoretically, therefore, the number of reported cases of gross violation of a woman's integrity may be substantially higher than the figure that is currently being recorded.[7]

The Swedish crime recording system records offences at an early stage of the legal process. Since gross violation of a woman's integrity consists of various individual offences, careful instruction is required to employ this code correctly. In the instruction booklet used by the police, it is stated that the individual offences (e.g. assault or threatening behaviour) should not be coded in the report in cases where the code for gross violation of a woman's integrity is employed. However, in about half of all police-recorded cases of gross violation of a woman's integrity, the underlying offences were also found to be recorded. Although this is unlikely to affect the criminal process, it is likely to exert a biasing influence on the crime statistics.

Figure 6.1 shows the monthly number of cases of gross violation of a woman's integrity recorded by the police.[8] By comparison with previous years, the number of gross violations of a woman's integrity recorded during 2004 has increased by a third. The main explanation for this increase is most likely to be that the police and prosecutors are becoming better at judging violence against women in accordance with the new legislation. Besides educating police officers in how to handle such cases, approximately half of the police authorities in Sweden have established special family violence units with responsibility for investigating violence against women. It is, of course, very important that patrol officers are also well trained in this issue, because evidence collected at an early stage may be very important to the continued investigation.

A comparison of recorded incidents for different regions shows[9] that different police authorities vary substantially in their use of the offence category 'Gross violation of woman's integrity' when recording crimes of violence against women. In Stockholm, for example, there was a 40 percent

---

7   Given 11,000 police-recorded incidents of assault of a woman by a current or former partner, with indications that these incidents are being repeated in at least half of the cases recorded, the number of recorded cases of gross violation of a woman's integrity could be more than twice that currently recorded.

8   Source: Official Crime Statistic published by the National Council for Crime Prevention (www.bra.se).

9   Corresponding tables are not presented here; data are available on-line at www.bra.se, differentiated by region, year, and offence type (continually updated; see also footnote 2).

increase in the number of police-recorded cases of gross violation of a woman's integrity between 2002 and 2003, mainly due to the establishment of a new family violence unit.

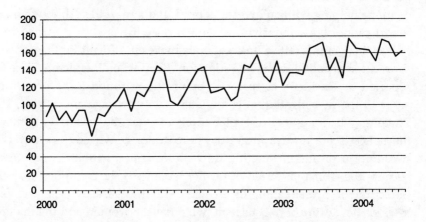

Figure 6.1   Cases of gross violation of a woman's integrity recorded by the police, monthly figures, January 2000 – June 2004

Over time there has been a relative increase in the number of offences being recorded by police authorities other than the three major metropolitan authorities (Stockholm, Gothenburg and Malmö). In 2003, the three major regions recorded approximately 56 percent of all cases, while in 2000 they had recorded 67 percent of all cases. Another regional difference is that the number of cases of gross violation of a woman's integrity per 100,000 women recorded by the police in Gothenburg is twice that recorded in Malmö (the actual geographical units involved relate to the counties of Västra Götaland and Skåne). However, the numbers of persons convicted of this offence are more or less equivalent in both areas. It is unclear whether this is due to 'better' investigations in Malmö, with a higher clearance rate, or whether the use of the code for gross violation of a woman's integrity is simply more inclusive in Gothenburg.[10]

---

10 Based on information on the number of police-recorded cases of assault on women, and interviews with police officers in Gothenburg, the second explanation seems most plausible.

Prosecuting Violence Against Women

Several Swedish studies have found that victims of violence, and in particular violence in intimate relationships, are not always willing to continue helping with an investigation (Lundberg, 2001). Although a crime report cannot be withdrawn in Sweden once it has been recorded by the police, the victim's refusal to co-operate makes it difficult for the police and prosecutor to continue the investigation. Even when the victim herself has reported the incident, as many as one-fifth are found to be unwilling to assist in the investigation at some later stage (Belfrage and Strand, 2003). There may be a number of explanations for this; the reason for contacting the police is not always to get the perpetrator convicted, but may rather constitute a means of quieting down a violent situation. It may also be because the woman is afraid of further violence if she continues to assist in the criminal investigation of a man who has already acted violently towards her. A further obstacle may be that the woman and the man have been involved in an intimate and emotional relationship, and may also have had children together.

Of all the cases of gross violation of a woman's integrity reported in 2003, approximately 40 percent resulted in prosecutions. Over the four years since 2000, the clearance rate, i.e. the number of offences being prosecuted out of all reported offences, for this category has increased substantially. Compared with other violent offences this is a very high percentage, which is due of course to the fact that the victim knows the perpetrator well[11] (Crime Statistics 2003). Table 6.1 presents the number of reported and cleared-up offences, as well as the number of men sentenced to imprisonment for gross violation of a woman's integrity.

---

11 One interesting development is the decline in the clearance rate since 1995 for the offence category 'assault of a woman by an acquainted person'. In 2003, about 23 percent of all reported cases led to prosecution. This figure had been 29 percent in 1995. A potential explanation may be that 'an acquainted person' in cases of assault is less likely to be a present or former partner.

Table 6.1 Number of reported and cleared-up offences, clearance rate and number of men sentenced for the offence 'Gross violation of a woman's integrity', 2000-2003

	2000	2001	2002	2003
No. of reported offences	1,147	1,512	1,571	1,860
No. of cleared-up offences	312	472	575	733
Clearance rate in percent	27	31	37	39
No. of men sentenced to imprisonment	80	136	165	212

Source: Crime Statistics (2003).

The most common reason given in cases where charges are dropped is that the evidence was deemed insufficient to establish that an offence had been committed. In an evaluation of the first eighteen months after the new offence of 'Gross violation of a woman's integrity' was introduced, the prosecutors were of the opinion that further evidence, such as medical certificates, is often required to support a prosecution in addition to the testimony of the complainant (Soukkan and Lindström, 2000). Although it is legally possible for the court to sentence a man for gross violation of a woman's integrity purely on the testimony supplied by the woman, very few such cases can be found (Karlsson, 2002, p. 46).

Court Judgments Concerning Gross Violation of a Woman's Integrity

It has been found that the most common combination of offences included in these court judgments comprises repeated assaults (Soukkan and Lindström, 2000; Karlsson, 2002). There is, however, no requirement of a certain number of acts that have to have been committed in order to constitute a gross violation of a woman's integrity. A general rule, according to prosecutors, is that if the incidents are less severe, there need to be several acts; whereas if the acts are severe, fewer are needed in order to constitute gross violation of a woman's integrity. The prosecutor is required to specify at least some of the individual offences in the allegation. Almost half of the acts cited took place within a period of four to six months. In the majority of cases, the timing of the acts is specified to the extent that they are dated to a specific day. The intention of the law to accept non-date-specified acts has not been used to any high degree. In half of the cases, the man admits either wholly or in part to one or more of the acts cited in the summons. In addition to the testimony of the complainant, there are often medical certificates and photographs to support the specific acts cited. This shows that, on the whole, the evidence in the cases coming before court is quite strong.

The sentence for gross violation of a woman's integrity is stipulated as imprisonment for a term of between six months and six years. Inspection of the crime statistics shows that approximately 85 percent of the men annually convicted of this offence were sentenced to imprisonment, for a mean term of eleven months. Fifteen percent of the men were sentenced to probation in combination with some form of treatment. Since the year 2000, there has been a large increase in the number of men sentenced to imprisonment for gross violation of a woman's integrity. In 2003, more than 200 men were sentenced to imprisonment for this offence (see Table 6.1), a figure that accounts for approximately four percent of all men serving a prison term of six months or over. As the police and prosecutors become more experienced in dealing with this offence, it is clear that more men will be imprisoned for domestic violence.

Part of the evaluation research by the National Council for Crime Prevention concerned an analysis of court sanctions passed on men in cases of repeated assault against women with whom they had been in a close relationship, comparing the situation prior to and subsequent to the introduction of the provisions on gross violation of a woman's integrity (Soukkan and Lindström, 2000). The results indicate that the proportion of prison sentences passed prior to the introduction of the provisions was more or less the same as it is for gross violation of a woman's integrity, but that the length of sentence was somewhat shorter for repeated assault. Looking back, the purpose of introducing the offence 'Gross violation of a woman's integrity' had been to upgrade the definition of less serious forms of assault and threats, so that when considered in the context of violence against a present or former partner they would be viewed as a serious crime. Both the study from the National Council for Crime Prevention in 2000 and a study by Karlsson (2002) have questioned whether this has happened, since the acts included in court judgments in general could be classified as 'normal to severe' incidents. As these studies do not include data after 2000, analysis of more recent data may lead to different conclusions.

The Perpetrators of Violence Against Women

The evaluation further showed that of all the men convicted of gross violation of a woman's integrity, 70 percent had a previous conviction for violent offences (Soukkan and Lindström, 2000). Of those with previous convictions, one-third had been convicted of offences against the same woman as was named as the victim in connection with the charge of gross violation of a woman's integrity. Drug or alcohol abuse was a common denominator linking many of the convicted men. According to interviews with police and prosecutors, the law on gross violation of a woman's integrity has not led to any major changes in the composition of the group of perpetrators. The change in the law has thus not meant that previously unknown offenders are reported to a greater extent.[12] On the contrary, it is often persons already known to the police, with an extensive criminal past and other social problems, who are charged with gross violation of a woman's integrity. A study of lethal violence against women in intimate relationship shows a similar pattern. In 60 per cent of cases, the perpetrators had previous convictions, predominantly for violence (Rying, 2000).

All in all, when handled before the court, gross violation of a woman's integrity is a serious offence and a large proportion of the men convicted of this offence were remanded in custody prior to their convictions. This outcome, however, only applies to a minority of the cases, as the majority of cases of domestic violence is not tried before court. In order to prevent further violence, restraining orders have become a popular measure employed by the criminal justice system.

Restraining Orders to Prevent Violence Against Women

Violence in intimate relationships is often repeated. In contrast to violence in other settings, the victim and the perpetrator may have a long history together and they will quite often have children in common. With this knowledge in mind, restraining orders were introduced in 1988 with the objective of improving the level of protection for individuals who are being persecuted and harassed. The use of restraining orders was introduced as

---

12 One expectation of the law was that lowering the threshold for the prosecution of violence against women would lead to more men without prior criminal records being prosecuted. There is no indication that this has occurred.

one of the efforts being made to restrict incidents of violence against women in the context of intimate relationships. Being issued with a restraining order means that a person may no longer visit or actively attempt to make contact in any other way with the individual that the order is intended to protect. The decision as to whether to issue a restraining order is taken by a prosecutor within seven days of an application being submitted. The police have an obligation to inform a victim of domestic violence that they can apply for such an order.

In 2003, the Restraining Order Act was changed so as to include also persons living at the same address, thus making it possible to force the person named in the restraining order to move. Furthermore, having consulted a prosecutor, the police could decide to issue an instant restraining order. These changes were inspired by legislation enacted in Austria. A restraining order may also be issued in connection with cases based on civil law, but this section will only discuss restraining orders issued by prosecutors in criminal law cases.

A Potential Preventive Instrument

The overall goal is that restraining orders should increase the levels of safety of those protected by the orders and serve to prevent crimes being perpetrated against them. In preparing the legislation, the risk was identified that restraining orders would not be respected. However, one intention was that the police should use the orders as a point of departure for their crime prevention work relating to domestic violence. By means of in-depth interviews with 40 women who had applied for restraining orders, and by examining the relevant statistics, the National Council for Crime Prevention evaluated the effect of restraining orders on safety and crime (Edlund and Svanberg, 2003). Over recent years, almost 7,000 individuals per year have applied for a restraining order, with just under half of these applications being approved. In just over 70 per cent of the cases, the applicant is a woman applying for an order to be issued to a man with whom she is or has been involved in an intimate relationship.

Effects of Restraining Orders

The evaluation shows that about 40 percent of the men issued with restraining orders were suspected of crimes against the person within a year of the restraining order being issued, and just over one in four were suspected of violating their restraining orders. These numbers should be interpreted with caution, however, since the data do not allow us to distinguish whether the crimes in question were committed against the woman whom the orders were intended to protect or against someone else. The conclusion of the study was that restraining orders may have a certain deterrent effect, even if only on a small group of individuals. This is primarily the case for men who have no previous criminal record. One explanation for this might be that these men perceive such orders to be a more serious measure than men with more experience of involvement in crime. The study leads to the conclusion that the effectiveness of restraining orders depends in general on two factors: which individuals are issued with restraining orders, and how serious the need for protection is among those applying for the orders. The number of restraining orders issued will be affected by the way that the police approach their duty to inform victims of their option of applying for a restraining order, and by the prosecutor's assessment of whether or not there are grounds for issuing such an order. The decision to issue or not to issue the restraining order is taken by the prosecutor, but a court may overrule this decision. The work conducted by the police and prosecutors in this regard is focused on relatively serious cases, where there is a clear risk that further crimes will be committed. The police primarily supply information on restraining orders to women who report crimes of violence and who have previously reported crimes, or where there are other factors present indicating that the offence being reported does not constitute a random incident.

In turn, the decision by the prosecutor to issue a restraining order appears for the most part to be based on whether the individual named in the application has previously been reported for crimes where there has been sufficient evidence to establish that an offence has been committed. Although during the preparation of the legislation, it was stated that this should constitute only one of a number of indicators of the existence of a continuing risk, the evaluation shows that it seems rather to have become a precondition for approving an application. The risk assessment rarely appears to be based on a careful consideration of the situation viewed in its entirety, and the grounds upon which prosecutors have based their decisions are often poorly documented. In recent years, the police and prosecutors have made an effort to develop better risk assessment instruments.

Interviews with police furthermore show that restraining orders, in contrast to their intended purpose, are rarely used as an instrument of crime prevention. The majority of police authorities report that they do not work proactively when an order has been issued, but rather wait until breaches are reported before acting. By the year 2002, only seven of Sweden's 21 police authorities had established routines for active and continuous follow-up work in connection with restraining orders in their area. Within these seven authorities, it is the community police officers or officers with special functions (e.g. police dog service) who carry out this follow-up work. Such work may, for example, involve the police making contact with the person who is to be protected and/or the person issued with the restraining order, in order to find out whether the order is being complied with and, if necessary, to introduce additional protective measures. Few police authorities have established routines that make information on restraining orders available within the agency.

Immediate interventions constitute another means of preventing crime that was emphasised in the preparation of the law. This involves the police intervening when an attempt is made to contact the person requiring protection, in order to avoid situations that might result in serious offences. The results of the evaluation show that interventions of this kind generally only occur if there is an evident risk that some other offence may be committed, and most often when the man is still to be found in close physical proximity to the woman when the police are called in.

Weak Effect

The interviews conducted with the women pointed to several aspects of how the justice system handles their reporting of violations, which they felt constituted a reason why they did not feel more secure. They stated that while the police encouraged them to report violations of the restraining orders, nothing happened when they did so. In many cases this meant that the women ceased to report such violations altogether, or only reported those involving serious incidents. The women also felt that the justice system failed to react against the man in question, and that the harassment therefore continued. The women also stated that there was a lack of continuity in their contacts with the police and that they had to describe the background to the restraining order every time they got in touch with them. Finally, slightly over half of the investigations conducted into violations of restraining orders were terminated without charges being brought. The most common motivation for this was that there was insufficient evidence to establish that the offence had been committed.

Concluding Remarks

Violence in almost all its forms is strongly condemned in contemporary western society and the right to a life without violence has become a human rights issue. Over the last 25 years, many countries have increasingly come to view violence against women and children in particular as a public rather than a private matter. This change in attitudes and levels of political interest places higher expectations on official authorities, including the criminal justice system, to tackle this social problem.

The number of incidents of violence against women in general, recorded by the Swedish police, has increased over the last decade. This trend may on the one hand be explained by higher levels of attention focused on such crimes in society at large. There may of course also be an underlying real increase, i.e. that more women are being made victims of violence, as has been found in surveys. One explanation for this increase appears to be that over time, more women run the risk of becoming victims of violence at work. For violence against women in the home, current data do not allow speculation about trends over time. Although the question of trends over time is important, this chapter has primarily focused on how the criminal justice system is currently dealing with violence against women in intimate relationships.

Violence against women in the home seldom occurs on a one-off basis. When a woman decides to contact the police, it is likely to be the result of a long period of abuse and violence. The ways in which the criminal justice system deals with these offences is a matter of major importance. By introducing the offence of 'Gross violation of a woman's integrity' into the penal code, Sweden has defined an offence that is quite unique from a European perspective, in that it views a number of less serious offences as a single unit of crime when they are judged in the context of a pattern of repeated victimisation. Starting with the police and prosecutors, it seems clear that violence against women is being given a higher priority, with increasing numbers of police authorities establishing special units to deal with family violence for example. There are also indications that patrol officers are receiving better training in how to handle such incidents.

The new provision was intended to treat less serious but repeated offences against the same woman as a single serious offence. It is still too early to draw any far-reaching conclusions as to how effectively this offence is functioning, one reason being that it has taken time for the criminal justice system to adapt its work fully to this offence. On the one hand, two studies have found that men convicted of gross violation of a woman's integrity have committed relatively serious offences and not, as intended, less serious incidents of domestic violence. However, both of these studies use data from 1998-2000 and it is possible that the situation is different today. On the other hand, the results also suggest that the courts have treated the gross violation of a woman's integrity as a particularly serious offence, as is demonstrated by the length of the prison sentences passed.

When it comes to working more proactively to prevent further violence, restraining orders may be one measure available to the police to bring this about. Over time, more and more women have been protected by restraining orders, although interviews with women show that this does not necessarily improve their sense of security. Many of the women interviewed stated that 'nothing happens' in terms of criminal sanctions if the man in question violates the order. There are, however, some interesting examples of more active work on the part of the police, including regular visits to the protected women, and occasionally even to the men. The final point to be made with regard to restraining orders is that it is reasonable to conclude that the police should assume a more active role in assisting women who are supposed to be protected by such an order.

By way of a final reflection, the criminal justice system often constitutes a rather blunt instrument for dealing with interpersonal violence, particularly when the victim and the perpetrator are, or have been, intimate, and not least if they have children in common. If a woman contacts the police because of an abusive partner, the police are obligated to initiate an investigation if they suspect that an offence has been committed, and the prosecutor has an obligation to prosecute if there is sufficient evidence. It is, on the whole, a positive thing that the decision as to what will happen in the criminal justice process is not placed on the victim's shoulders. The willingness of the victim to continue co-operating in a case is nonetheless a crucial element in this process. In reality, of course, the police occasionally become involved in some sort of mediation and no crime report may be made. Both the police and prosecutors, but also formal and informal social support groups, may have an important impact on the woman's decision. Having the man convicted for the offence may be one thing but the priority is, of course, that the violent behaviour ceases. If the couple intends to continue with their relationship, family counselling or other forms of therapy may then be a starting-point. Rather than closing the criminal case because the woman is not willing to continue with the process, a system of 'conditional prosecutions', which force the man actively to seek help to change his behaviour, or face prosecution, might constitute one possibility.

References

Belfrage, H. and Strand, S. (2003). Utveckling av ett riskinstrument för polisiär bedömning av risk för upprepat partnervåld (SARA:PV). Slutrapport från ett utvecklingsprojekt i Kalmar, Kronoberg och Blekinge län. Sundsvall: Mitthögskolan [Developing a risk assessment instrument for repeated violence in intimate relationships].

Carlstedt, M. (2000). *Repeat victimisation*. BRÅ-report 2001:3 (in Swedish with English summary). Stockholm: National Council for Crime Prevention.

Crime Statistics (2003). Stockholm: National Council for Crime Prevention.

Edlund, M. and Svanberg, K. (2003). *Restraining orders. An evaluation of the law and its application*. BRÅ-report 2003:2 (in Swedish with English summary). Stockholm: National Council for Crime Prevention.

Estrada, F. and Nilsson, A. (2004). Exposure to threatening and violent behaviour among single mothers. *British Journal of Criminology*, Vol 44 (2), pp. 168-187.

Karlsson, A. (2002). *Grov kvinnofridskränkning – en utvärdering*. Juridiska fakulteten. Uppsala universitet [Gross violation of a woman's integrity – an evaluation].

Lundberg, M. (2001). Vilja med förhinder: polisers samtal om kvinnomisshandel. Eslöv: Symposion [Will with obstructed: police officers' conversation about violence against women].

Lundgren, E., Heimer, G., Westerstrand, J. and Kalliokoski, A-M. (2002). *Captured Queen: Men's violence against women in 'Equal' Sweden: A Prevalence Study*. Stockholm: Fritzes Förlag.

Nilsson, L. (2001). *Violence against women in intimate relationships. An overview*. BRÅ-report 2002:14 (in Swedish with English summary). Stockholm: National Council for Crime Prevention.

Piispa, M. (2002). Violence against women as conveyed by surveys – the Finnish case. *Journal of Scandinavian Criminology and Crime Prevention* Vol. 3 (2), pp. 173-193.

Rosenfeld, R. (2000). Patterns in Adult Homicide: 1980-1995. Pp. 130-163 in A. Blumstein and J. Wallman. (Eds). *The Crime Drop in America*. Cambridge: University Press.

Rying, M. (2000). *Acts of lethal violence against women in intimate relationships*. BRÅ-report 2001:1 (in Swedish with English summary). Stockholm: National Council for Crime Prevention.

SCB (2004). Offer för vålds- och egendomsbrott 1978-2002 [Victims of violence and of property crimes 1978-2002]. Living Conditions Report no 104. Stockholm: Statistics Sweden.

SOU 2002: 71. Nationell handlingsplan mot våld i nära relationer. Delbetänkande av personsäkerhetsutredningen. [National Action Plan regarding Violence in close relationships]. Stockholm: Fritzes Förlag.

Soukkan, J. and Lindström, P. (2000). *Gross violation of a woman's integrity*. BRÅ-report 2000:11 (in Swedish with English summary) Stockholm: National Council for Crime Prevention.

Wennberg, S. (2000). Grov kvinnofridskränkning – en problematisk brottskonstruktion. Svensk juristtidning [Gross violation of a woman's integrity – a problematic offence construction].

Östberg, E. (1980). *Tveksam nytta av ändrad åtalsregel*. BRÅ-Apropå nr. 1 1980. [Doubtful use of changed prosecution rules]. Stockholm: Fritzes Förlag.

Chapter 7

Legal Processing of Domestic Violence Cases in the Italian Criminal Justice System

Anna C. Baldry

Introduction

When discussing violence in the family, a distinction needs to be drawn between 'domestic violence', referring to any violence perpetrated between intimate partners, and violence committed against children, parents, siblings or elderly people (Baldry, 2001). The latter type of violence is generally referred to as 'family violence'. Domestic violence refers not only to married couples but also to *de facto* relationships (Yllö and Bograd, 1988).

Many studies have been conducted in the field of family violence, and domestic violence in particular, addressing possible theoretical explanations of its causes and risk factors (Barnett, Miller-Perrin and Perrin, 1997). Findings from surveys of the nature and prevalence of domestic violence all over the world have indicated that one woman in four, or even one in two, is a victim of violence at the hands of a family member (Mirrlees-Black, 1999; Tjaden and Thoennes, 2000a, 2000b; Unicef, 2000).

Research in the Italian context is still scarce; data on the prevalence of domestic violence are based on shelter populations or on non-representative samples. Italy's National Institute of Statistics is currently conducting the first national survey on violence against women, with a representative random sample of 30,000 women. This survey should shed some light on the so-called 'dark number' affected by domestic violence (Baldry, 2003).

Domestic violence is characterised by a pattern of behaviours inflicted against a partner with the intention of humiliating, degrading or controlling the partner (Walker, 1979). Throughout this chapter, I will refer to domestic violence as any form of male violence (psychological, economic, physical and sexual) perpetrated against a female partner, as occurs in the majority of domestic violence cases. Cases of female violence against a male partner do take place, but these are fewer in number and less severe in their consequences (Crowell and Burgess, 1996).

This chapter will focus on current Italian legislation dealing with domestic violence. As will be noted, the Italian legislation does not always distinguish between family violence and domestic violence. Further in the chapter, I will also discuss the debate taking place within Italy on how to deal with this type of violence, and initiatives introduced by both law enforcement agencies and NGOs to combat domestic violence.

Italian Legislation in Cases of Domestic Violence

The Italian Criminal Code (C.C.) contains only a few provisions that deal specifically with family violence (and therefore with domestic violence); even fewer provisions refer specifically to domestic violence (Baldry, 2001). However, numerous crimes identified by the law can be applied in cases of domestic violence. In addition, a new legal provision enables restraining orders to be issued in cases where violence is committed within a family context. It is worth mentioning that all types of violence constituting 'domestic violence' (physical, psychological and sexual) are covered by the Italian criminal code. A woman affected by one of these types of actions can therefore report the violence to the police, who may send the case to the prosecution. Some crimes, to be prosecuted, must be reported by victims themselves. Other crimes in this domain, once known to the legal authorities, can be referred directly to the public prosecutor without the victim having to file a complaint. The different types of violence listed in Italian criminal law that may be relevant for the criminal prosecution of family violence are outlined below.

Psychological violence can be divided into three categories: *'Private violence'* (art. 610 C.C.), whereby a person may be convicted of psychological violence if he or she forces another, with violence or threat, to endure something – the perpetrator is punishable with imprisonment of up to four years; *'Threat'* (art. 612 C.C.), when someone threatens another, thereby causing damage; and *'Insult'* (art. 594 C.C.), when someone insults the honour or the dignity of another.

Physical violence is also divided into a number of categories: *'Assault'* (art. 581 C.C.), whereby someone hits another but no severe physical/mental consequences ensue – the perpetrator can be imprisoned for up to 6 months. Assaults are regarded as isolated events and a legal action is started only if the victim reports the crime to the police; *'Personal injury'* (art. 582 C.C.), when someone injures another, causing a physical or mental impairment – the perpetrator can be imprisoned from 3 months to a maximum of 3 years. If the victim reports an injury that will require up to 40 days to recover, the case can be prosecuted only if the victim reports the crime. If the injury is considered to be highly serious, and will require more than 40 days to heal, the legal authorities (police or public prosecutor) must initiate a legal action; *'Personal injuries'* can be 'serious' or 'very serious' (art. 583 C.C.), a crime punishable from 3 years to 7 years in the first case, or up to 12 years if, as a consequence of the 'very serious injury', a serious illness impairs the victim from leading a normal life.

Article nr. 572 of the Criminal Code refers directly to family violence and is identified as *'Maltreatment within the family'*. According to this provision, when somebody maltreats a family member, the punishment is imprisonment from 1 to 5 years. The article specifies that in order to proceed for a crime of 'maltreatment', the violence committed must include a set of violent acts (psychological as well as physical or sexual), committed repeatedly over an extended period of time, even if no violence takes place between one event and the next. Legal action by the authorities is mandatory. This means that the case will always be prosecuted, regardless of the victim's willingness to report it to the police. Maltreatment can apply to both married couples and 'de facto' relationships. In order to prosecute someone for maltreatment, there must be evidence that the physical and psychological violence has been inflicted repeatedly over an extended period of time.

In the Italian legal context, a suspect can also be charged with the crime of *'sexual violence'* (art. 609*bis* C.C.) within a family context. In 1996, a new law was introduced in the Italian penal code that addresses all forms of sexual violence. According to this law, 'whoever forces someone to do or suffer from a *sexual action* is punishable with imprisonment from 5 to 10 years' (emphasis added). All forms of sexual violence are included, ranging from sexual harassment to rape. These sexual crimes are punishable only if the alleged victim reports the crime. Once the victim has filed a complaint of sexual violence, she or he cannot withdraw it at a later stage. This is to prevent victims withdrawing a complaint from fear of the perpetrator's threats. If the victim is under-age, the prosecutor will officially start the legal action.

Obstacles Met While Collecting Evidence

A woman suffering from domestic violence can take different steps to protect herself, and seek help and assistance. She may, for instance, go to the police to report the crime or to hospital to have her injuries treated. For criminal proceedings to be instigated, it is important to collect sufficient evidence of the violence perpetrated. The obstacles described below may impede the gathering of evidence of the crime of violence within a family context.

- If a victim reports more than one violent incident to the police, each individual report may go to a different prosecutor, hindering the effective collection of evidence. It is, therefore, important that public prosecutors, the police and the victim's attorney assemble all reports of violence affecting the same victim, in order to have sufficient evidence of the multiple violent events that took place within a certain period of time. This multiple evidence may help demonstrate that a single act reported by the victim was only one of a series of violent acts. It also enables proceedings for the crime of 'maltreatment'.
- Medical reports of injuries suffered by a victim of violence can be collected. These reports, drawn up by a doctor, an emergency room or a hospital, may help the victim prove the violence when reporting the case to the police. It may happen, however, that a woman who is physically abused does not seek medical help, from fear of retaliation or because her abusive partner has actually prevented her from doing so. Some victims, even if they go to an emergency room, will offer another explanation for their bruises or wounds (e.g. fell down the stairs, bumped into a cupboard). The collection of evidence is impeded in such situations.
- Evidence to be obtained from witnesses is another obstacle in the criminal prosecution of domestic violence. In most cases domestic violence takes place behind closed doors, in a private setting or with only the children present. Witnesses can offer valuable support for the

women's claims, especially in cases where the only evidence is the victim's word against that of the alleged perpetrator. Nevertheless, particularly when the violent acts are repeated over time, some persons (relatives, friends, neighbours) are likely to be aware of what is taking place. They may have seen the bruises or heard the woman crying. The woman herself may have talked to people about the abuse. In some cases, therefore, witnesses are available.

To summarise, women often do not have sufficient evidence to prove legally what has happened to them (no medical reports, no witnesses, no other evidence) and the charge of maltreatment therefore fails in many cases. If the woman decides to report, it can happen that her case is not taken into serious consideration. The probability of this happening increases if she reported the violence to the police but later dropped the charge. There is a tendency to believe that women make up such stories in divorce cases, with the aim of obtaining custody over any children. To a certain extent, domestic violence is considered both by public opinion and by those working in the criminal justice system as a private matter, which needs to be resolved within the family context. This attitude is still held by many people, even by those working in victim protection. This suggests that family violence is underestimated, often considered as a private matter rather than a 'real' crime.

As mentioned before, some women report violence to the police but later withdraw the report. This may occur either because the woman is afraid of what might happen if the man is arrested, or because he has threatened her. Victims might even feel guilty because of what may happen to their partners as a consequence of their reporting the violence to the police (be sentenced, go to prison, lose their job).

Protection and Eviction Orders

In March 2001 a new Italian law was passed (Law nr. 154, 05/04/2001: '*Measures against violence within intimate relationships*') that deals specifically with cases of family violence. This law addresses the issue of victims' protection from a violent partner by enabling the court to apply a protection order when a person is accused of the crime of 'maltreatment'. Three types of orders are available: the obligation to live in a particular place or area, the prohibition to live at home and the prohibition to live in a certain community (art. 283 Code of Criminal Procedure). This law applies to married couples, as well as to *de facto* relationships, as long as the two partners live together. The order dictates that the violent person must leave the home and, in addition, comply with certain restrictions.

Both criminal and civil courts can issue the protection order. The victim of abuse can ask the civil judge to warrant the violent partner with an eviction order to leave the house, without needing to file a criminal charge. The civil judge can issue the order for up to six months. The judge can order that during this period the violent partner may not approach the places where the victim or her parents, children or friends live or work. The order can also dictate that the violent partner must stay away from the children's school.

The same restrictions can be applied in criminal proceedings to protect the woman's safety. The order forms a valid alternative to imprisonment. In these cases, the judge may also order that the perpetrator must still support the family financially. The criminal order is issued for a period of up to six months. If there is evidence that the situation remains dangerous for the victim, the period can be extended for a further six months. Along with the eviction order, the judge may order the intervention of special services, agencies, family mediation centres, or NGOs for the protection of abused women.

It is important to emphasise that this new law is producing positive effects for victims, because it allows them to continue living in their home without having to escape and find a place to live elsewhere with their children. This new law does not solve the problem of family violence, but it does constitute an efficient first-aid measure to reduce the risk of women and their children being revictimised. Unfortunately, protection orders are not always respected. In many cases, the violent man infringes the order and approaches the home, the woman's workplace or the children's school. Another problem is that judges do not use the law consistently across Italy. This problem is related to different attitudes held by judges themselves. It seems that some judges do not make use of the law because that would mean acknowledging the problem of domestic violence (Baldry, 2003).

The new law is an important outcome, achieved through the concerted efforts of some NGOs working for the protection of female victims of violence. The *Association Differenza Donna*, an association of women against violence against women, lobbied for the implementation of the law and is now helping victims who invoke the law in their case. In the city of Rome, in the two-year period since the law's implementation, there have been 30 requests for protective orders in the civil domain and 20 in the criminal domain. A high level of satisfaction is reported by victims who benefit from this procedure. Six months is not a long period for a restraining order but, in many cases, it is enough for a woman to organise her and her children's life, and seek alternative solutions (Baldry, 2003).

Powers of the Police and the Prosecutor

Once a case of domestic violence has been reported to the police, different paths can be followed depending on the severity of the case. Most cases of this sort are now dealt with by the so-called 'peace judge', who attempts to resolve conflicts. Trying to reach reconciliation between the partners may prevent less serious cases from coming before a court, which would reduce the court's workload. However, in my opinion, given that domestic violence tends to be downplayed as a crime, attention should be paid that the severity of these cases is not underestimated by having them dealt with by the peace judge. If the crime is considered more 'severe', competence is transferred to the criminal court to proceed for 'maltreatment'.

Before the hearing of the case at trial, the public prosecutor may ask the judge for a restraining order if the accused person is considered a danger to the victim or to society. In domestic violence cases, this order is not always issued, due to a general underestimation of the severity of the circumstances. It is often difficult to prove that the suspect is dangerous. The new protection order previously discussed (n° 154, 05/04/2001) enables the victim and children to stay in the home, while the defendant receives an order to leave.

Other precautionary measures can also be used in these cases. They vary according to the seriousness of the crime and the risk of reoffending. The 'obligation to sign' at a police station is one, requiring the offender to present himself at the police station and sign a register. This measure should help prevent the offender from leaving the city where he is resident or even the country. 'House arrest' is another measure that can be adopted. In the most severe cases, where the victim and society are considered to be at risk, 'preventive custody' can be imposed.

In some regions (Rome, Milan), special units of the public prosecution deal with cases of violence within the family (*Pool antiviolenza, sezione famiglia* – family section). These special units were created to facilitate a faster procedure for such cases, in view of the danger they may present if not dealt with in due time. Once public prosecutors working in these units take responsibility for a case, their focus is on shortening the time span between the preliminary hearings and trial of the case in court. In addition, the same public prosecutor hears all parties involved in the case, which enables the case to be processed quickly and efficiently.

Fast processing of this type of case is essential for victim protection. However, the number of domestic violence cases processed within the criminal justice system is still relatively small because professionals are not specifically trained on the issues and may consequently underestimate the seriousness of the case. It should be emphasised, however, that once a crime has been reported to the authorities, it is mandatory for them to proceed with it. No diversion (such as mediation outside the criminal justice system) may take place, meaning that all crimes, once known to the legal authorities, must be dealt with by the criminal justice system.

Police Initiatives in Domestic Violence Cases

Most domestic violence cases go unreported. In Italy, of all abused women who were admitted to a shelter in the year 1993, only 17.3% reported the crime to the police (Ventimiglia, 1996). The percentage of reported crimes has risen slightly, due to the police's increased sensitivity in dealing with domestic violence cases and a better social awareness of the problem. Of those abused women who do report the violence to the police, an unknown percentage subsequently withdraws the report due to fear of retaliation or reconciliation with the abusive partner. Children and financial constraints are often reasons for women deciding not to leave their partners.

The Italian police forces have as yet no specific units for dealing with domestic violence cases. However, so-called 'ufficio minori' (youth offices) deal with minors who have been victims of crime, and child abuse cases within a family context. These units receive special training and they are usually directed by a female chief inspector.

In 1994, the police department in Milan, Region Lombardia, developed a protocol for dealing with domestic violence cases and preventing an escalation of violence. The police generally do not keep track of emergency phone calls made from households. The project recommends forces to construct a data set, whereby all phone calls requesting police intervention in domestic conflicts are recorded. This is recommended in all cases, regardless of whether the police go to the site, arrest the man or do nothing, and whether the victim files a complaint or not. According to the protocol, the tasks of the police are as follows:

- Keep track of escalating conflicts and monitor them.
- At the third phone call from the same household for the same type of problem, regardless of whether the phone call has been made by neighbours or by someone living in the house, the police have the power to intervene. If multiple requests for help have been made, there may be evidence of 'maltreatment', a recurrent set of actions against another person within a family context. The victim is thus released from the burden of having to report her partner, and the case would be prosecuted without her official complaint being needed.
- Protect the victim and her children from any escalating violence.

The special family unit of the public prosecution gathers all information and uses it as evidence in case of a trial. Phone calls indicating family disputes are also recorded. Keeping records of all calls is essential to prove that violence occurred within the household. Unfortunately, data on the results of these police interventions are not yet available.

In my opinion, doctors and nurses working in the emergency rooms of hospitals should also be allowed to report any episodes related to family violence. Currently, the law specifies that doctors are only obliged to report to the police when injuries are assessed as needing 20 or more days to recover. This mandatory reporting is not always complied with, and many cases of child abuse and domestic violence are not reported.

Conclusions

In family violence cases in Italy, the most problematic aspect is that victims rarely report the violence they suffer to the police (Baldry, 2002). When they do so, they often only report the last episode and even minimise its seriousness. However, the reported incidents are often only the tip of the iceberg of what is actually taking place. If a woman reports, there should be an opportunity to find out whether other violence has occurred before. In this regard the police, as well as the public prosecutor, should be able to adopt special measures to find out whether previous to the last episode there have been others. Domestic violence cases are very likely to be characterised by repeated psychological, physical and even sexual violence.

Women go to the police only when they are very scared and fear for their lives and those of their children. When the authorities have knowledge of a case, they should deal with it with extreme caution, since many 'older' incidents of serious violence may be veiled behind it. Police officers and other professionals dealing with these cases should never underestimate them, and be satisfied with superficial and minimising explanations provided by one or both parties. Special organisations, shelters or centres for abused women play a fundamental role in this respect. They have the skills, experience and expertise to address violence against women and are able to help them disclose the whole story.

The police should be given more training in domestic violence cases. Training components should include the cycle of violence, consequences for abused women, risk assessment of recidivism, safety issues, and the needs of abused women and their children. Italy has no specific intervention programmes for abusers. There is a huge need for such programmes to treat violent men, even if their efficacy is not totally clear as yet (Dobash and Dobash, 2000).

The *Association Differenza Donna*, the association of women against violence against women, has just started a European project together with colleagues from Sweden and Greece. This project focuses on assessing the risk of recidivism, based on the Canadian model SARA (Spousal Assault Risk Assessment), and it is part of the European Daphne project for the prevention and reduction of violence against women and children. This project, the first of its kind in Italy, will provide training for police officers to help them assess the risk of recidivism. The training is intended to be used during the investigation phase. The project is aimed also at providing the offender with the best possible response to deal with his problem (treatment, restraining order, imprisonment). This project will be piloted with the partners of women who have sought help in the shelters for abused women in Rome. Subsequently, it will be extended to the whole country, provided that it receives support from the Ministry of Justice. The most effective response, however, is probably for violent men to seek help for themselves, take responsibility for their behaviour and try to change.

References

Baldry, A. C. (2001). Domestic violence in Italy. In R. Summers and A. Hoffman (Eds.) *Domestic violence: Global perspective.* pp. 32-45. Westport. Greenwood Publishing.

Baldry, A. C. (2002). Victimization of domestic and sexual violence in Western Europe. In P. Nieuwbeerta (ed.). *Crime victimization in comparative perspective,* pp. 249-264. Den Haag: Boom Juridische Uitgevers.

Baldry, A. C. (2003). La violenza in famiglia (Violence in the family). In M. Barbagli (a cura di). *Il rapporto della criminalità in Italia (Criminalità in Italy),* pp. 183-210. Bologna: Il Mulino.

Barnett, O. W. Miller-Perrin, C. L. and Perrin, R. D. (1997). *Family violence across the lifespan.* Sage, London.

Crowell, N. A. and Burgess, A. W. (Eds.) (1996). *Understanding violence against women.* Washington, DC. National Academy Press.

Dobash, R. and Dobash, R. P. (2000). Evaluating criminal justice interventions for domestic violence. *Crime and Delinquency, 46,* 252-270.

Mirrlees-Black, C. (1999). Domestic violence: Findings from a new British Crime Survey self-completion questionnaire. London: Home Office.

Tjaden, P. and Thoennes, N. (2000a). Prevalence and consequences of male-to-female and female-to-male partner violence as measured by the National Violence Against Women Survey. *Violence Against Women 6(2),* 142-162.

Tjaden, P. and Thoennes, N. (2000b). Full report of the prevalence, incidence and consequences of violence against women. Findings from the National Violence Against Women Survey. Washington, DC: National Institute of Justice and Centres for Disease Control and Prevention.

UNICEF (2000). Breaking the Earthenware Jar: Lessons from South Asia to end Violence against Women and Girls. UNICEF: Regional Office for South Asia.

Ventimiglia, C. (1996). *Nelle segrete stanze* [In secret rooms]. Milano, Franco Angeli.

Walker, L. E. (1979). *The battered women.* New York: Harper and Row.

Yllö, K. and Bograd, M. (1988). *Feminist perspectives on wife abuse.* London: Sage.

Chapter 8

Family Violence Against Women in Greece

Sevaste Chatzifotiou

Introduction

The study of family violence is a complex and multifaceted experience for any researcher. Every completed and published study can help us to learn more about the problem and respond to it more effectively. Yet the more we explore, the more relevant data there appears to be, bringing a risk of becoming overwhelmed with studies and their results.

This chapter presents and examines the topics of family violence that are commonly discussed among professionals and academics in Greece, from a variety of social and other perspectives. To identify the extent of the problem, I first discuss findings and results related to family violence against women in various European countries. I then present Greek data on family violence against women from a variety of sources, including findings from my own research studies. My analysis focuses primarily on the flourishing Greek socio-cultural perspectives that result from the patriarchal structure of Greek institutions and the system in general. Patriarchal societies stress the domination of males over females and view women in subordinate positions to men. The societal, legal and economic norms expressed by the laws and customs in society uphold this power difference between men and women, and legitimise the difference in their status. The chapter also presents victims' views: their experiences of violence at the hands of their partners and their cries for help to official institutions. I highlight the above by presenting a case study of a victim of violence, for whose support I personally testified as an expert witness. The chapter concludes by suggesting ways to better understand and combat the problem of family violence in Greece.

Family violence is a complex scientific area and only limited data are available in this field in Greece. This work could therefore be seen as an introduction. Yet, I believe, it should give the reader sufficient knowledge to understand the dynamics involved in family violence in Greek society.

The Problem of Domestic Violence Abroad: An Overview of its Extent

In the last two decades, numerous studies of prevalence have been conducted to measure the extent of the problem of domestic violence. As a result, the magnitude of the problem has now been well established in most European countries, as well as elsewhere in the world (Human Rights Watch, 2002; European Women's Lobby, 2000).

The first sources of data are national surveys using representative samples. In the United States, Steinmetz (1977) found that 3.3 million wives are severely beaten by their spouses. Also, Strauss, Gelles and Steinmetz (1980) estimated that over 1.7 million spouses had weapons used against them and over 2 million were beaten up. According to FBI findings, 50,000 women were murdered by their husbands in the USA in the 1980s (Asian Women and Domestic Violence, Information for Advisers, London Borough of Greenwich Women's Equality Unit, 1995: 2). Further, the first national study of wife battering in Canada, based on transition house records, estimated that at least 24,000 Canadian women were battered by their male partners during 1978 (Currie, 1990). The study was conducted on behalf of the Advisory Council on the Status of Women (CACSW) during 1979. At that time, the 73 safe houses that had been established provided the only source of data on wife battering (MacLeod, 1978 cited in Currie, 1990, 83). A more recent and larger Canadian survey of violence against women involved a telephone survey of 12,300 English-speaking and French-speaking women, 18 years of age and older, residing in households in ten provinces in Canada (Statistics Canada, 1993, 47 and 53). The data were collected through the random digit dialling approach and eligible respondents were randomly selected within the households contacted. According to this, one in six currently married women reported violence by their spouses, and half of the women with previous marriages reported violence by a previous spouse (Statistics Canada, 1993: 9).

In Britain, it is estimated that 48% of all murders of females are the result of women being killed by their partners. On average, two women per week are killed in England and Wales by their partners/ex-partners (Mirlees-Black, 1995). Also, according to British Crime Survey 1996, the largest increase in violent crime since 1981 has been in incidents of domestic violence (Home Office Research Findings, 1997). A number of local surveys in the UK show that between one in three and one in four women report having suffered domestic violence at some time in their adult lives (Women's Aid Newsletter, 1998: 6). A household survey of 430 women in a London borough found that one in three women had experienced domestic violence at some time in their lives, and 12% had been victims of domestic violence in the past year (Mooney, 1994). Another survey of 484 women in Surrey's shopping centres found that one in four women defined themselves as having suffered domestic violence by a male partner/ex-partner since the age of 18 years (Doming and Radford, 1996). Furthermore, a survey of 1,000 women in city centres in North England found that one in eight women reported having been raped by their husband or partner (Painter, 1991).

In 1996/97, nearly 55,000 women and children stayed in refuges in England and over 145,000 contacted Women's Aid for advice and support (Annual Survey, WAFE, February 1998: 2). The Women's Aid National Helpline receives nearly 400 calls a week from women seeking information, advice and support, as well as referral to a refuge or somewhere safe to stay. BT monitoring shows that over 2,000 calls are attempted (WAFE, 1998: 6). During 1996/97, the Women's Aid Federation of England received 145,317 calls, the Northern Ireland Women's Aid 14,948 calls, the Scottish Women's Aid 49,717 calls and the Welsh Women's Aid 17,500 calls. This puts the total number of contacts at 227,482, a number equivalent to 'one call every 2 and a half minutes, 24 hours a day, 365 days a year', and this does not include the many callers who were unable to get through (Economic and Social Research Council Report, 1998: 21). The Women's Domestic Violence Helpline in Manchester, UK, receives nearly 6,000 calls per year from women seeking various kinds of help and referrals to refuges (Women's Domestic Violence Helpline Manchester, Evaluation and Monitoring Report, 1995-6). Further, an average of 100 women are killed by partners or ex-partners in England and Wales every year (Home Office, 1996). Partners or ex-partners kill almost half of all female victims of homicide in England and Wales, compared to 6% of male victims of homicide (WAFE, February 1998: 1).

Ireland has no national statistics determining the prevalence of violence against women. However, data from the independent report to the 4th UN world conference on women reveal that the Women's Aid National Helpline received 17,510 calls from March 1992 to May 1995, from women who were being physically, sexually and mentally abused by men in intimate relationships (National Women's Council of Ireland, 1995: 15).

Police reports on assaults and murders are another source of data. However, they can sometimes be incomplete because the police do not always encourage legal prosecution. Still, according to Edwards (1989), the Metropolitan Police receive over 1,000 phone calls a week from women experiencing domestic violence. West Yorkshire Police took 2,675 calls related to domestic incidents in a three-month period (Leeds Interagency Project Progress Report, 1996: 11). And in Ireland, the Special Domestic Violence and Sexual Assault Unit, set up by the Gardai (police) in the Dublin Metropolitan Area, received 5,000 calls in a four-month period (National Women's Council of Ireland, 1995: 15).

While exact statistics are probably impossible to obtain, it is evident that marital violence is predominantly violence against 'wives' and that it affects a large number of individuals/victims, who pay a high personal, physical, psychological, mental, familial, social and financial price for surviving the violence (Stanko, Crisp, Hale and Lucraft, 1997). Child abuse, and child behaviour and developmental problems are associated risks. Research found that 90% of the women's children are either in the same or the next room when violence occurs. One third of the children witness the abuse, try to protect their mother and may be abused themselves (Asian Women and Domestic Violence, Information for Advisors, 1995: 2; Women Against Rape, 1998: 1). The abused woman's fear that things will get worse if she takes action and seeks help from outsiders constitutes an important factor in stopping her reporting the violence, making her decide to stay in the violent relationship, suffer the violence and not seek help.

The Patriarchical Culture of Violence

The importance of social and cultural factors in forcing an abused woman to consider her decision to seek external help and/or leave her violent husband is also well stressed at the international literature (Mahoney, 1994, 60; McWilliams and McKiernan, 1993, 50-55; Dobash and Dobash, 1979; Kirkwood, 1993). Traditional values in patriarchal societies suggest that being a wife and mother are the most important roles for a woman. Moreover, Muslim and Arab societies also believe that one cannot be a full woman unless married (Human Rights Watch, 2002). Not surprisingly, such societies place the burden of family harmony on the woman, with the implication that a failed marriage is her fault. This suggests that 'commitment' to the relationship constitutes a salient factor in the decision to keep silent, suffer the violence and not seek help for a long time (Strube and Barbour, 1983: 786). Thus, the deeply ingrained idea that a marriage should be preserved at almost any cost, for the sake of the family, is compounded by the stigma associated with a wife's status as a divorcee, and by the notion that she is the one to blame for the marriage split-up. All these ideas are urged upon her by friends, relatives and representatives of social agencies, and they constitute important reasons that deter a woman from seeking external help and leaving a violent relationship (Chatzifotiou and Dobash, 2001; Chatzifotiou, 2003b).

The difficulties that abused women face in respect of the response from so-called 'support' agencies are encountered in many research findings too (Dobash and Dobash, 1979; Mullender, 1996; Hague and Malos, 1993; Maynard, 1985; Pahl, 1985; Mama, 1989; Hanmer et al., 1989; Heise, 1996, 10). In general, service delivery is frequently not co-ordinated, many agencies deal only with particular aspects of the problem, and formal and informal liaison among agencies is not optimal. In addition, many professionals continue to underestimate the severity of the violence experienced by their clients. The majority of 'support institutions' remain passive or naive bystanders to the problem of violence against women and the abused women's needs. Institutions such as the police and the medical profession are often male-dominated and patriarchal in their structure and function. They tend to promote the reproduction of the sexual division of labour, and rationalise the exploitation and oppression of women. In other words, they indirectly participate in the social construction of the battered woman's social isolation and continued suffering as her attempts to seek help go in vain. Flitcraft and Stark (1980), referring to the medical 'support' profession in relation to battered women seeking help, put it as follows:

> Medicine's role in battering suggests that the service's function is to reconstitute the 'private' world of patriarchal authority. (Flitcraft and Stark, 1980: 81)

And elsewhere:

> Medicine's purposive failure to make wife battering visible is the patriarchy's success. (p. 83)

In the last decade, countries outside Greece have taken a number of initiatives to tackle domestic violence at both local and national level. These include changes in police responses to domestic violence and the development of domestic violence units, the introduction of legal remedies and amendments focusing on marital relationships, and the development of over 200 multi-agency forums in the UK to improve local responses (WAFE, July 1997, 2). Also, pioneering projects are currently being conducted in the UK, some particular examples in places with an excellent past record of countering violence against women. One such project is being carried out in the Hammersmith and Fulham area of West London, inspired by and based on the work of projects conducted elsewhere, such as the Domestic Abuse Intervention Project in Duluth USA. The project aims to establish the best possible integrated and co-ordinated community and criminal justice response to domestic violence, through learning lessons from America (Hammersmith and Fulham Violence Forum, 1998). Also, evaluation reports from various past projects, such as the Domestic Violence Intervention Project (DVIP) in West London, have been published. These aim to improve knowledge and understanding of the issue of violence, from the point of view of women themselves, their abusers, and the professionals and agencies under consideration (Burton, Regan and Kelly, 1998).

Despite all these initiatives, there is established evidence that escaping domestic violence is still as hard for many women and children as it was twenty years ago. Recent attitudinal surveys have confirmed that many agencies and individuals still misperceive domestic violence as a personal or relationship problem, or an acceptable element of contemporary gender relations (WAFE, November 1997). Further, a significant gap between policy and practice still exists for many of the social agencies, such as the police and their domestic violence units. More analytically, a recent report on 'Policing Domestic Violence' reveals that 38 of the 42 forces in England and Wales that participated in the study had published a domestic violence policy document (p. 5). However, 39% of policy makers, 48% of line managers and 65% of operational domestic violence officers within the police (p. 19) felt that there was a 'significant policy/practice gap' (Plotnikoff and Woolfson, 1998). Gaps between policy and practice are documented throughout the literature on policy implementation, but in cases of domestic violence the divide seems even more prominent.

Two important factors play a role here. First, that police involvement and rights to intervene are not specified or supported by the law at all times. And second, that domestic violence is still regarded as a family and thus private issue. As far as multi-agency work is concerned, independent research reveals that despite the many domestic violence forums that have been set up across the UK, no single model of practice can be identified. The groups operate in different ways, according to their leadership or make-up (Hague, Malos and Dear, 1996). This lack of consistent structures or guidelines for practice across services hinders the comparison of results and the setting of shared goals that the various groups involved in combating domestic violence can use as a common frame of reference.

> Unless laws, regulations and practice are changed and a lead taken by government in terms of co-ordination and setting policy priorities in this area... the improved response of many individual agencies and multi-agency forums will only have a limited effect, despite the enormous commitment of many individuals working within them. (WAFE, October 1998, p. 2)

The Greek Context and Culture of Violence

The exact degree to which family violence against women exists in Greek society is difficult to establish for a variety of reasons (Chatzifotiou, 2002; Spinellis, 1997: 231). I briefly describe the situational, cultural and structural contexts below. Firstly, the lack or inadequacy of data provided by the different institutions contacted by women survivors of violence inside or outside the family makes it very difficult to assess the extent, nature, severity and effects of this phenomenon in Greece. Secondly, violence against women within the family is under-reported because it has often been accepted within societies worldwide, particularly those with very strong traditional values concerning the sex role differentiation and power distribution. In this context, social values and attitudes support the man in his position as head of the family, whose absolute power cannot be questioned by anybody. Also, the legal professions have avoided involvement in what they consider a private matter, while legal and social agencies have been concerned mainly with family preservation.

In Greece, the women's independence movement has been raising the question of violence against women since 1978. It is due to this movement that the issue has become public, that consciousness has been raised and that the public authorities have become more sensitive and responsive. According to the National Report on Physical and Sexual Violence Against Women in Greece (Ministry to the Presidency, December 1990, 5), the level of scientific research in this domain remains low. Still, the number of publications on this and similar matters, mainly produced by female scientists, has slowly but steadily been increasing (Artinopoulou and Farsedakis, 2003; Chatzifotiou et al., 2002; Chliova, 1992: 21-30; Chatzi, 1990: 1-15; Chatzi, 1992: 16-29).

It is consequently very difficult to develop an official estimate of the extent, nature, importance and consequences of violence against women in Greece. Practitioners agree that while the research data may be limited, the extent of the phenomenon is much greater and much more acute. For example, according to the Director of the centre for battered women in Athens (Reception Office), around 120 women visited the centre for help in 1996. The centre received almost four times this number in phone calls, which were not presented anywhere in official statistics or papers as cases (personal communication, December 1996). In 2002, 300 women asked for help in person, and 500 phone calls were received (personal communication, March 2003).

Existing Services to Date

Greece has very few specialised services where battered women may seek help (see more in Chatzifotiou, 2003b: 244). The main service dealing with the issue of domestic violence in Athens is the Centre for battered women. It was established on the initiative of the General Secretariat for Equality (G.S.E.) and has been operating in Athens since October 1988. The Centre runs two services. The Reception Office for battered women offers free legal advice, psychological support and information on other available services. The Refuge for battered women has operated in Athens since 1993, in co-operation with the G.S.E. and the Municipality of Athens. The Refuge offers hospitality to women and their children, as well as psychological support and information on other available services.

Two other refuges were recently established in Greece, one in the city of Heraklion on the island of Crete, and the other near the port of Piraeus. The latter is, however, understaffed and has only a small capacity. Finally, a family support centre offering shelter to battered women has recently opened in Athens. This runs under the auspices of the Athens Archdiocese.

In Thessaloniki, (Northern Greece), the only specialised agency in operation is the Office for Women's Issues. It was established in 1994 and is run with the support of the Municipality of Thessaloniki. An independent women's group ran an SOS call service for battered or raped women, from October 1990 to 1996, and from 1998 to 1999. The service started up again in

2003, having secured funding for 14 months. It provides free legal advice, psychological support and general information to women.

The Extent of the Problem in Greece

It is commonplace that the majority of domestic violence incidents never come to the attention of the authorities (Spinellis, 1997, 232; Mouzakitis, 1989, 219). The 'dark figure' of female victimisation within the family is usually investigated through specially designed victim surveys (National Report of Greece, 1990). Police statistics or criminal court statistics do not provide a complete picture of the existing situation, since they do not include information on the victims of crimes, i.e. number of victims, gender, and relationship between victim and offender. Thus, for example, arrests or convictions of perpetrators of wife/partner battering or homicide cannot be identified among the existing data.

At the same time, public or private grants for social research are limited in Greece. This has resulted in a paucity of data in the area of family conflict and female victimisation. Most existing research, as a consequence, is based on small samples or samples of convenience. Despite the limited research studies, there is a consensus among researchers that violence against women in the family is likely to be greater and more acute than suggested by what relevant but scattered data there is (Epivatianos and Basiliadis, 1981, 1051; National Report of Greece, 1995).

In May 2003, the findings of the first national survey using a representative sample of 1,200 Greek women from the urban and semi-rural areas were presented. The survey was supported by the General Secretariat for Equality of the Sexes, a governmental body that runs under the auspices of the Ministry of Internal Affairs and Decentralisation. It was conducted by a scientific team from the centre for research on women's issues (Artinopoulou and Farsedakis, K.E.TH.I., 2004). According to these findings, out of 1,200 women, 3.6% revealed physical violence by their partners, 56% suffered psychological and verbal abuse, whereas 3.5% of the sample experienced at least one episode of sexual abuse by their partners (Artinopoulou, 2003). This survey constitutes an important work, with hopefully more of the same to follow.

At the same time, other limited and small-scale research (mainly in the form of pilot studies) on marital violence against women in the home was conducted by independent researchers, most of whom were working in the research setting. That research derives from various sources: research conducted by physicians, forensic doctors and students in the course of their degrees; research conducted in hospitals, police stations and women's organisations; and research conducted by the press. Those sources provide some enlightening information about the situation (Agathonos, 1990, 92). For example, according to Fereti (1990), only one in four battered Greek women reports the violence to the police, whereas 21% seek medical treatment. Also, about 15% of the battered women are granted a divorce because of maltreatment and abuse, while 23% of the women's sample is victim of their husbands' violence (cited in Agathonos, 1990, 92).

Furthermore, a survey conducted in an Athenian General State Hospital for a six-month period in 1986 revealed that each month an average of 14 cases were classified in the hospital's books as 'beating'. The patients' injuries ranged from minor to serious. All were females, most of them married and with limited income. Other cases reached the Hospital with the same 'symptoms' but they were classified as 'accidents' and therefore not counted (Malli, cited in Spinellis, 1997, 236). Similar 'accidents' were revealed in another independent study, in a state hospital in the city of Ioannena, which has a population of 45,000. None of the women involved called themselves 'battered wives'. According to the researchers, the women were too ashamed or afraid to reveal the causes of their injuries (Kastanou, cited in Spinellis, 1997, 236).

In conclusion, it can be said that Greece, like most European countries, is slowly but steadily gathering scientific data that will recognise and reveal the problem of violence against women in their homes. It is now more than certain that the problem is acute, but that the public and other services are not yet ready to deal with it in the most efficient and adequate way. This is not to say that the professionals who work in those services are indifferent to this new reality. Indeed, they can be highly committed and effective as long as they know what they need to do and how. Recognition of the magnitude of the problem in Greek society is a key step towards creating the organised agendas needed to deal with and combat the problem.

The Role of Law and the Police

The law 1329/1983 made certain amendments to the Greek Civil Code and in particular to the section of Family Law. The amendments aimed to respect the constitutional principle of equality of men and women and in that way work towards the harmonisation of husband-wife relationships.

However, scholars believe that the law's recognition of the individual needs of women renders the family a source of conflicting attitudes and interests (Koumantos, 1988, 10). Responsible for this would be the negative influences of the pre-existing 'male-oriented system of law which created relations of dependency, submission and rivalry (which) may be considered as one of the factors of victimisation of women within the family which still occurs in Greece as well as in other societies' (UN, 1989). Among other amendments to the section of Family Law, Laws 1288/1982 and 1558/1985 declared the establishment of a General Secretariat for Equality of the Sexes (G.S.E.S.). This independent government agency would take a number of concrete measures towards effective intervention in cases of female victimisation within or outside the family (National Report of Greece, 1990). Greece has only broad constitutional and legal protections for women (Greece: Human Rights Practices 1995 report, section 5), and the various types of violence against women in the family do not constitute a separate offence under Greek criminal law (Kravaritou, 1996; Spinellis, 1997, 242). So, the question is to what extent the existing general provisions of the Criminal Code, the Code of Criminal Procedure and other laws adequately protect female victims of family violence.

In Greece, as in other countries, police have been sharply criticised for their indifference to the problem of battered wives, for their lack of preparation in handling victims of family violence, for not taking seriously their complaints and needs, and for tending to regard incidents of family violence as not 'real' police work (Fragoudaki, 1987, 2; Zorba, 1991; Agathonos, 1990, 47; Tsikris, 1996). The G.S.E.S. asserts that police tend to discourage women from pursuing domestic violence charges and instead undertake reconciliation efforts, although they are neither qualified for, nor charged with, this task. The G.S.E.S. also claims that the courts are lenient when dealing with domestic violence cases (Greece: Human Rights Practices 1995 report, section 5).

An ongoing research project, conducted in various police stations in Athens and in the municipality of Heraklion at Crete (Chatzifotiou, 2004), shows that police stations in Athens may handle two to four cases a day. The police stations in the greater area of Heraklion handle the same number of cases per week, or elsewhere per month. Current data, derived both from the women who asked for the police's help and from police responses, reveal that women from major cities are more likely to come forward and report the violence to the police. Women from the areas around Athens and Heraklion (i.e. smaller localities with village-like cultural and social characteristics), in contrast, seem to consider it 'culturally inappropriate' to report the 'father of their own children' to the police. They only report in cases of emergency; life or death situations for themselves or their children. In addition to these cultural differences, women in large cities may have better opportunities to stay elsewhere, to escape scrutiny by their local community, to find a better trained police officer when they go to the police, and to have less conservative neighbours and bystanders who might keep them from reporting.

The results also show that the police often made clear to women that they view the matter as a private affair rather than one of their areas of competence. Most police officers were of the opinion that 'reporting to the police must be a wrong response to the matter'. Others stressed their concern that most female victims of domestic violence are psychologically and economically involved with the perpetrator and, as a result, do not press charges. Consequently, the victims' reports often do not result in a prosecution (Chatzifotiou, 2003a; Chatzifotiou, 2004).

Results from ongoing research bring to light a different dimension of the police's attitude towards the same issue. During my Ph.D thesis on abused women's barriers to reporting violence to the formal agencies (finalised in 1999), interviewees [that is, abused women] told me that 'the police believed that a man can do anything he wants, not only with his own life but with his family's members lives too. Men are like that and as such they can never be the ones to blame'. My current research, however, quotes a woman who could represent the average response of the sample so far: 'I felt sorry for the man [policeman]… He wanted to help but did not know what to do, if he could do it and how….' The difference in women's evaluations of the police response at different periods of time (1999 and 2003) suggests a change in the way Greek men think; that they are now more sympathetic and understanding of the complexity of the issue of male violence against their partners. Of course, this claim remains to be further explored.

A Case Study Presentation

In spite of potential recent changes suggested by my research in Athens and Heraklion, it must be said that this does not appear to reflect the situation for all professionals in the country. Many women still struggle to find support and get help from services, and they still have many complaints about the adequacy of support provided. In order to highlight this, I include the writings of an American woman who experienced long-standing violence by her abusive Greek husband and did not receive the support she would have expected.[1] She tells her own story and describes the responses of the Greek services that she approached for help in escaping her abuser while living in Greece. Her story characteristically combines the common problems that abused women experience and the inability of the system to be there for her and provide the services that she needs at every step of the way. Kristi Mchaney, whose husband accused her of child abduction, went through The Hague Convention Court and won her case.

> I met and fell in love with a young man from Athens, Greece in 1983 while attending Michigan State University. We were married in 1986 in Columbus, Ohio where I was finishing my degree from The Ohio State University. We lived for a time in Rochester, Minnesota where my husband finished his post-doctorate work at the Mayo Clinic. Upon completion of this assignment, we moved to Morristown, New Jersey where he worked as a scientist for a pharmaceutical company while I worked in the hospitality industry. We lived there until 1997.
>
> From 1986 until my escape in January 2000, I was subjected to the masterfully executed actions and techniques of an abuser. He was so good at it that I never realised what was happening. First I was isolated from my family. I was brainwashed to believe that I was nothing without him. He was superior. I knew nothing and he knew everything. I was isolated from having any friends. I was not allowed to make telephone calls without his permission. I was punished for making long distance calls. I was lightly but physically punished for my mistakes. He would snap my ear with his fingers. Later he would slap the back of my head. According to him these actions were innocent and designed to make me a better person. Even then they were humiliating and degrading but I had become a prisoner within my own life.
>
> In 1992, we had a son. I thought that now things would get better and the life that I had expected would flourish. In 1995, I became pregnant with a daughter. When he found out, he

---

1   Unpublished writings by Kristi Mchaney and Associates (permission granted).

punched me in the stomach. I was at fault because another child was not part of his master plan. In 1997, I again became pregnant with another son. I was once again rewarded by the cowardly punch in the stomach. It was my fault for both punches because I had disappointed him and caused his plans to be revised. I kept the abuse to myself. I hid the bruises and never told anyone about the dark side of my life. I was not worthy and the children depended on me for support. I had to be strong for them.

The pressures at his work seemed to be mounting and I was more and more becoming the physical and mental outlet for him. The small physical abuses continued to mount. The mental abuses seemed to be escalating. We lived in a one-bedroom apartment with three children. The children slept in the living room and so did I. My night job was to keep the children quiet while he slept. I was punished for my failures. In 1997, he announced that he was going to leave his employment in New Jersey and take a short-term assignment in Greece. The move would be an adventure for the family. It would be the cultural experience of a lifetime. The children would learn about the culture and history of their father's homeland. We would have an opportunity to get a larger apartment and have a better life with less stress while he recovered from the pressures of pharmaceutical industry.

The only part of that picture that came true was the larger apartment. The abuses continued and escalated month by month. I became a prisoner in Greece rather than New Jersey. I was isolated. I was given a list of daily duties and punished for failure to complete or comply. I was a twenty-four hour mom and servant to my husband. His physical and mental abuse was also directed at our sons. He did not strike our daughter. Our youngest son was subject to screaming and physical abuse. He never slept through the night without night terrors until after our escape. At age six our oldest son was forced to do four hours homework every night and humiliated for his mistakes. He was beaten for his failures and punished for not being the best or the smartest.

All of these things were part of my daily life but I still tried to maintain our family and preserve the marriage. I guess that I just held out hope that life would improve. It didn't! Between Christmas and New Year's Eve 1999, my husband caught the youngest boy climbing on a chair to retrieve a toy from the bookshelf. He screamed and ran to the boy picking him up by the hair and throwing him across the room. Fortunately, the youngster landed on the couch. However, his father ran across the room and beat his two-year old son with both fists. The next day my husband severely beat my oldest son and me. He threatened to kill me and told me to take the two youngest and get out of the house. These events cleared my mind and I knew that my hopes and dreams would never come to be and I had to do something quickly to save my children.

The following morning, I got up early and hid my oldest son with a friend. I went back home to take care of the younger children and do my early morning duties. When my husband went to work, I took some clothes and my two youngest children and reunited with my oldest son. I called my parents and told them what was happening. They were supportive and told me to continue hiding. My dad told me to go the police and report the incident and ask for help. I did exactly that and was told by the police that I should go back home and try to be a better wife. Since I was afraid for my life and the lives of my children, I did not take the advice of the Greek Police. I remained in hiding.

Since I only had one friend, my husband continued to harass her family while trying to locate us. We were moved to another location to provide some security for my friend and her family. We stayed at the new location until after New Year's Day. We tried to find shelter in Athens so we did not become a burden to our friends but no one answered the phones at the shelters. We called many times for three days and never got an answer. We finally moved to another location within the city.

My mother flew to Greece to be with us and help us through the Greek legal system. She planned to be with us for at least three months to help us get settled in a new apartment in a free and safe environment. Prior to her getting there, we were very active in looking for help. We went to the United States State Department and asked for help. They told us to stay in the country and get an attorney. We went to the hospital to get help and report our injuries. They gave us the shelter telephone numbers that never answered our calls. They could offer no other help. The attorney recommended by the State Department tried to negotiate a return to the family apartment and support from my husband. He declined. The attorney said that she was afraid of my husband and was of no further help.

When my mother arrived, we found a new attorney who informed us of the process. We would be required to return to the apartment and live with my husband who threatened to kill me while the judicial process took its course. The attorney said that it would take at least three months to get a restraining order and he [my husband] would know that I was trying to get one while I was still living in the apartment. That was not a safe alternative for my family. We were advised to get out of the country as soon as possible.

My mother called my father and told him that the U.S. State Department and the Greek government could not offer any help or security for the children or me. The social system in Greece was merely a thought and non-funded future undertaking. Our only alternative was to escape Greece and the system that protected the abuser. Knowing that I could not leave Greece with the three children without the written permission of their abusive father created an obstacle but certainly not an impossible task.

My dad called the airlines and purchased round trip tickets for all of us with each set of tickets to be picked up at each departure ticket counter. The first leg of the flight departed from Athens to Amsterdam. The plan in Athens was to split up the family in the terminal. My mom would take the oldest and I would take the two youngest. We would wait for a large noisy group (not difficult in the Athens Airport) and my mom would get in front of the group while I got near the end of the group. Hopefully, the noise, distractions and impatience of the group would create enough confusion that we could make it through the security and boarding process. My mom made it through without a problem. We saw her move through security.

When our turn came, we were detained for questioning. We were held up, questioned and questioned, checked on the computer and forced to wait. It was almost time to close the door when I told the Officer to check my tickets one more time. They were round trip tickets to Amsterdam. I told him that my husband was on assignment for the EU and that we wanted to surprise him with a visit because he missed the children. We were allowed to pass through security and get on the flight just before the door closed. We picked up our new set of tickets in Amsterdam and flew to Kennedy in New York. We repeated the process and flew from here to there across the US until we arrived in Spokane, Washington.

It is now September 2003. We are together in a safe environment. We have not heard from the abuser for more than ten months. The children are healthy and happy. They are loved. They are no longer abused. They are all in school and doing very well. They sing, dance, practice karate (no one will ever abuse

them again), do chores around the house, do homework when it
is required, play, take good care of each other and their mom.

One might say that the experiences of this well-educated American woman are characteristic of the problems that Greek women usually face when they try to seek help, even though we may not hear their stories. Greek men, like males in other societies, use physical force to control their partner's behaviour. Their right to do so has been condoned and reinforced by social, historical and cultural attitudes, still prevalent in Greece, which place women in a subordinate position to men in the family and in society.

Although cultural change is happening in Greek society, one still wonders what is stopping modern Greek women from seeking help. Greek family life is characterised by the principle of exclusive personal loyalty (Hart, 1992: 171). The solidarity, material stability, social integrity and advancement of the family are axiomatic in Greece. The pervasive emphasis on the priority of males over females is a constant reminder to Greek women of the limitations on their movements and self-expression in public. Greek culture expects women to treat men with deference, to protect them from 'stress', to follow their orders, and so on. These socially constructed behaviours, and the patriarchal ideology of the privacy of the family home, are further reinforced by widely-held individual and societal beliefs, ideas and attitudes with regard to male-female relationships. If a woman acts contrary to these ideas, she will encounter the general disbelief and disapproval of the public. If she tries to leave, she will either be stigmatised or judged for breaking up the family. If she stays, she must continue living in fear and misery.

Even when women are able to come to terms with personal shame and societal disapproval, they must still weigh up their chances of receiving the support they need from public sources of help, that is institutions such as the police, courts, doctors, etc. Previous research has shown (Chatzifotiou, 2002) that women's perceived lack of trust and/or negative previous experience of agency responses make them very concerned about the actual help they could expect to receive if they decide to bring their problem to light. Agencies are seen as a reflection of prevailing societal norms and attitudes, and from that perspective the benefits might seem outweighed by the risks of going public. Women were therefore either kept from reporting, or they did report but received an unsatisfactory response.

In short, the image of the woman as a self-sacrificing martyr is one that holds considerable emotional currency in Greek gender ideology (Hart,

1992). Women have strongly internalised Greece's specific social, political and cultural norms, and ideas of the sanctity of the family and marriage. The patriarchal ideology embodied in community attitudes, and institutional policies and practices that assign responsibility to women for keeping the family together, are other reasons why Greek women have often felt restrained from disclosing their experiences and seeking help. Nowadays, it should be recognised that the Greek state is striving to change these attitudes and stereotypical views that polarise the roles of the sexes. For instance, campaigns and seminars on family violence and gender equality issues have been organised (K.E.TH.I., 2004). That said, there is a great deal of work yet to be done.

Furthermore, one should be aware of the process of violence and the stages that women go through before they can find the strength to break down the restraints of silence and suffering. Research has found (Chatzifotiou and Dobash, 2001) that women living in a violent relationship only gradually start to realise that the violence is not a one-off event. In some cases, the injuries might become more severe, so inevitably the problem cannot be kept private any longer. The women have to face the fact that the situation is only getting worse, and that it may have affected the children in the home. Accordingly, women find that potential catalysts in their decision to seek help from formal agencies included the realisation that their partner would not change and that he was not able to keep his promises. Another catalyst seems to be a heightening sense of physical danger, and a re-assessment of themselves and the situation they have been living in for years. At this stage, women actively sought the assistance of public agencies dedicated and committed to helping people in need.

The police are the number one port of call that women turn to. Should they continue to appear ineffective in their work with abused women (e.g. as we saw in the case study presented above), they risk being accused of condoning wife beating, by failing to protect wives and punish husbands. Nevertheless, some Greek police forces are already found to be purposefully reconstructing their patriarchal attitudes (Chatzifotiou, 2004). This is a case for optimism, suggesting that the police's more focused and gender-specific work will be more effectively oriented towards women's best interests.

Discussion

As stated previously, women in Greece go through various stages of awareness before disclosing their experiences of violence to others. Certain findings suggest changes for the better, though these have yet to be stronger supported and validated (Chatzifotiou, 2004). Nevertheless, women still seem to face inadequate agency responses. These include trivialising the problem, projecting a lack of concern about women's needs and requests, and encouraging them to 'go back and sort things out'. Future research should stress the fact that domestic violence oppresses women and that it is a human rights crime. Researchers should not view violence against women simply as an individual problem. They should also see it as a structurally gendered issue, which is related to the subordinate position of women in the family and in society in general. In light of this, one should be more oriented towards applying gender-specific methods and research tools while planning and adopting a research design on family violence. Future research should not be gender-neutral; it should properly address gendered structural inequalities in society.

Changes and improvements also need to be made in various policy areas and legislation. The general public's awareness and interest in domestic violence should be continuously raised by grassroots groups and by professionals working in this area. Greater attempts should be made towards understanding its prevalence, causes and consequences across many dimensions. More community-based and nationwide programmes, aimed at protecting women's rights and directly addressing domestic violence, should be developed and run all over Greece, covering urban as well as rural areas. More services for battered women should be established and social services should expand their range of responsibilities and provisions. Although some female victims of spousal abuse can seek generic social services from public centres or women's centres, it is important to know that women's needs change over time according to the psychological stages they are going through. I would argue that greater numbers of appropriately staffed organisations specialising in domestic violence must open in Greece. Collaboration between all parties providing support to female victims of domestic violence should become the preferred method of service delivery.

The funding of service organisations and research projects on family violence is a major challenge. Until recently, Greece had no strategic focus or co-operation between women's groups and professionals working in services for domestic violence victims. Although some progress has been made (K.E.TH.I., 2004), much remains to be done to present an even greater challenge to the cultural norms, attitudes and beliefs that contribute to domestic violence.

In the same vein, the women's need for 'more services and better responses' appears to be as great in Greece as it is internationally. I would argue that 'better responses' should mean encouraging women to recognise and disclose violence, and promoting more constructive, feminist-oriented and less victim-blaming attitudes among professionals as well as among family members, friends and the community at large.

Further, every agency's policy and practice agenda should have as a starting point the principle that women suffer violence by men, and that abusive men should be held accountable and responsible. This will grant women the rights they deserve. Not being held responsible for their own abuse, they will be able to step forward and report their experiences publicly. Men might then think twice before choosing to use violence against their partners. Also, women's safety should be the priority in every policy-making document. To best serve the needs of women, a large network of agencies providing help and support should be established. Refuges for example, although not a panacea to the problem, are key agencies in combating violence against women, providing them with an immediate safety place and enabling them to leave the violent man. Still, a refuge alone is not enough. A woman who experiences violence by her partner needs a safety net, something that only inter/multi-agency work can provide. So refuges (although one may not exist in every neighbourhood) need to co-operate with other services and agencies, such as the local authority; the housing department; women's aid; social, legal, health and medical services; the police; helplines; support centres for women and children; voluntary sector groups; other women's and community organisations, etc. An integrated approach like this is found in the good practice examples of other countries (see for example Hague and Malos, 1993; Hague et al., 1996). It provides well-established elements that indicate the great benefits of such a network. It is expected that such an approach would bring the same benefits when applied in the Greek context.

One should recognise that Greece is currently working hard to bring the issue of family violence against women further into the public arena.

Still, the hope is that more co-ordinated research will increase people's awareness of this type of violence and instigate zero tolerance towards it. The Greek state should support studies that will permit cross-cultural comparability, thereby highlighting the universality and commonality of women's issues all over the world. Let us all hope that the Greek state will be a good listener and organiser of the above, so that eventually there will be fewer and fewer cases like Kristi's.

References

Baldry, A. (2002). Victimisation of Domestic and Sexual Violence in Eastern Europe. Pp. 249-264, in Nieuwbeerta, P. (Ed). *Crime Victimisation in Comparative Perspective*. Den Haag: Boom Juridische Uitgevers.

Burton, S., Regan, L. and Kelly, L. (1998). *Domestic Violence: Supporting Women and Challenging Men: Lessons from the Domestic Violence Intervention Project*. London: The Policy Press.

Chatzifotiou, S. (2002). Keeping Domestic Violence in Silence: The Case of Greece. International Conference Proceedings *Family Violence: A Plan for Action*. Nicosia, Cyprus, 2000, pp. 113-121.

Chatzifotiou, S. (2003a). Towards an International Approach for the Measurement of Violence Against Women: The Case of International Violence Against Women Survey. Expert meeting proceedings. Conference under the auspices of the Greek European Presidency on Combating Domestic Violence and the Trafficking of Women, Athens 30-31 May 2003.

Chatzifotiou, S. (2003b). Violence Against Women and Institutional Responses: The Case of Greece. *European Journal of Social Work*, Vol. 6, No 3, pp. 241-256.

Chatzifotiou, S. (2004). Researching Police Attitudes on Family Violence Against Women in Greece (Unpublished ongoing research project).

Chatzifotiou, S. and Dobash, R. (2001). Marital Violence Against Women in Greece. Seeking Informal Support, Special Issue, Global Examples of Violence Against Women. *Violence Against Women*, Vol. 7, No. 9, pp. 1024-1050.

Chatzifotiou, S., Dobash, R. with Tsougas, M. (2002). The Last Violent Event: The Experiences of Greek Battered Women. *Journal of South European Society and Politics*, Vol. 6, No 3, pp. 55-78.

Currie, D. H. (1990). Battered Women and the State: from the Failure of Theory to a Theory of Failure. *Journal of Human Justice*, Vol. 1, pp. 77-96.

Dobash, R.E. and Dobash, R. (1979). *Violence Against Wives: A Case Against Patriarchy*. Sussex: Open Books.

Dominy, N. And Radford, L. (1996). Domestic Violence in Surrey: Towards an Effective Inter-Agency Response. Surrey Social Services, Roehampton Institute.

Economic and Social Research Council Report, Violence Research Programme, (October 1998). Taking Stock: What do we know about violence? ESRC Violence Research Programme, Middlesex: Brunel University.

Edwards, S. (1989). *Policing Domestic Violence*. London: Sage.

European Women's Lobby (2000) http://www.euwl.violence.com.

Flitcraft, A. and Stark, E. (1980). Notes on the Social Construction of Battering, *Antipode*, Vol. 10, pp. 79-84.

Hague, J. and Malos, E. (1993). *Domestic Violence: Action for Change*. New Clarion Press, UK.

Hague, G., Malos, E. and Dear (1996). *Multi-Agency Work and Domestic Violence: A National Study of Inter-Agency Initiatives.* School for Policy Studies, University of Bristol.

Hammersmith and Fulham Domestic Violence Forum (1998). Work to Combat Domestic Violence in Hammersmith and Fulham. Community Safety Unit, Hammersmith Town Hall.

Hanmer, J. Radford, J. and Stanko, E. (1989). *Women, Policing and Male Violence: An International Perspective.* London: Routledge.

Hart, L. K. (1992). *Time, Religion, and Social Experience in Rural Greece.* USA: Rowman and Littlefield, Inc.

Heise, L. L. (1996). Violence Against Women: Global Organising for Change, pp. 7-34, in: Edleson, J. L. and Eisikovits, Z. C. (Eds). *Future Interventions with Battered Women and their Families.* London: Sage.

Home Office Research Findings. Findings from the 1996 British Crime Survey, No 16, Home Office 1997.

Human Rights Watch/Africa (2002). Violence Against Women in South Africa: The State Response to Domestic Violence and Rape. London: Human Rights Watch.

Kirkwood, C. (1993). *Leaving Abusive Partners: From the Scars of Survival to the Wisdom for Change.* London: Sage.

London Borough of Greenwich Women's Equality Unit, Greenwich Asian Women's Centre, and Greenwich Asian Women's Project (Kranti) (1995) *Asian Women and Domestic Violence: Information for Advisers,* pp. 1-31.

Mahoney, M. R. (1994). Victimization or Oppression? Women's Lives, Violence, and Agency, pp. 59-92 in Fineman, M. A. and Mykitiuk, R. (Eds). *The Public Nature of Private Violence: The Discovery of Domestic Abuse.* London: Routledge.

Mama, A. (1989). The Hidden Struggle: Statutory and Voluntary Sector Responses to Violence Against Black Women in the Home. London: The London Race and Housing Research Unit.

Maynard, M. (1985). The responce of social workers to domestic violence. In: Pahl, J. (Ed). *Private Violence and Public Policy: the Needs of Battered Women and the Response by the Public Services.* London: Routledge and Kegan.

McWilliams, M. and McKiernan M. (1993). *Bringing it out in the Open: Domestic Violence in Northern Ireland.* Belfast: HMSO.

Mirrlees-Black, C. (1995). Estimating the Extent of Domestic Violence: Findings from the 1992 British Crime Survey. Home Office Research Bulletin No. 37.

Mooney, J. (1994). *The Hidden Figure: Domestic Violence in North London.* Centre for Criminology, Middlesex University, Islington Council. London: Islington Police and Crime Prevention Unit.

Mullender, A. (1996). *Rethinking Domestic Violence: The Social Work and Probation Response.* London: Routledge.

National Report of Greece (1990). The Physical and Sexual Violence Against Women in Greece (Ministry to the Presidency, December 1990).

National Women's Council of Ireland (1995). An Independent Report to the 4th Conference on Women: Beijing and Beyond, Achieving an Effective Platform of Action. Dublin, Ireland.

Pahl, J. (1985). *Private Violence and Public Policy: the Needs of Battered Women and the Response by the Public Services.* London: Routledge and Kegan.

Painter, K. (1991). *Wife Rape and the Law Survey: Key Findings and Recommendations.* Manchester: Department of Social Policy and Social Work, University of Manchester.

Plotnikoff, J. and Woolfson, R. (1998). Policing Domestic Violence: Effective Organisational Structures. Home Office, Policing and Reducing Crime Unit, Police Research Series, Paper 100.

Spinellis, C. D. (1997). *Crime in Greece in Perspective.* Athens: Sakkoulas.

Stanko, E., Crisp, D., Hale, C., and Lucraft, H. (1997). *Counting the Costs: Estimating the Impact of Domestic Violence in the London Borough of Hackney.* Swindon: Crime Concern.

Statistics Canada (1993). Violence Against Women Survey Highlights and Questionnaire Package. Canadian Centre for Justice Statistics, Canada.

Steinmetz, S. K. (1977). *The Cycle of Violence: Assertive, Aggressive and Abusive Family Interaction.* New York: Praeger.

Strauss, M. A., Gelles, R. J. and Steinmetz, S. K. (1980). *Behind Closed Doors: Violence in the American Family.* New York: Anchor.

Strube, M. J. and Barbour, L. S. (1983). The Decision to Leave an Abusive Relationship: Economic Dependence and Psychological Commitment. *Journal of Marriage and the Family,* Vol. 45, pp. 785-793.

United Nations (1989). Violence Against Women in the Family. New York: Centre for Social and Humanitarian Affairs.

Women Against Rape. A Few Home Truths About Domestic Violence (30.10.1998).

Women's Aid Federation of England (WAFE). Families Without Fear: Women's Aid Agenda for Action on Domestic Violence: Recommendations for a National Strategy. WAFE (October 1998).

Women's Aid Federation of England. Vulnerable and Intimidated Victims: Improving Safety and Protection for Women and Children Experiencing Domestic Violence. Briefing for the Working Party from the Women's Aid Federation of England. WAFE (November 1997).

Women's Aid Newsletter. Domestic Violence – Fact Sheet. November 1998, pp. 6-7.

Women's Domestic Violence Helpline (Manchester). Evaluation and Monitoring Report 1995-1996. Manchester (UK): Women's Domestic Violence Helpline.

Greek Literature

Agathonos-Georgopoulou, H. (1990). E Via stin Ikogevia [Violence in the Family], *Sigrona Themata,* Vol. 47, pp. 78-100.

Artinopoluou, V. (2003). Combating Family Violence in Greece: The First National Study. Paper presented at conference 'Combating Family Violence in Greece and the Trafficking of Women'. Expert Meeting proceedings, under the auspices of the Greek European Presidency, Athens 30-31 May 2003. Greek General Secretary of Equality publication.

Artinopoluou, V. and Farsedakis, I. (2003). *Family Violence in Greece.* Centre for Research on Women's Issues, K.E.TH.I. (http://www.kethi.gr).

Bouri, G. (1998). Ksenovas Kakopiimenon givekon [Refuge for Battered Women]. Presentation on one-day Seminar on Violence, 4.6.1998, organised by the General Secretariat for Equality, Athens, Greece.

Chatzi, T. (1990). Paraviasis tis somatikis eleftherias ton givekon [Intrusions of the Physical Freedom of Women]. Presentation in Workshop on Violence, University of Athens, Athens, Greece.

Chatzi, T. (1992). Erevna epi tis seksoualikis eleftherias ton ginekon [Report on the Sexual Freedom of Women]. Presentation in Workshop on Violence, University of Athens, Athens, Greece.

Chliova, A. (1992). Ekthesi gia tin somatiki kai seksoualiki via kata ton givekon stin Ellada [Report on the Physical and Sexual Violence Against Women in Greece]. Presentation in Workshop on Violence, University of Athens, Athens, Greece.

Epivatianos, P. and Basiliadis, N. (1981). E chtipimeni sizigos stin Ellada [The Battered Wife in Greece]. *Galinos*, Vol. 23, Part 6, pp. 1047-1052.

Fragoudaki, A. (1987). E Askisi Vias kata ton Ginekon: Ekthesi tou Evropaikou Kinobouliou [Violence Against Women: The Report of the European Council]. *Dine*, Vol. 2, pp. 7-12.

K.E.TH.I. (2004) Centre for Research on Gender Equality Issues, http://www.kethi.gr.

Koumantos, G. (1988). *Ikogeniako Dikeo* [Family Law], Vol. I, Athens, Greece.

Kravaritou, G. (1996). *Filo ke Dikeo* (Gender and Law]. Athens, Greece: Papazisi.

Mouzakitis, C. (1989). Sizigiki Via: Etiologia, Epiptosis, Paremvasi [Spouse Abuse: Etiology, Effects, Intervention]. In *Kinoniki Ergasia* [Social Work], Vol. 16, pp. 217-227.

Ta Nea, Via Kata ton Ginekon [Violence Against Women], 5.7.1993, pp. 20-21.

Tsikris, A. (1996). *Viasmos* [Women and Rape]. Athens, Greece: Sakkoulas.

Zorba, H. (1991). Somatiki Kakopiisi kata ton Ginekon: Erevna sto Nosokomio tis Nikeas, Athens. [Physical Violence Against Women: Research in the Hospital of Nikea, Athens]. *Sigrona Themata*, Vol. 48-49, pp. 14-26.

Chapter 9

(Un)Organised Responses to Domestic Violence: Challenges and Changes in Switzerland

Corinna Seith

Introduction

Domestic violence has returned to the forefront of public debate in recent years. Appeals for law reform to improve the protection of survivors and calls for repressive measures directed at prevention are being heard globally. Anglo-American countries have a longer and stronger tradition of state responses to domestic violence, including intense scrutiny of the criminal justice system for over two decades. A significant body of research (for an overview, see Holder 2001; Seith 2003) now indicates a need for the implementation of legal and institutional reforms to be evaluated. Few statute reforms or policy changes have been implemented consistently, with taken-for-granted practices and deliberate evasions undermining both legislators' intentions and attempts to organise coherent and consistent responses. Across Europe – with the possible exception of the UK – legal and institutional reforms have taken longer. Since the mid 1990s, however, a new dynamism has transformed laws, practices and, in particular, statutory agencies (see Kelly, this volume). At the heart of these changes stand the twin challenges of improving women's safety and ensuring perpetrators are no longer afforded special leniency.

This chapter explores these issues in the context of international political initiatives, channelled primarily through the United Nations and the Council of Europe. These initiatives recognise violence against women, and domestic violence in particular, as human rights violations. As a direct consequence, abused women can now articulate their claims to protection and justice through citizenship rights. Renée Römkens, locating these moves in a wider context, suggests that domestic violence can be considered 'the premier civil rights issue' in late modern societies.

> The call to law and legal rights and their concomitant progress narratives figure centrally in late modern society. This pull is particularly characterized by an appeal to law as an instrument to bring about recognition of various social and political problems as civil rights issues. In many respects, domestic violence can be considered the premier civil rights issue in this context.
> (Römkens 2001: 265)

Responses to domestic violence are explored here, from two rights-based dimensions: 'the right to support' and 'the right to protection and justice'. Swiss legislation granting victims of crime a legal right to support will be critically examined, as will recent legal reform in German-speaking countries that prioritises protection for victims of domestic violence. These innovations will be placed in a wider context of discussions about (a) safety being the priority need when victims approach the police and other agencies, (b) prosecution as a route to sanctions and justice, and (c) the need for support to expand battered women's agencies, so that the women can exercise their citizenship rights and establish autonomous lives. It will be shown that securing these outcomes requires the development of proactive interventions by state and voluntary agencies (NGOs).

Data and Sources

The data presented in this chapter are primarily drawn from a study of the police, social services[1] and a domestic violence shelter in the French-speaking canton[2] of Fribourg in Switzerland (Seith 2001, 2003). The study was funded by the Swiss National Science Foundation, within National Research Programme 40: *Violence in Everyday Life and Organised Crime* (www.nfp40.ch). Its aim was to analyse the extent to which agencies deal with domestic violence and their responses to it. Inter-institutional

---

1 In Switzerland, material aid (income support) and personal support are supplied by the same service, henceforth called the social service agency or social services.
2 Switzerland consists of 26 cantons, each of which has legal and administrative autonomy.

responses were also observed, to identify whether the problem of domestic violence was recognised at all.

A multi-methodological design was chosen, with a combination of quantitative and qualitative methods. The data consist of: 300 cases dealt with in 1996 (see Figure 9.1), with information drawn from 2570 pages of anonymised documents (e.g., case files, police reports, lawsuits) produced by the three institutions; expert interviews and 24 in-depth interviews with practitioners and victims of domestic violence; policy documents, laws and official statistics. Data collection was carried out in two phases during 1997 and 1998. Quantitative data was recorded in a customised database and included: socio-demographic data, the type, extent and context of violence, contact between clients and institutions, and institutional responses. The sampling frames and qualitative analysis drew on a combination of Grounded Theory (Strauss and Corbin, 1990) and Objective Hermeneutics (Oevermann, 1979, 1996).

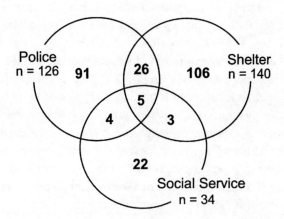

Figure 9.1 Domestic violence cases (N=300) by institutions in 1996
Source: Seith (2003: 60)

Unlike the majority of research studies, which draw on data from a single agency, this project, by examining three institutions, could consider the complexity of the cases and the multi-layered needs of some women. As Figure 9.1 shows, it also enabled tracking of the extent to which cases overlapped. Contrary to suggestions in the literature that most women are in contact with multiple agencies (Mullender, 1996), the vast majority were found to be in contact with only one, and only five of 300 cases involved all three agencies. This demonstrates the need for multiple entry points into systems of support and intervention.

Support: Towards a Rights-Based Provision

As EU-funded projects (EWL 2001) and Council of Europe policies (Kelly 1997) demonstrate, the support requirements of domestic violence victims encompass protection, psycho-social support, legal advice and economic assistance. The diverse needs of female victims cut across a range of institutions, often making it difficult to ensure that all needs are met consistently. While many Swiss responses correspond with those in other countries, some variations and innovations are less common, and reflect a rights-based approach.

The Swiss Victim Support Law (VSL) is innovative not only in defining the rights of victims to support in statute, but also by setting national standards to regulate support, advocacy and compensation for victims of crime. It clarifies the responsibilities of the criminal justice system and mandates NGOs to deliver a range of support services and legal advocacy. In the European context the Victim Support Law may be unique, offering a national rather than local route to recognising gender injustice through the criminal justice system. The ways in which Swiss shelters have adapted their provisions to this law are explored below, as are current limits and challenges. In addition, the links between domestic violence, poverty and welfare will be explored. The right to financial support under welfare state provisions is a significant element of Western democracies, and has proved important in enabling women to end violent relationships.

The Swiss Victim Support Law: a Window to the Gendered Nature of Victimisation and Support

The Victim Support Law (VSL) came into force in 1993, seeking to strengthen the position of victims in legal procedures.[3] It forms the basis of a comprehensive policy for providing support (medical, social, material),

---

3 Bundesgesetz vom 4. Oktober 1991 über die Hilfe an Opfer von Straftaten (Opferhilfegesetz, OHG) [Federal Law in Support for Victims of Crime, October 4th 1991].

protection and legal advocacy to ensure that victims can exercise their rights in criminal procedures, including claims for compensation. Victims of crime have the right to information, regardless of whether they make a claim for compensation. All Swiss cantons are obliged to provide support for victims, and this should deliver medical, material and legal assistance on a 24-hour basis. In 2001, 65 centres provided mandated services to different target groups (women, children and men) (Bundesamt für Statistik, 2002). Feminists successfully lobbied for women-only services for victims of gender violence. Existing service providers could apply to be mandated to provide the new services. The question of accepting a state mandate generated considerable debate within the feminist NGO sector. Both shelters and rape crisis services had been very critical of the original proposals. The fundamental tensions centred on issues of autonomy and integration (Seith, 2003). The advantages of increased integration were clear: financial security and recognition from mainstream institutions. The potential dangers were less obvious, it being unclear how joining the state-funded and legally based provision would affect the valued autonomy of women's NGOs. Not surprisingly, no consensus was reached and existing services took different decisions about being contracted under the Victim Support Law. Shelters could apply in two ways: either to provide safe housing only; or to expand to include an open advice service. The latter model is referred to as 'VS-services'. Not all shelters decided to integrate a VS-service into their provision. The shelter in the canton of Fribourg did extend its provision under the Victim Support Law; the VS-services in Zurich, Bern and Lucerne are separate agencies. Some are run as women-only services. Others provide services for women, children and men, allowing clients to choose a staff member of the same sex. Whatever the local outcomes, this critical reflection undoubtedly contributed to a more gender-sensitive implementation of the Victim Support Law overall.

Although the law is gender-neutral and was not designed primarily to help victims of gender violence, the latest data from the Federal Office of Statistics demonstrate that victimisation is gendered (BFS 2002).[4] In 2001 the 65 centres recorded 21,255 consultations, of which 20,269 were analysed in detail: this represents an increase of a quarter on the previous year. The following statistics show the extent to which the Victim Support Law is

---

4   Agencies are obliged to gather and submit data, which is collected nationally by the Federal Office of Statistics. While undoubtedly not all victims are included, the data are nonetheless an important addition to the current knowledge base.

responding to gendered patterns of victimisation, much of which occurs in a familial context.

-   The majority of service users were female (72.5%, 14,885 of 20,269), and most (56.8%) used the service several times.
-   Over two-thirds (68%) were victims of interpersonal violence,[5] and 71 per cent of this category is defined as family violence.
-   Women/girls made up: 75 per cent of victims of offences against the sexual integrity of children; 88 per cent of victims of offences against sexual integrity: 69 per cent of victims of bodily harm; and 60 per cent of victims of attempted murder.

As there is no specific domestic violence law in Switzerland, the VSL data is the best national indication of the number of cases where support and intervention is sought in any one year.[6] Recalculation of data supplied by the Office of Statistics shows that adult women make up over 93 per cent of those using VS-services because of sexual violence and bodily harm that happened in familial contexts.

The Victim Support Law also provides the possibility of compensation and reparation.[7] According to the Federal Office of Justice, victims can claim compensation from the state:

> ... for the financial and moral damage they suffered if they cannot obtain such compensation from the offender. Compensation for material damage is limited to 100,000 Swiss Francs and takes into account the damage suffered and the financial means of the victim. Compensation for moral tort [in this chapter called reparation] is granted regardless of financial means: requirements are that the victim has to deal with severe suffering.[8]

The Victim Support Law compels the criminal court to hear and decide on any claims made by victims of crime in relation to compensation and

---

5   This is the category used by the Office of Statistics. The category covers violence in adult relationships and across generations (e.g. child sexual abuse), with a sub-category called family violence.
6   This should change, since on 1.4.2004 a new law was introduced that codifies repeat common assault and bodily harm as a state offence. Because this codification attributes more importance to offences in the context of domestic violence, it is hoped that data collection will also improve.
7   In German: Entschädigung und Genugtuung.
8   http://www.bj.admin.ch/e/index.html.

reparation. In addition, victims of violent or sexual offences are entitled to free legal advice from a lawyer about the claim and also representation when the matter is heard. Somewhat uniquely in European law, the Victim Support Law specifies that victims of serious sexual or violent offences have the right to request that their case be heard by a judge of the same sex.

In 2001, the authorities and cantons dealt with 986 requests for compensation and reparations (BFS 2002). Compensation was awarded in 18 per cent of these cases. Reparations were awarded in 67 per cent. Interestingly, the system seems to work better for men, despite the fact that female victims represent the majority of service users. Eighty-two per cent of male applicants were awarded compensation, compared with 67 per cent of women. One can observe the familiar pattern of rights being realised to a lesser degree where victimisation takes place in an intimate or family violence context. These findings call for a more detailed analysis of the practices and general outcomes of compensation claims.

People were referred by the police or justice system in less than a fifth of all VS-cases (17%), and in just over a third (38%) was a charge pressed. This suggests that many cases are not reported to the criminal justice system, and that the police and the criminal justice system do not consistently refer to the VS-services. This result in turn emphasises the importance of non-legal support services. It is difficult to quantify the hidden figure of those who contact the police but are not referred, and of those victims who make no contact at all. However, research on police responses to domestic violence suggests that the number of potential victims who could apply for support under the Victim Support Law is higher (Seith, 2003, 122). Analysis of case files and interviews with police officers revealed that the police acted as gatekeepers in a double sense. They were inconsistent in giving victims information about the law. And they interpreted its provisions narrowly, as only applying to victims of severe bodily harm and sexual violence.[9] According to the domestic violence case file records, the police provided information to women in very few of the cases where there was an intervention – only in 3.8 per cent (3 of 80 cases). Since the local shelter had an integrated VS-service, this clearly illustrates how individual practice, in the form of professional discretion, can undermine attempts to enable women to exercise their full rights as victims of crime.

---

9   The law defines entitlement in terms of 'all victims of crime who are directly affected with regard to their physical, sexual and psychological integrity' (OHG Art. 2,1).

While the law was intended to ensure that the police link crime victims to support services, current practice requires victims to consent to the police referring their contact details to a VS-service. Recent research findings suggest that this is neither the most efficient process nor what victims themselves want. Access is currently limited by varying definitions of eligibility used by individual police officers (Seith, 2003). Furthermore, English research that asked abused women and recent rape victims about their preferences found that the majority welcomed automatic, proactive contact (Burton et al., 1998, Lovett et al., 2004). These findings challenge orthodoxies, which have relied on arguments about data protection and self-determination, and refuse to countenance automatic referral and re-contact. The female victims' data raise the question of whether service providers beyond the women's sector have responded on the basis of their own construction of victims, as persons who need protecting from further intrusion. While understandable, this has the unintended consequence of also constructing these women as a class of people less able than others to accept or refuse the offer of support. It certainly has narrowed the extent to which victims of crime are receiving support 'as of right', which was the intention of the legislation.

Shelters: Recognised, Stabilised and Challenged

As in other countries, specialist women's support services in Switzerland were developed by committed women linked to the women's movement. The first Swiss shelter opened in Geneva in 1978. Recent years have seen changes and differentiations, over and above the fact that some services have ceased to exist and some geographical areas have never had a shelter.[10] The orthodoxy in the shelter movement, requiring women to leave their home to achieve safety, remained the normative model. This reflected the classical function of providing a safe place and psycho-social support in dealing with the violence.

Differences between Swiss shelters exist not only in terms of having an integrated VS-service, but also in terms of whether workers provide 24-hour cover (another model would involve an emergency 'on call' system). Organisational structures also vary, with some maintaining the democratic or flat model, and others moving to more mainstream management

---

10 One such region is the Canton of Wallis. A community-based strategy has emerged recently, whereby committed people offer unoccupied holiday homes as 'safe houses'.

structures. The need for the safe house has not lost its importance, but the introduction of the Victim Support Law has encouraged an expansion of the support services on offer.[11] These services are now extended to women before they end the relationship and after they leave the shelter.

The research on institutional responses included analysis of the shelter files. In 1996, the shelter in Fribourg provided support to 140 women. Forty-five women took refuge in the shelter, and five others found an external place to stay (Seith 2003). More recent data indicates continued expansion. In 2003, 402 women used the service: 89 took refuge and 19 found an external solution.[12] Having accepted a mandate under the Victim Support Law, this shelter now supports three times as many women as in the year covered by the research data. Figure 9.2 illustrates that provision in 1996 covered telephone advice, face-to-face counselling and residential services, and that women used variable combinations of the options on offer.

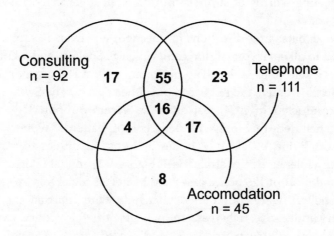

Figure 9.2 Services provided by the Fribourg shelter in 1996, based on case files (n=140)
Source: Seith (2003: 66)

---

11 The Victim Support Law has stabilised the financial base of some groups. For example, since mandated under the VSL, about two-thirds of the Fribourg shelter's running costs are covered under the law (Seith 2003, 175).
12 Written communication, June 11, 2004.

New Challenges – The Question of Proactivity

The provision of support for battered women has changed in terms of both form and content. Women no longer have to stay in, or even come to, the shelter. Support and legal advice has been offered much more systematically since the Victim Support Law was introduced. At the same time, many women's support services continue to uphold a reactive working principle, requiring women to seek support or, under the VSL, explicitly consent to contact. A proactive approach (see Burton et al., 1998) is not yet part of the provision. In this respect the Swiss situation has very much in common with other German-speaking countries, and it must be questioned whether this is an adequate response to women's needs. Historically women's NGOs have stressed the importance of women making their own decisions and, as a consequence, have relied upon them making and maintaining contact with services. More recent research demonstrates that women do not resent proactive contact. In fact, many welcome it, indicating their difficulties with prioritising their own needs and in feeling worthy of support (Burton et al. 1998; Kelly, 1999; Lovett et al., 2004).

New debates and directions are needed, however, if support is to be extended to all survivors of domestic violence. Shelters and victim support services reach only a small proportion, and certain groups, such as professional women, are not accessing either option. The Swiss prevalence study, conducted in 1994, just after the Victim Support Law came into force, concluded that only 12 per cent of battered women contacted agencies (Gillioz et al., 1997). Research on institutional responses to domestic violence demonstrates (see Figure 9.1) that shelter involvement was found in 31 of 126 police cases and in 8 of 34 social service cases (Seith, 2003). Shelters were found to deal mainly with married mothers with children under 16, whereas the clients of the police were more heterogeneous (50% married, 25% divorced and 25% not married). Limitations within the shelter data collection meant it was not possible to compare clients with respect to their professional status.

Reactive principles, justified with reference to notions of autonomy, become even less convincing when their effect of undermining women's agencies is recognised. As noted already, research suggests that women appreciate agencies taking responsibility for maintaining contact. If all police domestic violence cases were referred to shelters and VS-services, the victims' rights to support, protection and justice could be better assured. To achieve this, however, would require an amendment to the Victim Support Law through an agreement that women's right to support and protection is a higher priority than orthodoxies of autonomy and data protection. Proactive approaches have yet to be adequately tested in Switzerland, and women should be explicitly consulted about their preferences. Retaining reactive principles limits the potentially transformative influence of the Victim Support Law.

'Women – A (violent) Husband away from Poverty': The Link Between Domestic Violence, Poverty and Welfare

Social work responses take place within social, legal, institutional and regional contexts. The Law on Social Assistance for the canton of Fribourg defines social assistance not only as financial and personal assistance, but also as a measure to enable independence (Art. 4, 1-4 SHG). The requirement in law to combine material assistance, personal support and prevention has both progressive and preventative potential, although this potential may not be fully realised. The statute, which came into force in 1994, requires social services to be provided and staffed by qualified personnel in each district. The costs of the service and social assistance are to be shared equally between the canton and local municipalities.

While the rights of people without means to financial support is not contested in Western democracies, there are debates as to the kind of support they should receive, who is regarded as the 'deserving poor' (Maeder and Nadai, 2004) and how they can be moved out of poverty. The support of welfare recipients who are affected by domestic violence requires knowledge about this group, but official statistics and research reveal little if anything.[13] Switzerland is undoubtedly a rich country, although national data for 1992 suggest that between 5.6 and 10.3 per cent of households could be defined as poor. These percentages would produce a total of 390,000 to 710,000 people (Leu, Burri and Priester, 1997; cited in Nadai, 2004). A recent analysis of the Swiss workforce survey for 1999 produced a poverty rate of 10.6 per cent, with variations across regions and

---

13 An emerging literature from the United States has begun to document the extent of domestic violence against women receiving public assistance (see Raphael and Tolman, 1997 for a summary) and the intersections between battered women, poverty and welfare cutbacks (see Brandwein, 1999). Most of these studies, however, are less concerned with the responses of welfare agencies to abused women than with evaluating the impact of special programmes, such as welfare to work, in the context of domestic violence.

social groups. Single mothers had the highest poverty rate (20%) and represent a sixth of those classed as poor.[14] However, it has not been possible to examine these figures further to assess how many recipients of public assistance have experienced domestic violence. In the study of institutional responses (Seith, 2001, 2003), a random sample of case files (see Figure 9.3) revealed that domestic violence had occurred in every seventh case (14%).[15] Some 8 per cent of the cases involved physical violence (every twelfth case). Projecting this incidence to the total of 1,010 case files in the city of Fribourg yields an approximate annual figure of 141 cases in which the social workers would be faced with domestic violence. Eighty-one of these would involve physical violence. Extrapolating to the cantonal level results, 348 cases would involve domestic violence (n=2.485 case files). At the national level, between 55,000 and 99,000 of the poor in Switzerland would be affected by domestic violence, with children involved in the majority of cases.

Domestic violence was recorded in more detail in 34 cases.[16] Study of these cases revealed that most women (80%) had children and fell into one of two main groups. Four in ten were married women in the 'working poor' category, since at least one of the partners was in paid work. The other, larger group involved women who had separated from their violent husband. In the latter case, financial assistance was needed because they had lived in a traditional relationship, where the man was the breadwinner and the woman looked after the children. Thus women had either not been in paid employment during the marriage or, if they had, their income was too low to enable financial autonomy.

---

14 Other social groups particularly affected by poverty are people with less education and training, families with large numbers of children, the long-term unemployed, migrant families and the working poor.

15 For various reasons these results are likely to be an under-estimation: case workers do not record every indication of violence; not every counselling session, which might be violence-related, leads to a case file being opened; a considerable proportion of abused women who live in rural areas, where social control is high and anonymity is minimal, shy away from either contacting the social services or revealing violence if they do. The data, therefore, reflect what has been officially recorded: the minimum incidence rate within social services case loads.

16 The case files were selected through a combination of random sampling and social workers identifying cases known to involve domestic violence. The combined selection process produced 39 cases involving violence. Twenty-two of these were drawn randomly, and 17 were selected by social workers. Since five of the 39 were overlapping, a total of 34 case files were analysed in depth.

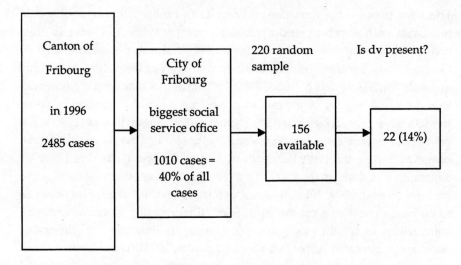

**Figure 9.3   Findings from random sampling of social service cases in
Fribourg, Switzerland**
Source: Seith (2003: 65)

Feminist research on gender and the welfare state has focused on women's
life chances, identifying the tensions between dependence and
independence (see, for example, Lewis, 1992; Ostner, 1995; Riedmüller,
1984). In the context of the bourgeois model of work and marriage, in
which social security and employment are closely associated, a married
woman's entitlement to social security hinges upon her husband's ability to
play his role as the breadwinner. If he fails to fulfil his side of the bargain,
or if the couple separate, the woman may face sudden poverty and social
marginalisation. The phrase, 'women — a husband away from poverty'
(Ostner, 1995, 3) evokes the fragility of this economic position.

Analysis of social services case files (Seith, 2001, 2003) confirmed that
following the bourgeois model can become a trap for women, especially
since attempting to re-enter the labour force as a single parent is difficult.[17]
Interviews with social workers also revealed the role of the Civil Court in
deciding who will become a welfare recipient. In a separation context
where family income is insufficient to sustain both parties, courts prefer
only one to receive welfare and tend to maintain the man's autonomy.

17 Switzerland does not have a strong record with respect to state provision of
childcare.

Thus, for many women, separation results in exchanging dependence on husbands with dependence on public assistance. While the latter is often connected to marginalisation and stigmatisation, recent scholarship in Germany and Switzerland questions an entirely negative story of welfare dependence. Mädje and Neusüss (1996) attribute an emancipatory potential to social assistance for single mothers, viewing it as a third option between the labour and marriage markets (Nadai, 2004). From this perspective it offers both a route out of marriage and the possibility, for a certain time, of not shouldering the twin burdens of paid work and child care. Welfare assistance can thus create space for a 'breather in the everyday struggle to survive' (Nadai, 2004, 10). This space is partly possible because there seems to be broad consensus on the legitimacy of supporting single mothers. In comparison with other categories of claimants, they are the 'deserving poor' and are treated better (Maeder and Nadai, 2004). These findings both echo and expand the domestic violence research with respect to abused single mothers claiming public assistance (Seith, 2001; 2003).

For welfare to function effectively as a third option for abused women requires more than an emancipatory potential within systems of social assistance. Specifically, the police and the criminal justice system must intervene effectively. The Swiss data demonstrate that separation did not always create safety, since in at least a third of the cases (35%) violence continued, in the form of stalking/post-separation violence (Seith, 2001; 2003, 149). Former husbands and ex-partners adapted their violence to the new situation, employing tactics such as telephone terrorism, stalking, causing scenes in public, denouncing women to their employers or to the authorities, threatening to kill them and, in the most extreme cases, attempting to murder them. Such tactics of attrition may last for a protracted period, and can be extremely dangerous. In such contexts, anxiety and the depletion of emotional resources can undermine social workers' investment in attempting to expand skills, confidence and autonomy.

Practices of Welfare Agencies

The feminist welfare debate needs to be expanded when considering abused women. The conditions for autonomy are not only economic independence, but also freedom from violence and the creation of conditions to secure long-term safety. Policy and institutional interventions should aim to achieve all three conditions. Social workers therefore need to discover, monitor and deal consistently with gender-related violence. Research on institutional responses showed that social workers proactively or systematically asked about domestic violence in less than one in five domestic violence cases (18%). Violence was rarely monitored continuously. In fact, the outcome remained completely unknown in a number of cases (Seith, 2001; 2003). Even in cases where married women referred to marital problems and mentioned their intention to separate, social workers frequently failed to note the underlying issue of domestic violence. In some cases, the violence appeared in the case files years after it began. The issue may have been lost when cases were transferred to other workers. This may also have occurred when other institutions that defined the problems as violence-related were involved. In two-thirds of the cases studied, civil and/or criminal law was involved, that is, the women had contacted lawyers and filed for divorce, and/or brought a criminal charge against their partner. In half of the cases, the women's shelter (13 of 34) or the police (4 of 34) had already been involved.

Further indications of a tendency to avoid evidence of violence, and a failure to monitor it, were found in the notes on meetings with clients. In a fifth (21%) the violence was not addressed at all; in a third (34%) only one meeting took place where violence was addressed; in less than half (45%) was violence explicitly addressed on more than one occasion. Since most welfare recipients have been social service clients for quite some time[18] and can be required to attend meetings, this limited attention cannot be explained by a lack of time or opportunity. Interviews with social workers suggest that while passivity, indifference and suppressed awareness played their part, uncertainty and lack of training were also key factors. Some social workers mentioned difficulties in knowing how to begin or continue to address violence, exacerbated for some men by an awareness of their gender. Others referred to the necessity of keeping an emotional distance and remaining neutral.

This reluctance and ambivalence with respect to uncovering and addressing domestic violence was also evident in how the violence was defined in the case files. In less than half (40%) did the social workers' case notes identify the situation as 'violence inflicted by man on his (female) partner'. In the remainder, either gender-neutral descriptions were used,

---

18 Some of the files covered 13 years. Only a quarter had been opened within 12 months of the data collection, meaning that three quarters covered more than a year of agency contact.

such as 'disputes between spouses/partners', or the violence was defined as 'personal problem/one person's particular behaviour'. These latter categories normalise abuse, making it difficult if not impossible to frame domestic abuse as a violation of women's psychological and physical integrity, that is, as a breach of the law. In such cases, professionals are as likely to blame the woman as see this as a context where citizenship rights have been breached. Normalisation of violence was likely to result in referrals to a marriage counselling service, offers that abusive men hardly ever took up.

The ways in which social services in Fribourg responded to cases involving domestic violence highlight problems, contradictions and inconsistencies. It was largely down to the individual professional whether violence was identified, and whether the risks involved and the complexity of the situation were adequately understood. Combating domestic violence requires strategies that take into account both the dangers involved and the women's need for safety. The social service data clearly demonstrate the importance of coordinated inter-agency approaches, since the success of financial and personal empowerment strategies used by social services depends, at least in part, on how the criminal justice system deals with domestic violence. A non-intervention policy against perpetrators undermines the professional work of social services. Social workers can support women. But as long as the violence is not confronted or stopped, all social support that aims to increase the woman's contact with an agency risks failure. This failure is, all too often, then interpreted as the woman's inability to be clear about what she wants. What is regarded as individual failure in fact turns out to be the (unintended) consequence of structural (legal and institutional) obstacles.

Protection and Prosecution: the Role of the Police and the Criminal Justice System

While creating safety for women is increasingly recognised as the central issue in domestic violence, no Western society can claim to have transformed police and criminal justice practices to the extent that every woman can expect a consistent response. Inconsistent responses are the outcome of various factors, including: an unwillingness to place perpetrators at the centre of interventions; lack of legal regulations and powers; unwillingness to ensure widespread implementation, including effective monitoring mechanisms to overcome the tendency to revert to traditional practices. The depth of resistance to change can be seen in research from the USA, where despite considerable legal, institutional and policy reforms, violent husbands and ex-partners continue to be treated less seriously than those who commit assaults in public. A recent study (Avakame and Fyfe, 2001), drawing on secondary analysis of the National Crime Victimization Survey (NCVS) from 1992-1994, confirmed that perpetrators of domestic violence are still treated with special leniency. The inertia within police forces (see also Hague et al., 2001 for Canada; Holder, 2001 for Australia; Kelleher and O'Connor, 1999 for Ireland; Kelly, 1999 for the UK) reflects deeply embedded aspects of Western liberal democratic culture, including the value attributed to protecting the private sphere against state interventions, and continued practices and presumptions of gender inequality in intimate and familial relationships.

For most of the twentieth century, women in Switzerland were seldom protected in their own homes. Just as in other Western societies, safety was difficult to find before shelters were established.[19] During the 1980s, the notion gained acceptance that women could take refuge in a shelter. This turned around the earlier perception that women had a duty to stay in their marriages; that their self-sacrifice was expected. The contemporary Swiss women's movement, like its counterparts across the globe, has subjected these cultural expectations and constructions of femininity to intense critique. It is undoubtedly the case that women gained increased possibilities for autonomy. For example, they face less stigma as single mothers and have individual entitlements to welfare payments. But these new 'freedoms' can force women to confront new expectations. So, if they do not follow advice to leave – the standard response in a reactive legal context, they risk losing the support and understanding of their family as well as that of agencies. This demonstrates how fragile modernised thinking can be and how easily it can revert to familiar victim-blaming patterns. Once this familiar terrain emerges, uncomfortable questions and reflections on structural barriers and institutional resistance can be avoided and the perpetrator easily disappears from view.

The absence of both legislation and policy to encourage proactive legal responses explains why protection for women was weak and why perpetrators were seldom subjected to criminal sanctions. In Switzerland,

---

19 That some women were able to escape, especially when divorce became easier, and even that a few pursued criminal charges does not alter the overall picture: no institutions or procedures existed to address an extremely common event.

somewhat later than in some other European countries, law and police intervention have been reviewed at the federal level, and within certain cantons, with a view to increasing women's safety.[20] The generic problems that inhibit better protection and more consistent prosecution cover several areas. Although in principle the police can make arrests and protection orders can be granted under the civil code, the German-speaking countries (Austria, Germany and Switzerland) have a limited tradition of using these legal powers. By contrast, Anglo-American countries have seen a strong push for 'pro-arrest' strategies, though interestingly this measure remains contested (see Buzawa and Buzawa, 1996; Holder, 2001). It is, therefore, unsurprising that the police in Switzerland have been reluctant to use arrest in domestic violence cases. Moreover, a significant barrier to prosecution has been that repeat common assault and bodily harm taking place in the context of an intimate relationship was not defined as state offence. As a direct consequence, women have filed most charges themselves[21] (Seith, 2003: 89, 105).

It would not, however, be appropriate to reproach the police for 'not doing anything', when in fact they are acting in various ways. Analysis of 126 case files and interviews with police officers reveal that they provide information about legal rights and procedures, refer to relevant institutions, suggest safety measures and even on occasion arrest perpetrators (Seith, 2003: 118). The focus, however, continues to be on restoring the peace and offering support to the victim. Interventions intended to prevent repeat victimisation through repression and prosecution were rarely and reluctantly deployed. The police did remove the man in over a quarter (28%) of cases, but apart from the small number of arrests that lasted only for 12 hours, a third were brought to the police station to explore whether psychological problems were involved. The

---

20　Included here are legal reforms at the federal level – making domestic violence a state offence (came into force April 1, 2004), the Law for the Protection from Violence (Gewaltschutzgesetz) is under discussion in parliament. Several cantons have changed the Police law (St. Gallen, Appenzell Ausserrhoden). The canton of Zürich has launched an integrated proposal for a 'Gewaltschutzgesetz' (see Kranich et al., 2004). At the policy level, several cantons, for example, Basel, Bern, Zurich, have funded intervention projects that work on the system level (http://www.equality.ch/d/aktivitaeten/gewalt-intervention.htm). The police ran a national campaign in 2003 and introduced specialist police training.

21　The exceptions here would be where (a) the assault was considered more serious – such as severe bodily harm and attempted murder, and (b) the police took the decision to charge.

threshold for arrest was very high and required that a number of factors be present: a history of violence, previous calls to the police and more than one previous charge. Additional factors that increased the likelihood of arrest were: women showing clear signs of victimisation and powerlessness, such as having been thrown out of the house, wearing hardly any clothes, having no money and being injured; threats to third parties; child protection issues; or threats with weapons. Alcohol and drug use, in addition to disturbing the peace, also moved police towards arrest.

The intervention style of the police has been described as more a 'secret social service' than an instrument of crime control (Seith, 2000, 2003). Police officers emphasised that dealing with these situations required 'being a little bit of a psychologist', but were frequently fatalistic about the possibilities for protecting women. Framing domestic violence as a social problem that requires soft skills reinforced the reluctance to arrest, and often resulted in a failure to deliver protection. Police officers claimed that they were now able to refer women to the shelter. However, the rather astonishing finding from the case files was that referrals were recorded in only six per cent of cases.

As in other countries, there is no deliberate policy in Switzerland to treat abusive men more leniently. This was nonetheless the outcome, since so few were arrested, prosecuted and convicted – despite the fact that in all instances, unlike most other crimes, the identity of the perpetrator is known, and repeat victimisation is common. Gloor et al. (2000) tracked charges through the justice system and found that the City of Basel prosecutors closed over three-quarters (76%) of domestic violence cases, with less than one in twelve (7.9%) resulting in a conviction.

This failure to prosecute and sanction violent partners has been more and more contested, with legal reforms reflecting this political shift. The two major legal changes in Switzerland involve codifying domestic violence as a state offence and introducing a Protection from Violence Law (Gewaltschutzgesetz), similar to those in force in Austria and Germany (see Kelly this volume; Seith 2003, 2004). When the Swiss parliament recently debated the re-definition of repeat common assault and bodily harm as a state offence, few politicians argued against this move to criminalisation. That the principle was not accepted previously is clear; it took eight years for this relatively simple reform to be enacted from Magrith von Felten's original initiative in 1996. The response of the Swiss criminal justice system can be seen as a form of structured conservatism, in that the discrepancy between women's safety needs and what was provided did not result in an internal impetus for change. Rather, the challenge came – again – from outside, in this instance from research (Büchler, 1998; Gloor et al., 2000; Seith, 2000, 2003), from politicians, from intervention projects, and from equal opportunity offices. These actors, drawing on new knowledge, the earlier critique of shelters and the broader women's movement, campaigned for the introduction of a Protection from Violence Law, versions of which are operating in some Swiss cantons already, through reform of the police law (Seith, 2003, 2004).[22] The proposed federal Protection from Violence Law, often referred to as the 'removal law', represents an evolution of the eviction orders known in many countries. It is an improvement in at least three ways. Firstly, the removal is immediate, since neither the police nor the victim has to apply to the court for the initial period of 10-14 days. Secondly, it delivers the protection that is often missing when arrests are made. And lastly, by placing these actions within routine police powers, the requirement for women/victims to initiate legal processes is removed. In comparison with the classic arrest, the Protection from Violence Law can be seen as soft. Nonetheless, it asserts the right of women with children to remain in the family home and exerts a sanction on violent men by temporarily removing their much defended property rights.

The strong hope is that the combination of these two fundamental changes will result in fewer women remaining in abusive relationships for long periods of time, partly due to increasing perceptions of a right to protection and safety. Removal laws can be said to deliver the kind of protection that women seek when calling the police: they want the violence to stop. However, questions remain as to whether protection and rights of residence may be bought at the cost of prosecution. So, while safety may increase, it may remain the case that few perpetrators are convicted of violent offences. Quite how these two reforms – the creation of a state offence and police powers to remove perpetrators of domestic violence – initiate change will be a matter for empirical enquiry.

---

22 The first local implementation was in St. Gallen (1.1.2003), followed by Appenzell Ausserrhoden and other cantons.

Conclusion

A recurring theme in domestic violence literature is criticism of institutional responses that fail to meet the needs of victims and afford leniency to perpetrators, consistently across national contexts. Moving beyond these deficiencies often includes a call for legal reform in addition to changed institutional practices. There is undoubtedly a new openness in rethinking (un)organised responses to domestic violence, and this openness is in turn increasingly reflected in legal and institutional reforms.

The appeal to law as an instrument to afford recognition to social and political problems – like domestic violence – as civil rights issues is central for modern societies. Substantial law making and reform has taken place in various countries. This chapter has used the example of Switzerland to argue that a legal framework that regulates the provision of support and protection is instrumental in meeting the civil rights claims of abused women. The major legal steps to improving support, protection and prosecution include:

- domestic violence being recognised as a state offence – a pre-condition for the state and its agencies to respond in a proactive way;
- the police, the criminal justice system and shelters supporting a proactive policy;
- police powers to remove the perpetrator enhanced, and these powers transformed into protection orders (Protection from Violence Law);
- legal entitlements for victims of crime to support, advocacy and compensation, and the provision of gender-specific services;
- legal and financial provisions that ensure equal rights to support and protection for migrant women who separate from abusive spouses, i.e. reporting domestic violence should not compromise their right to stay.

As legal reform gathers pace, intended outcomes and unintended consequences need to be monitored and evaluated. The Swiss Victim Support Law was not enacted to address gender violence, but in effect has undoubtedly improved the position of shelters and women's support services. The extent of this effect can be seen in the proposed revisions, which include a requirement that each canton provide services specifically for women. Analysis of the unintended consequences of legal reform rarely encompasses positive outcomes such as this. The next phase of assessment in Switzerland will be to examine how treating assaults in the context of domestic violence as state offences affects the level of prosecutions and convictions. It remains to be seen whether the police join the ranks of change makers rather than upholders of tradition, and whether the rates for charges and prosecutions increase, as has happened, for example, in Canada (Owens, 2000; Seith, 2003 for an overview; Statistics Canada, 2000).

While prevention through repression is an important principle, it should not detract from the necessity of providing support. The fact that women enter through various access points in the domestic violence arena highlights the importance of informed responses from all agencies. Research on the responses of social services and the health and education sectors is still scarce in German-speaking contexts. However, their role in detecting violence and enabling women to secure safety and regain autonomy is vital. The current challenge to these agencies is whether they regard domestic violence as important enough to allocate resources to detection and early intervention. In addition to these moves, the question of extending the reactive approach of shelters and women's services to a more proactive one is central. The adoption of a more proactive approach would not only allow services to reach more women, but also hopefully reduce the length of time that women remain in violent relationships.

References

Brandwein, R. A. (Ed.) (1999a). *Battered women, children, and welfare reform: The ties that bind*. Thousand Oaks, CA: Sage.

Büchler, A. (1998). *Gewalt in Ehe und Partnerschaft. Polizei-, straf- und zivilrechtliche Interventionen am Beispiel des Kantons Basel-Stadt*. Basel: Helbing und Lichtenhahn.

Bundesamt für Statistik (2002). Schweizerische Opferhilfestatistik (OHS) 2001: Beratungen, Entschädigungen und Genugtuungen. Rechtspflege Nr. 19. Neuchâtel: Bundesamt für Statistik [cited as BFS 2002].

Burton, S., Regan, L. and Kelly, L. (1998). *Supporting women and challenging men. Lessons from the Domestic Violence Intervention Project*. Bristol: Policy Press.

Buzawa, E. S. and Buzawa, C. G. (1996a). *Domestic violence: The criminal justice response*. Thousand Oaks, CA: Sage.

Buzawa, E. S. and Buzawa, C. G. (eds.) (1996b). *Do Arrests and Restraining Orders Work?* Thousand Oaks, CA: Sage.

Buzawa, E. S., Hotaling, G. T., Klein, A. and Burna, J. (1999). Response to domestic violence in a proactive court setting. Research Report, National Institute of Justice, U.S.

European Women's Lobby (2001). Towards a common European framework to monitor progress in combating violence against women: Proposals for a policy framework and indicators and case studies of models of good practice. Brussels: EWL.

Gillioz, L., Puy de, J. and Ducret, V. (1997). *Domination et violence envers la femme dans le couple*. Lausanne: Payot.

Gloor, D., Meier, H., Baeriswyl, P. and Büchler, A. (2000). *Interventionsprojekte gegen Gewalt in Ehe und Partnerschaft. Grundlagen und Evaluation zum Pilotprojekt Halt-Gewalt*. Bern: Haupt.

Gloor, D., Meier, H. and Verwey, H. (1995). *Frauenalltag und soziale Sicherheit. Schweizer Frauenhäuser und die Situation von Frauen nach dem Aufenthalt*. Chur/Zürich: Rüegger.

Hague, G., Kelly, L. and Mullender, A. (2001). *Challenging Violence Against Women. The Canadian experience*. Bristol: Policy Press.

Holder, R. (2001). *Domestic and Family Violence: Criminal Justice Interventions*. Issues Paper 3. Sydney: Australian Domestic and Family Violence Clearinghouse.

Kelly, L. (1997). Final report of activities of the EG-S-VL including Plan of Action for combating violence against women. Strasbourg: Council of Europe.

Kelly, L. (1999). Domestic Violence Matters. An Evaluation of a Development Project. Home Office Research Study 193. London: Home Office.

Kelly, L. and Humphreys, C. (2001). Supporting women and children in their communities: outreach and advocacy approaches to domestic violence. Pp. 239-274, in J. Taylor Browne (Ed.). *Reducing Domestic Violence: What Works?* London: Home Office.

Kelleher, P. and O'Connor, M. (1999). Safety and Sanctions. Domestic Violence and the Emforcement of Law in Ireland. Dublin: Women's Aid.

Lovett, J., Regan, L. and Kelly, L. (2004). Sexual Assault Referral Centres: Developing Good Practice and Maximising Potentials. Home Office Research Study 285. London: Home Office.

Maeder, C. and Nadai, E. (2004). *Organisierte Armut. Sozialhilfe in wissenssoziologischer Sicht.* Konstanz: UVK.

Mädje, E. and Neusüss, C. (1996). Frauen in der Sozialpolitik- und Armutsforschung. Pp. 206-222, in: T. Kulawik and B. Sauer (Eds). *Der halbierte Staat: Grundlagen feministischer Politikwissenschaft.* Frankfurt/M.: Campus.

Maynard, M. (1985). The response of social workers to domestic violence. Pp. 125-141, in: J. Pahl (Ed.). *Private Violence and Public Policy. The needs of battered women and the response of the public services.* London: Routledge/Kegan Paul.

Mullender, A. (1996). *Rethinking Domestic Violence: The Social Work and Probation Response.* London: Routledge.

Nadai, E. (2004). Viel Monat übrig am Ende des Geldes – Arme in der Schweiz. *Frauenfragen. Eidgenössische Kommission für Frauenfragen,* Vol. 27,1, June 2004, Bern, pp. 9-12.

Oevermann, U. (1996a). *Konzeptionalisierung von Anwendungsmöglichkeiten und praktischen Arbeitsfeldern der objektiven Hermeneutik. Manifest der objektiv hermeneutischen Sozialforschung.* Frankfurt/M. (Manuskript).

Oevermann, U. (1979). Methodologie der objektiven Hermeneutik und ihre allgemeine forschungslogische Bedeutung in den Sozialwissenschaften, pp. 352-434, in: H.-G. Soeffner (Ed.). *Interpretative Verfahren in den Sozial- und Textwissenschaften.* Stuttgart: Metzler.

Ostner, I. (1995). Arm ohne Ehemann? Sozialpolitische Regulierung von Lebenschancen von Frauen im internationalen Vergleich. *Politik und Zeitgeschichte,* B36-37, 3-12.

Owens, T. (2000). Do prosecutors have a role in the co-ordination of services between the police, correctional, health and social service agencies? Paper at Metropolitan Police Conference 'Domestic Violence: Enough is Enough'. October 2000. London.

Rapheal, J. and Tolman, R. M. (1997). *Trapped by poverty, trapped by abuse: New evidence documenting the relationship between domestic violence and welfare.* Chicago: Taylor Institute.

Riedmüller, B. (1984). Frauen haben keine Rechte. Zur Stellung der Frau im System sozialer Sicherheit. Pp. 46-72, in: I. Kickbusch and B. Riedmüller (Eds.). *Die armen Frauen.* Frankfurt/M.: Suhrkamp.

Römkens, R. (2001). Law as a Trojan Horse: Unintended Consequences of Right-Based Interventions to Support Battered Women. *Yale Journal of Law and Feminism,* Vol. 13, 265-290.

Seith, C. (2000). Institutionen und Gewalt im Geschlechterverhältnis – Ergebnisse einer quantitativen und qualitativen Untersuchung im Kanton Freiburg. *Olymp.*

Feministische Arbeitshefte zur Politik. Männer-Gewalt gegen Frauen: gesellschaftlich, grenzenlos, grauenhaft. 12, 52-64.

Seith, C. (2001). Security Matters: Domestic Violence and Public Social Services. *Violence Against Women,* 7, 7, 799-820.

Seith, C. (2003). *Öffentliche Interventionen gegen häusliche Gewalt. Zur Rolle von Polizei, Sozialdienst und Frauenhäusern.* Frankfurt/Main: Campus.

Seith, C. (2004). What counts: legal reforms, data collection and decision making with respect to sexual and domestic violence in German speaking countries. In Jaspard, M. and Condon, S. (Eds.). *Genre, Violences sexuelles et Justice.* Actes de la journée-séminaire du 20 juin 2003. Documents de travail 121. Paris: Institut National d'Etudes Démographiques.

Statistics Canada, Canadian Centre for Justice Statistics (2000). *Family Violence in Canada: A Statistical Profile 2000.* Ottawa: Statistics Canada (cited as Statistics Canada 2000).

Strauss, A. and Corbin, J. (1990). *Basics of Qualitative Research: Grounded Theory Procedures and Techniques.* Newbury Park, Ca: Sage.

Ursel, J. (2000). Family Violence Courts. Pp. 45-48, in Family Violence in Canada: A Statistical Profile 2000. Canadian Centre for Justice Statistics. Ottawa: Statistics Canada.

Chapter 10

Abuser Programmes and Violence Against Women

Russell P. Dobash and Rebecca Emerson Dobash

Abstract

Using the findings of the Violent Men Study,[1,2] we explore the impact of various criminal justice interventions, particularly court mandated abuser programmes, on men's subsequent use of violence against a woman partner. The three-year evaluation study examined the relationship between various criminal justice sanctions against domestic violence (abuser programmes and other interventions such as fines, warnings, probation) and men's subsequent use of violence and controlling behaviours. In addition, we examined the sustainability of change over a period of one year. The findings suggest that all types of intervention from the justice system are associated with some reduction in violence over a short period of time, but abuser programmes are associated with greater levels of reduction and these are more likely to be sustained over a period of one year. Reductions in physical violence are also associated with reductions in other forms of controlling behaviours. While marital status and employment also appear to be related to outcome, successful participation on an abuser programme is an important factor in reductions in violence and controlling behaviour and in the sustainability of change.

---

1   This chapter is a much revised version of a chapter titled 'Interventions Against Violent Men' that initially appeared in M. Eliason (ed.). *Assessing the Impact of Court Mandated Abuser Programmes on Subsequent Violence and Controlling Behaviour.* Uppsala: University of Uppsala Press.
2   The Violent Men Study was funded jointly by the Home Office (London) and the Scottish Office (Edinburgh). Principle Investigators: (Professor Russell P. Dobash and Professor Rebecca Emerson Dobash). Researchers: Dr. Kate Cavanagh, University of Stirling and Dr. Ruth Lewis.

Introduction

The growing body of evidence regarding the efficacy of treatment programmes for men who have been violent to a woman partner derives mostly from research based in the United States and focuses mostly on voluntary programmes and those providing services to a combination of voluntary and court mandated participants. In Britain, there is considerable debate about the efficacy of criminal justice based abuser programmes, and across Europe there have been few attempts to assess the work of such programmes. Here, we present the results of a three-year evaluation study of two British, court mandated abuser programmes. We develop the theoretical and empirical rationale for the efficacy of court mandated intervention and present evidence regarding the impact of such programmes on subsequent violence and controlling behaviour of men who have been convicted of assaulting a woman partner.

Any attempt to eliminate intimate partner violence should require an intervention that addresses constituent elements of the problem at the individual, cultural and institutional levels. It is unlikely that successful intervention can be achieved through any single intervention within criminal or civil justice. Neither 'arrest' nor 'civil injunctions' are likely to solve the problem on their own without subsequent action. We maintain that criminal and/or civil justice interventions are more likely to contribute to a reduction in men's violence if they contain elements of 'control' and 'surveillance' as well as positive forms of 'reform'. All of these elements are contained in the combination of *arrest* and *prosecution* combined with a cognitive-behavioural community based *abuser programme* whose contents are tailored to this particular form of offending behaviour. The findings in this research support this approach and provide evidence about the effectiveness of court mandated, cognitive behavioural programmes compared with other forms of intervention within the justice system.

The Violent Men Study addressed a number of questions: (1) What is the relationship between various types of criminal justice sanctions and subsequent violent behaviour? (2) What are the relative effects of court mandated abuser programmes compared with other sanctions over a short time period of three months compared with a longer period of one year; and (3) Is there a relationship between a reduction in acts of physical violence and other forms of intimidating and controlling behaviour?

In examining these questions, we also consider differences in outcome that might be associated with other factors including socio-demographic characteristics of offenders, previous arrest and a history of repeat offences of violence against an intimate partner. The study compared court mandated abuser programmes with other forms of court sanctions (fine, admonish, probation) in which violent men and women partners were studied at three points over a period of one year. In discussing the necessary elements of an effective intervention, we review literature about the violence itself, informal community interventions, the formal intervention of arrest and, finally, the nature of pro-feminist, cognitive behavioural programmes for violent abusers.

The Violence

Evidence strongly suggests that over time and across cultures, violence against women in intimate relationships exists within a nexus of male power, control and authority (Counts, Brown and Campbell, 1992; Dobash and Dobash, 1979; Gordon, 1988; Levinson, 1989; Pleck, 1987; Wilson and Daly, 1998). Systematic surveys conducted in Britain, USA, Canada, Australia and several European countries reveal that during their life time approximately one-quarter of all women will experience at least one incidence of violence at the hands of their partner (Johnson, 1996; Tjaden and Thoennes, 2000; Heiskanen and Piispa, 1998; Australian Bureau, 1996; Mirrlees-Black, 1999; Medina-Ariza, 2002; Medina-Ariza and Barbaret, 2003). The violence includes a wide range of violent acts from slapping to homicide, is often systematic, severe and persistent and may also include sexual assault and rape (Campbell, 1999; Daly and Wilson, 1988; Dobash and Dobash, 1984; Kelly, 1988; Tjaden and Thoennes, 2000; Wilson, Johnson and Daly, 1995; Medina-Ariza and Barbaret, 2003). Findings from the Canadian National Violence Against Women Survey reveal a pattern of repeat victimisation throughout the married life of a considerable proportion of the women who reported violence by an intimate partner, '63% of women who had been assaulted reported more than one episode and 32% more than ten' (Johnson and Sacco, 1995: 297). An estimate from the US National Crime Victimization Survey indicates that nearly a third of all female victims of intimate partner violence were assaulted at least twice during the six months prior to the research (Greenfield et al., 1998).

Physical violence that is systematic and severe often occurs in a context of various forms of threat, intimidation and other coercive acts (Wilson, Johnson and Daly, 1995). In the research reported here, we differentiate between acts of physical violence and other forms of controlling and intimidating behaviour. We refer to this combination as the 'constellation of abuse' and in this chapter we examine the links between physical violence and other forms of controlling and intimidating behaviour (see Dobash, Dobash, Cavanagh and Lewis, 2000; Dobash and Dobash, 2004).

Violence against intimate women partners has traditionally existed within a social and institutional context of relative 'tolerance' or indifference. At best, most societies maintain a moral ambivalence toward the use of such violence; often merely setting limits with respect to the level of severity that might be tolerated. Most societies exhibit cultural beliefs and practices with respect to the relationship between husband and wives that reinforce a man's authority over his wife (Dobash and Dobash, 1979; Campbell, 1992; Pleck, 1987; Levinson, 1989). In support of that authority, many societies either explicitly condone the use of violence in the exercise of male authority or respond with ambivalence that reflects a legacy of legal and social tolerance of such behaviour.

Theoretical perspectives as diverse as feminism and evolutionary psychology emphasise the functional aspects of this violence and suggest that it works to sustain men's authority and to ensure the delivery of domestic and sexual services. Since violence provides such rewards, it easily becomes habituated and routine (Dobash and Dobash, 1998; Wilson and Daly, 1998). Within the wider cultural context, individual men legitimise their violence by invoking culturally prescribed scripts that justify its use and deflect responsibility onto others (Dobash and Dobash, 1998; Leibrich, Paulin and Ransom, 1995; Ptacek, 1988; Pence and Paymar, 1993). The point here is that violence against women within intimate relationships is, for the most part, embedded within wider social and institutional conditions and traditions, and this makes it a form of behaviour that remains entrenched, complex and ambivalent even within societies working toward its elimination.

Responding to Violence Against Women: Surveillance, Control and Sanctions

Evidence from small, kinship-based societies suggests that reduced levels of wife beating occur in communities where there are effective sanctuaries for abused women and meaningful sanctions for abusers. These responses include various forms of informal surveillance and control used by kin and community to oversee relationships and inflict 'costs' on the perpetrators for the continuation of violence. This may involve indirect disapprobation such as shaming as well as threats and/or coercion directed at the perpetrator who continues to use violence (Counts, Brown and Campbell, 1992; Baumgartner, 1993; Descola, 1996: 182-200). It appears that sanctions involving costs to the offender and informal methods of surveillance and control may have a deterrent effect on men's use of violence against intimate partners. In contemporary urban-industrial societies, the social control functions of kin and community have generally diminished or disappeared and have largely been replaced by institutions of the state (Dobash and Dobash 1981; Pahl 1985; Hoff 1990; Fagan 1992). Over the last two decades, women's groups throughout the world have pressed institutions of the state to alter policy and practice and to become more responsive to the issue of violence against women. In the US, one important focus of such efforts has been on the sanction of arrest.

In the 1980s, the National Institute of Justice sponsored several evaluations of the effect of arrest on subsequent acts of violence (see Sherman, 1992 and Garner, Fagan and Maxwell, 1995 for an overview). The findings have been mixed, ranging from early declarations of effectiveness that suggested a pro-arrest policy, to later findings of 'no effect' or even negative effects (Sherman and Berk 1984; Sherman, 1992). Interpretations of why that might be so have also varied from views that arrest may only work for those with a sufficient investment in the community (through employment) to make an arrest socially or personally costly (Sherman and Smith, 1992; Berk, Campbell, Klap and Western, 1992a), to notions that it will not work on repeat offenders (who are disproportionately unemployed and black) (Sherman, 1992, 1995) and, finally, to speculations that arrest may actually lead to an increase in violence among certain men especially the unemployed and/or repeat offenders (Sherman, 1992). In some locations, these shifts in position have led to a reversal of proposals away from pro-arrest in favour of selective arrest (with no arrest for the most 'hardened' repeat offenders and its possible use among those more embedded in work, marriage and the community). In addition, some commentators have proposed a move away from the use of the justice system toward a greater reliance on informal methods (Braithwaite and Daly 1994; Sherman, 1995; Masters and Smith, 1998; see Stubbs, 1995; Lewis, Dobash, Dobash and Cavanagh, 2000 for a critique).

A quite different interpretation of the arrest studies has also been drawn, suggesting that arrest on its own does not work because more rather than less criminal justice intervention is required in order to generate an effect (Berk et al., 1992a; Berk, Campbell, Klap and Western, 1992b). Berk and his colleagues state that the findings of the various evaluations 'provide no sound rationale for abandoning arrest, even presumptory arrest, as a policy option' (Berk, et al., 1992a: 706; see also Hart, 1993; Stark, 1993). They further suggest that 'bail could be much higher' and that police and the community might provide more assertive interventions to assist victims through the use of orders of protection and shelters or refuges.

Court Mandated Programmes for Violent Abusers

Pro-feminist cognitive-behavioural programmes for abusers are based on the understanding that this form of violence is strongly linked to differentials of power and authority in intimate relationships. As such, the content of such programmes addresses both the violent behaviour and supporting beliefs and attitudes. Hundreds of abuser programmes now exist in the US and Canada along with a few in Europe, New Zealand, Australia and Britain (Dobash and Dobash, 1992; 2000a). The general orientation is one in which abusers are deemed to be acting within a culturally constructed context of relationships between 'husbands' and 'wives' in which the man has greater power and authority over the woman and violence is used to control and punish. Violence is seen as learned, purposeful behaviour, usually occurring against a background of intimidation, coercion and other forms of control (Adams, 1988; Pence and Paymar, 1993). While some abuser programmes are voluntary, others are located within a criminal justice context. In the US many voluntary or 'mixed' programmes have become dedicated criminal justice interventions.

Theoretically, court mandated programmes combine a number of important strands that might be viewed as essential for developing and sustaining non-violent approaches to intimate relationships. Through arrest and prosecution, they increase the cost to the man of using violence and provide a limited form of potential deterrence incorporating a short period of surveillance and control by criminal justice authorities. Going beyond arrest and other short-term interventions such as injunctions and fines (the usual sanction in Britain) probation adds the elements of a longer period of surveillance, control and support focused specifically on the offender. Court mandated abuser programmes add a focus on changing the specific offending behaviour while the individual remains within the necessary nexus of official surveillance and control. Abuser programmes deal directly with the violence and with underlying beliefs and justifications as well as with other forms of intimidating and controlling behaviour with the explicit aim of their elimination. In this respect, they offer men new ways of thinking and behaving that allow them to build and sustain relationships free of violence and intimidation. Finally, such interventions constitute a symbol of the rejection of intimate partner violence both within the community and to the individuals directly involved. This creates a wider context of disapprobation both for the offender and throughout society. Overall, this combination of factors would seem to increase the possibility of sustained change within individuals and move away from traditional tolerance of violence within the wider community and the justice system.

The two Scottish programmes considered here, CHANGE and the Lothian Domestic Violence Probation Project (LDVPP), were the first dedicated criminal justice based abuser programmes in Britain and, to our knowledge, in Europe. They build upon model programmes from the US, particularly the influential Domestic Abuse Intervention Programme from Duluth Minnesota and the Man Alive programme of Marin, California (Pence and Paymar, 1993; Sinclair, 1989). The two programmes were firmly established throughout the duration of the research and while there was some variation in their content, this was more a matter of detail of delivery than of overall content or philosophy (Dobash, Dobash, Cavanagh and Lewis 1999, 2000; Morran and Wilson, 1994; 1997). Like their North American counterparts, these programmes focused specifically on the offender, his violent behaviour and his need to change. They did not accept voluntary referrals as this would exclude the criminal justice system with all the essential components contained within it. The men on the abuser programmes had been found guilty of an offence involving violence against their woman partner and, having been assessed as appropriate for the programme, participated as a condition of a probation order. Men sentenced to programme participation were required to attend weekly group sessions for six months. Group work was 'challenging', aimed at creating alternative styles of thinking and reducing violent and controlling behaviour.

Evaluations of Abuser Programmes

Since the 1980s, there have been a number of attempts to assess the efficacy of abuser programmes and several reviews have summarised Canadian and American research (Burns, Meredith and Paquette, 1991; Eisikovits and Edleson, 1989; Gondolf, 1997). Various types of interventions have been studied including voluntary and court mandated programmes, and various methods have been used to evaluate their efficacy including self evaluations, quasi-experimental designs and randomised experimental designs.

Early evaluations found that abuser programmes had some impact on subsequent violent behaviour and that a considerable proportion of programme participants remained violence free after intervention (Bersani, Chen and Denton, 1988; Dutton, 1986, 1995; Edleson and Grusznski, 1988; Edleson and Syers, 1991; Gondolf, 1988, 1991, 1999; Saunders, 1996; Saunders and Hanusa, 1986; Tolman and Bennett, 1990). While the majority of these evaluations assessed voluntary programmes, the few studies that assessed court mandated programmes using subsequent arrest as the assay of failure also found successful outcomes (Chen, Bersani and Denton, 1989; Dutton, 1995; Hamm and Kite, 1991). They also suggested that court mandated participants were more likely than volunteers to complete a programme and that offenders who complete are less likely to re-offend (Gondolf, 2002).

Recent evaluations have used quasi-experimental designs and a few have used randomised experimental designs but they all face a variety of challenges in design and implementation and debates remain about appropriate methods and the veracity of evidence. Because of the nature of the issue itself as well as the interventions, many studies suffer from a number of limitations including small sample sizes (usually not more than fifty respondents at the onset of a longitudinal study, see Hamm and Kite, 1991 for details), a lack of comparison groups, no baseline measures at intervention, and reliance on the self-reports of offenders and/or re-arrest as the sole indicator(s) of subsequent violence. The absence of comparison groups threatens the validity of findings because similar outcomes might have been achieved using some other form of intervention or by doing nothing. Despite their widespread use in criminal justice evaluations, research in this domain suggests that police reports or self-reports of offenders are exceedingly unreliable methods for assessing subsequent incidents of violence because many incidents go unreported to police and abusers persistently fail to acknowledge the full extent of their violence (Dutton and Hemphill, 1992; Pence and Paymar, 1993; Heckert and Gondolf, 2000). Most recent evaluations have used self-reports of victims in addition to men's reports and records of re-arrest, although self-reports of women partners are not routinely included in evaluations of criminal justice based programmes. Other problems include the lack of follow-up period(s) or follow-up periods that are very short, usually not more than six months. High rates of attrition are customary in these follow-up studies, ranging from 60-80% (Tolman and Bennett, 1990). These problems present challenges to all research on this topic whether the method selected for study is self-evaluation, quasi-experimental or experimental.

With respect to the efficacy of abuser programmes, quasi-experimental evaluations have generally found more positive results while those using randomised experimental designs have produced more negative results.

While randomised experimental designs are not generally used in the evaluation of abuser programmes, the few that have been conducted appear to show that they are no more effective than other forms of intervention (Taylor, Davis and Maxwell 2001; Dunford, 2000), although this conclusion is not universally agreed by those who have used this method (Palmer, Brown and Barrera, 1992). Randomised experimental methods, like quasi-experimental approaches, encounter problems associated with implementing rigorous designs in natural settings. Some of these include: small numbers of participants, high attrition rates, compromised randomisation procedures, unrepresentative samples and problematic settings of programmes such as those delivered within the controlled environment of the military (Berk, Smyth and Sherman, 1988; Gondolf, 2001: 51-61).

The Study

Research Design

The Violent Men Study reported here builds on existing North American evaluations of abuser programmes and attempts to deal with some of the limitations described above. It was designed to assess the impact of a range of criminal justice sanctions on violent behaviour and the constellation of abuse over a one-year period. As noted above, the issue of valid evaluation design is subject to debate and some argue that the strengths of randomised designs warrant the exclusion of all others (Sherman, 1992). A randomised design was not used in this research because it was considered to be unworkable, impractical and potentially unethical (for a fuller discussion see Dobash and Dobash, 2000b).

The quasi-experimental method used in this research – sometimes called the 'non-equivalent control group' design (Campbell and Stanley, 1966; Chen et al., 1989) – compared the effects of criminal justice interventions on two naturally occurring groups of offenders. The Programme Group included men sentenced to one of the two court mandated programmes for violent men, CHANGE and the LDVPP; the Other Criminal Justice Group, included men sanctioned in other ways (80% received fines although a few were placed on probation). Men and women partners included in the study were interviewed at Time 1 (usually immediately following an intervention) and sent postal questionnaires at Time 2 (three months after interview) and Time 3 (twelve months after interview). Interviews were both intensive and extensive and covered a wide range of issues in order to establish a multi-dimensional baseline for assessing change over time (for details see Dobash et al., 2000). At Times 2 and 3, postal questionnaires were used to assess changes in the criterion behaviours and orientations. Court reports of subsequent arrest during the follow-up period were also used to monitor re-offending over a one-year period.

The main limitation of the non-equivalent control group design is that it cannot deal with the selection bias that might be introduced through criminal justice processes. For example, Scottish judges might have sentenced to the Programmes only men who committed less severe violence and/or those with histories of 'minimal' violence (i.e., men assumed to be most likely to respond positively to any intervention). In addition, programme staff might accept only those offenders they consider most likely to succeed. Post-hoc aggregate matching was used to evaluate potential biases that might have been introduced through the processes whereby men were 'chosen' to participate in abuser programmes.

Throughout the course of the study, relevant cases were obtained through systematic monthly scrutiny of pending cases in the courts of Central Region and Edinburgh (the locations of the programmes). As there is no offence category 'domestic assault', all pending cases were examined and those involving violence in marital and marital-like relationships were identified. Official charges in these cases ranged from 'assault' and 'assault to severe injury' to 'breach of the peace' – the majority (over 80%) involved convictions for assault.[3] The achieved sample at Time 1 included 122 men convicted of an offence involving violence against a woman partner and 134 women who had been the victim of an incident involving domestic violence and whose partner had been processed through the courts. Within this sample there were 95 intact couples. Most men and women were white and had Scottish, English or Irish parents, and thus were representative of the court cases examined in the two jurisdictions. The analysis presented here is based on these two naturally occurring comparison groups – Programme and Other CJ sanctions. The Programme group includes 51 men and 47 women partners and the Other CJ group is comprised of 71 men and 87 women partners.

Measuring Criterion Behaviour

It was important to obtain valid estimates of the levels of violence at Time 1 for comparison with the subsequent follow-ups at Times 2 and 3. It was also important to create a method that would produce valid and reliable data from both men and women across three periods of time and to deal with the potential reluctance of men to discuss their violence. Past research by Dobash and Dobash (1983; 1984) used a context specific approach focusing on discrete violent events – the first, the worst and last – which yielded a wealth of quantitative and qualitative data from women who had been physically abused. Building on this, a form of event analysis was used that included systematic questions seeking open-ended answers in combination with more standardised, quantitative forms of data collection. In order to assure the collection of systematic data for comparisons across the three time periods and to encourage maximum disclosure from both men and women, five indexes were developed and used to examine 'violence', 'injuries', 'controlling behaviour' and 'quality of life' for men and for women (the quality of life indexes are not discussed here).[4]

---

3   It should be noted that this evaluation differs from most North American studies of arrest and abusers' programmes, in that cases of serious violence – 'felonies' – were included here whereas they are usually excluded in most North American research.

4   At interview, the indexes were used only after men and women had responded to systematic, open-ended questions about the violence and its consequences. Immediately following these open-ended questions, respondents were handed a 'cue card' containing the VAI, IAI or CBI. The interviewer then read out only the letter corresponding to a particular violent act or injury and the respondent was asked if, for example, 'A' had occurred. Thus, both the respondent and the interviewer did not have to articulate the words describing the particular type

The Violence Assessment Index (VAI) included twenty-six distinct acts ranging from aggressive threats and restraint to punching and kicking and the use of a weapon.[5] The twenty-one-item Injury Assessment Index (IAI) assessed specific injuries and their locations on the body, ranging from bruising of the body to lost hair to internal injuries. The Controlling Behaviours Index (CBI) contained 22 specific acts such as verbal forms of intimidation and coercion including 'swear at her' and 'questioning her activities' and more indirect acts such as 'putting her down in front of others' and physical aggression such as 'making to hit'. Using these three indexes, men and women were asked to indicate how often during a specific violent event and throughout the relationship the man had used (or his partner had experienced) each of the particular acts and injuries.

The straightforward disaggregated percentage outcomes of the specific items used in these indexes have been reported elsewhere (Dobash, Dobash, Cavanagh and Lewis 1998), but in order to conduct more parsimonious comparisons between the two groups, the results of the VAI, IAI and the CBI were converted into summary scores for each index. Cronbach's Alpha was used to assess the internal consistency of each index (Carmines and Zeller 1979). Using the responses of both men and women at Time 1, the results revealed strong internal consistency for each index with Alphas of .93 for VAI, .90 for IAI and .90 for CBI. Each index was refined using established procedures and a specific assessment was made for each respondent by averaging the number of items they responded to on each of the indices. Scale scores were calculated for each index for each time period: one for the *prevalence* of the acts (at least once) and the other for the *frequent* occurrence of these acts (five or more incidents).[6]

---

of violence or injury. Comparing information from the indexes with the transcribed text of responses to the open-ended questions showed that this method enabled men to disclose much more about such events.

5   The three indexes were developed from earlier research by the authors that focused on the violent events and violent relationships of a sample of 109 women who had abused by their male partner (Dobash and Dobash, 1979; 1984). The interviews with abused women revealed a wide range of violence, injuries and controlling behaviours, and the most frequently occurring and/or consequential items were incorporated into the three indexes. For details of the validation procedures see Dobash et al., 2000.

6   It was often impossible for women and men to provide the precise number of times they had perpetrated/experienced a specific type of violence or injury. As such, it was not possible to use a straightforward procedure of simply adding all items for a given individual in order to calculate a frequency score. Therefore data were gathered on the following basis: 'never', 'rarely' (once every six months); 'sometimes' (once every 3 to 6 months); 'often' (once every 3 months);

The Follow-up Periods

Postal questionnaires were used to assess changes in the behaviour and orientations of men and the predicament of women at follow-up. In order to assess possible 'separation effects' women were asked about their living arrangements during each period of follow-up and, if separated from the man who committed the assault, to indicate how much contact they had during the specific follow-up period. Women and men were asked to record the number of incidents of violence in the specific follow-up period, to provide details of violence, injuries and controlling behaviour using the VAI, IAI and CBI and to assess changes in other relevant areas.

Reasonably good levels of retention were achieved over the two follow-up periods. At Time 2, 80% of men and 83% of women in the Programme group and 72% of men and 77% of women in the Other CJ group returned a questionnaire. Attrition rates were calculated as a proportion of those interviewed at Time 1 and included non-returns as well as those who could not be traced. The rates of return at Time 3 were calculated similarly. Fifty three per cent of men and 60% of women in the Programme group and 49% of men and 57% per cent of women in the Other CJ group returned questionnaires at Time 3. The rate of return after one year is predictably lower than after three months; although the rates at both follow-up periods are at least as good as those achieved in similar studies in this area and well within acceptable levels (Ribsil et al., 1996). The characteristics of those who returned questionnaires at the two points of follow-up were compared to those of the entire sample; there were no statistically significant differences on a number of pertinent variables.

Results

Here, the findings of the Violent Men Study are used to consider questions of selection bias, the effects of criminal justice interventions, the impact of other relevant factors and the relationship between violence and controlling behaviours. In order to consider selection bias, we assess differences in background characteristics and levels of violence, injuries

---

and 'very often' (once a month). Individual scores for *frequent* violence were obtained by summing the categories 'often' and 'very often' for all items in an index and calculating the percentage of items identified in this way.

and controlling behaviour between the two groups at Time 1. The effects of criminal justice interventions upon subsequent violence and controlling behaviour are examined by comparing the two groups across the three time periods. We then consider the possible impact of other relevant factors upon violence and controlling behaviour regardless of group membership. Finally, the relationship between violence and controlling behaviour is examined across the entire sample for all three time periods. Throughout most of this analysis, *women's reports* are used.[7] This was considered to be particularly important when considering changes in violence and controlling behaviour since we consider their reports to reflect the most stringent test of changes in men's behaviour. We now turn to a discussion of the results, beginning with a discussion of selection bias that also provides a description of the sample.

Investigating Selection Bias

The intensive data gathered at Time 1 allow for comparisons of the men in the two groups on a wide range of social and demographic characteristics that might influence their offending behaviour. The average age of the men in both groups was 32 years, and most grew up in households with both natural parents. There were no statistically significant differences between the two groups on a range of variables associated with violence in their family of origin. A considerable proportion of men in both groups reported a fair amount of physical chastisement at the hands of their fathers during childhood. Forty-four percent of Programme men and 47% of Other CJ men described this chastisement as 'serious' or 'very serious', and about one-quarter in both groups said they were often hit 'too much' and 'unfairly'. About the same proportion of men in both groups (40% Programme/52% Other CJ) grew up in a family in which their mother was subjected to physical violence at the hands of their father. The majority of these men (79% Programme/62% Other CJ) judged the violence used against their mothers as 'serious' or 'very serious', although a much higher proportion of Programme men defined such violence as 'very serious'. There were two statistically and theoretically significant differences between the two groups from the outset. A higher proportion of men in the Other CJ group

---

7   Some might criticize the use of men's reports for any information. However, it was important to include men's reports of their own biographical details, such as father's occupation and previous criminal convictions since many women had little or no knowledge about the man's past.

were unemployed (72.9% vs. 51.9%) and fewer were in state sanctioned marriages (61.5% vs. 35.7%). Most men, whether cohabiting or in state sanctioned unions, were in long-term relationships with the woman they had assaulted. Another difference between the groups that nearly reached statistical significance was religious affiliation, with a higher proportion of men in the Programme group identifying themselves as Protestant.

Histories of criminal justice experience were broadly similar for men in the two groups. Comparisons were made on previous arrests for an offence, including violence perpetrated against a previous partner, number of previous convictions and number of times in prison as well as previous police intervention in connection with incidents involving their current partner. A general feature of both groups was a history of contact with criminal justice: only two men in the Other CJ group had no previous record while well over 80% of men in both groups reported two or more convictions, and approximately the same percentage reported previous police intervention in connection with violence against their current intimate partner. No statistically significant differences emerged in these comparisons, though a higher proportion of Programme than Other CJ men reported a previous arrest for violence, including violence against a partner (72.5% vs. 60.9%). Men in the Other CJ group were more likely to report 20 or more previous convictions, primarily for public order offences such as breach of the peace often associated with public drunkenness (23.5% vs. 9.8%).

In order to extend the investigation of selection bias, the scale scores of men's violence (VAI), injuries (IAI) and controlling behaviour (CBI), as reported by women, were compared for the two groups at Time 1. It can be seen in Table 10.1 that there were no significant differences in the mean scores of the two groups at the beginning of the research. About three-quarters of women reported that a male partner had used violence against them sometime during their relationship (*prevalence*), and over one-third of these acts occurred *frequently* (five times in a typical year of the relationship). Using the IAI, women also reported a range of injuries inflicted by male partners. For both groups, nearly two-thirds of the men inflicted at least one injury during the relationship (prevalence) and nearly one-quarter did so on a frequent basis during a typical year. The prevalence and frequency of controlling behaviours (CBI) was nearly identical for both groups, with women reporting that about three-quarters of the controlling acts had been used against them by a male partner at least once in their relationship and nearly a quarter experienced this on a frequent basis.

Table 10.1   Average Scores of Programme Group (n=47) and Other Criminal Justice Group (n=87) at Time 1 on Three Indexes (prevalence ever and frequency; women's reports)

	Prevalence Score		Frequent Score	
	Programme	Other CJ	Programme	Other CJ
VAI-Violence Assessment Index	0.73	0.72	0.39	0.39
IAI-Injury Assessment Index	0.65	0.60	0.22	0.24
CBI-Controlling Behaviour Index	0.71	0.75	0.22	0.24

Note: There were no statistically significant differences on any of these comparisons.

Based on women's reports, there were no significant differences between the two groups in the prevalence and frequency of violence, injuries and controlling behaviour at the outset of the research (Time 1). In other words, the two groups of men in the study did not differ before the research began, thus making it more likely that any subsequent differences might be related to the intervention received rather than to initial characteristics. Various comparisons show few differences in the current status, family backgrounds and criminal careers of the men but, as stated above, men in the Other CJ group were more likely to be unemployed at the point of intervention and they were more likely to be living in non-state sanctioned relationships (cohabitation). Existing research shows that employment may be an important indicator of a personal 'anchor' within or connection to the community and this, in turn, may have important implications for the potential impact of arrest on subsequent violence. Furthermore, living in a non-state sanctioned relationship has been shown in other research to be an important risk factor for violence against women (Wilson, Johnson and Daly, 1995). The impact of these variables on reductions in violence and controlling behaviours will be explored more fully when considering the effects of Programme participation and other sanctions.

Effects of Criminal Justice Interventions on Violence and Controlling Behaviour

On the basis of the theoretical contention that successful interventions will incorporate elements of continuous control and reformation, we would expect to find important differences in the levels of violence and controlling behaviour in the two groups at the two periods of follow-up.[8] Straightforward assessment of court records revealed only minor, non-significant differences in the prevalence of re-arrest between the two groups following a criminal justice intervention. Of those cases we were able to assess during the course of the research, only 7% of the Programme Group and 10% of the Other CJ group were re-arrested during the standardised one-year period of follow-up. On the basis of these results we might assume that all forms of criminal justice intervention have a significant effect and that the abuser programmes are only slightly more successful than other types of interventions in this respect. Reports of women tell a very different story.

The reports of women at Time 1 indicated that all male partners in both groups had committed at least one violent act in the year before the research began. At Time 2 (3 month follow-up), women's reports indicted that 29.6% of programme men had committed a subsequent violent act while 61.0% of men in the Other CJ Group had done so, a statistically significant difference.[9] Considering the cumulative failures at Time 3 (12 month follow-up), 33.3%[10] of programme men had committed a violent act while 69.4% of men in the Other CJ Group had done so; again, a statistically significant difference between the two groups.[11] It should be noted that all of these men had committed at least one violent act in the year preceding the study and that many had committed five or more such acts (26% of Programme Group and 31% of Other CJ Group, a non-significant difference).

The results show that men in the Programme Group were more likely to stop using violence during the one-year period of follow-up and were also more likely to reduce controlling and intimidating acts. Table 10.2 presents the average *prevalence* and *frequent* scores on the CBI for the

---

8   All of the men included in the Programme group at follow-up had successfully completed an abuser programme. Nine men initially assigned to the Programme group were reassigned to the Other CJ group at follow-up because they did not attend any of the programme sessions. It should also be noted that the results of the VAI and IAI at follow-up are not reported here. Women who reported no violence at follow-up, rarely completed these two indexes because there was nothing to report. As such, it is obvious that a comparison would be a relatively meaningless exercise, yielding a zero sum outcome.

9   Chi Square p< .001.

10   The cumulative failures were calculated across Times 2 and 3 in order to include all men who failed at either point but to avoid double counting across the two points. The denominator was based on the n's at Time 2.

11   Chi Square, p< .001.

two groups at all three time periods based on the reports of women who returned questionnaires at all three periods of assessment. One year after the intervention women reported that men on the abuser programmes were more likely than men in the Other CJ group to have reduced their controlling behaviours.

Table 10.2   Average Scores on Controlling Behaviour Index (prevalence and frequent) at Three Time Periods (women's reports)

	CBI- Prevalence		CBI- Frequent	
Time	Programme	Other CJ	Programme	Other CJ
Time 1	0.70	0.75	0.38	0.48
Time 2	**0.52**	0.68	0.22	0.33
Time 3	**0.53**	0.71	**0.20**	0.36

Programme group n=21; Other CJ group n=44 (includes only cases where women returned questionnaires at Time 3 and completed the CBI at Times 1, 2, and 3). Chi Square, bold: $p < 0.05$.

Of the men reported upon at Time 3, those in the Other CJ group had reduced only marginally their *prevalence* scores on the CBI across the twelve-month period (from .75 at Time 1 to .71 at Time 3). Although the men in the Programme group began with a somewhat lower average score at Time 1 than men in the other group (.70 vs .75), their average scores were reduced significantly by Time 3 (.53 vs .71). A similar pattern is apparent when considering the differences between the two groups in scores for the *frequent* occurrence of controlling acts over the three time periods. Here, the scores for men in the Other CJ group show a marginal reduction over one year (.48 at Time 1 to .36 at Time 3). While the average score for the Programme group at Time 1 is somewhat lower than the Other CJ group (.38 vs .48), this is not a significant difference, and by Time 3 there is a statistically significant reduction in CBI scores for men in the Programme group (.38 at Time 1 to .20 at Time 3). The CBI results suggest that while men in both groups reduced the use of controlling behaviour after one year, men in the Programme group were much more successful in this respect than men in the Other CJ group. It is important to note that men in the Programme group had not completely stopped using controlling and coercive behaviour, but the reports of women partners suggest that the range of these acts had been reduced and that they occurred on a less frequent basis.

Effects of Background Characteristics and Previous Criminal Justice Experience upon Violence and Controlling Behaviour at Time

Violence at Follow-up

The results at follow-up would seem to indicate that the men in the programme group were more likely to reduce or eliminate their violence and controlling behaviours over a period of one year. However, it is important to ask whether such differences are a result of participation on the programme or if they might be attributed to other factors such as personal characteristics that are not related to the programme such as age, employment and marital status. For example, ending violence may not be associated with having participated on an abuser programme but, rather, to having a job or some other factor. In order to consider this, we focused on Time 3 and combined *all* men from both groups (n=65) in order to examine the relationship between personal characteristics and violence (at least one incident) after one year (Time 3). In addition, we also examined each of the personal characteristics in relation to the average CBI scale score.

The results in Table 10.3 suggest that the continuation of violence after a criminal justice intervention may be associated with certain background characteristics beyond what might have been associated with the intervention. While it might be expected that young men would be more likely to use subsequent violence and/or controlling behaviour, there was, in fact, no statistically significant differences by age. By contrast, all of the men in the study, regardless of the type of intervention, were significantly more likely to use subsequent violence if they were cohabiting (79.2%) rather than married (46.7%). The unemployed were also more likely to use subsequent violence (72.4%) than the employed (48.0%). Religious affiliation and the number of children in the relationship seemed to have no impact on failure at follow-up. In addition, personal characteristics appeared to have little or no effect on the CBI scores at Time 3.

Table 10.3 Percentage violent and CBI Scores at Time 3 by background characteristics of offenders (women's reports)

	Percent violent	*CBI scores*	N
Background Characteristics			
Age of offender			
17-25	72.7	0.71	11
26-30	69.2	0.77	13
31-40	53.5	0.58	38
Employment			
Employed	48.0	0.62	28
Unemployed	72.4	0.68	34
Marital status			
State sanctioned	46.7	0.62	33
Non-state	**79.2**	0.69	27
Length of relationship			
<2 years	50.0	0.54	9
2-5 years	82.4	0.76	20
5-10	64.3	0.65	14
>10 years	40.0	0.59	19
Man's religion			
Protestant	58.1	0.66	34
Roman Catholic	75.0	0.69	13
None	54.5	0.58	15
Number of children			
One	66.6	0.61	12
Two	53.3	0.66	15
Three	70.0	0.75	17
Four	70.0	0.62	10
Five	60.0	0.58	8

N=65, Chi Square, bold: $p < 0.05$.

Differences in previous experiences with the criminal justice system did not seem to be related to subsequent violence at Time 3. At Time 3, men who had been previously arrested for offences that included assaults were only slightly more likely to have assaulted their partner than the few men with no history of previous arrest and those with previous arrests for non-violent offences (Table 10.4). Men who reported a history of at least one police call-out regarding violence in their current relationship (the majority) were no more likely to fail than those men who reported no such previous incident. The number of previous convictions did not appear to be linked to subsequent violence at follow-up, although it should be noted that all of the men with more than 21 previous convictions for any type of offence were reported to have committed violence at follow-up. That is, men with a large number of previous charges for any type of offence, appear to persist in violent offending. With respect to controlling behaviour, with one exception, previous criminal justice experiences seem to have no significant effect on average CBI scores at follow-up (Table 10.4). The exception is associated with previous convictions. Men with 21 or more convictions were significantly less likely than men with fewer previous convictions to reduce their controlling behaviour at Time 3.

Table 10.4   Previous Criminal Justice Experience by Violence and CBI scores at Time 3 (women's reports)

	Percent violent	*CBI scores*	N
Criminal justice experience			
Arrest record			
No previous	50.0	0.71	2
arrests (no assault)	58.3	0.64	17
arrests (incl. assault)	62.5	0.65	43
Number previous convictions			
0	50.0	0.72	2
1	42.9	0.54	11
2-5	40.0	0.50	17
6-10	66.7	0.75	13
11-20	57.1	0.63	8
>21	100.0	**0.83**	11
Police call-out to current relationship			
Yes	61.7	0.62	48
No	57.1	0.85	7

N=65, Chi Square, bold: p < 0.05.

In summary, after one year, men in the Programme group were more successful than men in the Other CJ group in reducing violence and other controlling behaviour. The results presented in Tables 10.3 and 10.4 further suggest that successful cessation of violence is also associated with marriage and employment. Married and employed men are more likely than cohabiting and unemployed men to reduce their violence. Other socio-demographic variables had almost no effect on violence and controlling behaviours at follow-up. In addition, previous criminal justice experiences did not appear to be linked to violence and controlling behaviour, although men with over 21 previous convictions did have higher levels of repeat violence and controlling behaviour than men with fewer convictions regardless of the type of intervention.[12]

Relationship Between Violence and Controlling Behaviour

Although some background factors appear to be linked to repeat incidents of violence, a reduction in violence and controlling behaviour seems to be linked to successful participation on an abuser programme. One might ask if an offender reduces his controlling behaviour for whatever reason (either with or without participation on an abuser Programme or any other form of CJ intervention) will he also reduce or eliminate his use of violence. In order to consider this possibility we investigated the direct relationship between controlling behaviours and violence by comparing *prevalence* and *frequent* scores on the CBI at Times 1, 2 and 3. Given the theoretical account presented at the outset of this chapter, we would anticipate that men who continue to use violence at follow-up also continue to use controlling behaviour.

Table 10.5 shows a significant relationship between reduction in violence and the *prevalence* and *frequent* use of controlling behaviour across all time periods regardless of the type of intervention. For those men who subsequently used violence by Time 3, it can be seen that their CBI scores (*prevalence* and *frequent)* remained virtually the same across all three-time periods. The men who did not use violence by Time 3, began with slightly lower CBI scores than their counterparts at Time 1, but by Time 3 the men in this group had significantly reduced their CBI scores both in terms of *prevalence* (.65 to .46) and *frequent* use (.35 to .10).

---

12 Conventionally, the next step in teasing out importance of various factors associated with observed effects would be multi-variate analysis. Logistic regression was used to assess the impact of various variables, including type of intervention, on repeat incidents of violence (Hosmer and Lemeshow, 1989; Farrington, 1997), however, because the numbers achieved across the three times periods were relatively small the statistical results were unstable and thus unreliable. Although larger numbers would be required in order to yield more stable results, the results of the logistic regression were nonetheless basically in line with the bivariate findings and confirm the observed effects of programme participation as well as the nature of relationship on reduction of violence.

Table 10.5 **Violence at Time 3 by CBI scores (prevalence and frequent) across the three time periods (women's reports)**

Time period	Time 1	Time 2	Time 3
Violence at Time 3:			
CBI (prevalence)	0.78	0.78	0.78
CBI (frequent)	0.48	0.43	0.44
No violence at Time 3:			
CBI (prevalence)	0.65	*0.39*	*0.46*
CBI (frequent)	0.35	*0.06*	*0.10*

Note : Includes only cases where women returned questionnaires at Time 3 and completed CBI at Times 1, 2, and 3. Chi Square, bold italics: p< 0.01.

These findings lend support to the theoretical concept of a 'constellation of abuse' which includes both physical violence and other forms of controlling and intimidating behaviour. Given the relationship between these two sets of behaviour, it is difficult to judge whether a reduction in violence leads to a reduction in controlling behaviour or *vice versa*. Concurrent reduction seems most likely but this needs further investigation. The results also suggest that a reduction in violence and controlling behaviour is more likely to occur among men who have successfully completed an abuser programme.

Summary and Conclusion

This chapter compared the relative effectiveness of two court mandated abuser programmes with other forms of criminal justice sanctions for men who are violent to an intimate partner. The abuser programmes in the study were highly structured, cognitive-behavioural interventions based on group work that focused explicitly on the offence, the offending behaviour and associated behaviours and beliefs. Offenders were mandated to participate in these programmes as a result of conviction and a probation order which offered a strong sanctioning potential if they failed to comply. Both of the programmes were well founded and were variously linked to other services in the wider community including those for woman who had been abused.

The findings suggest that men who successfully complete an abuser programmes are significantly more likely to reduce violence and controlling behaviour than men sanctioned in other ways. In addition, violence and controlling behaviours appear to co-vary. That is, regardless of the nature of criminal justice intervention, men who stop using violence are also more likely to reduce their controlling behaviour during a one-year follow-up period. Certain socio-demographic characteristics – nature of relationship and employment – also appear to be associated with reductions in violence and controlling behaviour following a criminal justice sanction.

There was some selection bias in the sample, as marital status and, to a lesser extent, employment status differentiated the two groups at Time 1 and was, to a degree, associated with failure rates at follow-up. It may be that employment is an indicator of 'embeddedness' within the community. Men who are employed may have more to lose through the continued use of violence, including the loss of their job and/or the approval of colleagues. State sanctioned marriage may be a factor because it seems to involve a greater commitment of the couple to one another and also because marriage usually incorporates a wider network of individuals involved in the support and management of the intimate life of the couple. On the other hand, it may be that cohabitation is, in fact, a marker for poverty and youthful relationships both of which are related to violence. Programme participation is likely to be a useful intervention even for repeat offenders although the most persistent of offenders appear to be resistant to change.

The limitations of this study include the selection bias noted above and the attrition of cases over a one-year period. Nonetheless, on the basis of the quantitative and qualitative results presented here and in our other publications (Dobash et al., 1998, 1999, 2000) as well as findings from other evaluations of abuser programmes (Gondolf, 2002; Palmer, Brown and Barrera, 1992), there appears to be a relationship between successful participation on an abuser programme and a reduction in subsequent violence and controlling behaviour. Additionally, these conclusions are broadly in line with other evaluations of cognitive behavioural programmes focusing on domestic violence and other types of offending (McGuire, 1995; Andrews et al., 1990; Gendreau, Cullen and Bonta, 1994; Gondolf, 1997, 1999; Marshall, 1999; Saunders, 1996). Whatever the results of various treatment programmes, debates will continue about the most appropriate and/or valid design. This study used a quasi-experimental design. While we do not reject the use of randomised controlled experiments, our research experience suggests that this method is unlikely to be achieved in natural settings (see Gondolf, 2002) and presents a number of ethical problems, particularly that of obtaining 'informed consent'.

Based on these findings, we suggest that the violence and abuse perpetrated against women in intimate relationships might profitably be conceptualised as a 'constellation of abuse' that includes both physical acts of violence and other forms of intimidation and controlling behaviour. This 'constellation of abuse' must be addressed in order to effect a meaningful reduction in acts of physical violence, particularly if changes are to be sustained beyond a short period of time. Findings from the Violent Men Study presented elsewhere (Dobash et al., 2000) suggest that abuser programmes that address the beliefs that support and justify this violence are more likely to be effective than those that address more general issues such as 'anger control' or focus solely on physical violence.

The results also indicate that the justice system provides a crucial and indispensable element of an overall response to abusers in terms of surveillance, condemnation of violence, control of violent behaviour and costs for its continued use (see also Dutton, 1995; Ford, 1991a, 1991b; Fagan, 1992). In this respect, arrest and prosecution appear to be necessary components of an effective intervention but, on their own, are not sufficient to effect change that can be sustained over a period of time once short-term surveillance and potential costs to the offender have passed. The findings of this study lend support to the contention that more rather than less intervention may be required in cases of domestic violence (Berk et. al., 1992a).

While contained within the nexus of criminal justice control, court mandated abuser programmes provide elements additional to the necessary components of surveillance, control and cost contained within arrest and prosecution. These relate specifically to the offence itself and to its elimination. By providing the opportunity for the offender to make positive changes in beliefs about 'wives', women, domestic authority and the use of violence, and in their behaviours with respect to the use of violence and intimidation, abuser programmes provide additional and vital components that extend the efficacy of intervention beyond short term effects. This would appear to provide a foundation for change that is sustainable beyond that which can be achieved within the period immediately following arrest. The combination of arrest, prosecution and an abuser programme focused on the specific offence and the offending behaviour appear to provide an intervention that is more effective than other responses without such a targeted focus.

References

Adams, D. (1988). Treatment models for men who batter: A profeminist analysis. In K. Yllo and M. Bogard (Eds). *Feminist Perspectives on Wife Abuse*. Beverly Hills, CA: Sage.

Andrews, D., Zinger, I., Hoge, R. D., Bonta, J., Gendreau, P. and Cullen, F. T. (1990). Does correctional treatment work? A clinically relevant and psychologically informed meta-analysis. *Criminology*, 28, 369-404.

Australian Bureau of Statistics (1996). Women's safety survey, Australia, 1996. Canberra: Commonwealth of Australia.

Baumgartner, M. P. (1993). Violent networks: The origins and management of domestic conflict. In R. B. Felson and J. T. Tedeschi (Eds.) *Aggression and Violence: Social Interactionist Perspectives*. Washington, DC: American Psychological Association.

Berk, R. A., Smyth G. K. and Sherman, L. W. (1988). When random assignment fails: Some lessons from the Minneapolis spouse abuse experiment. *Journal of Quantitative Criminology*, 4, 209-23.

Berk, R. A., Campbell, A., Klap, R. and Western, B. (1992a). The deterrent effect of arrest in incidents of domestic violence: A Bayesian analysis of four field experiments. *American Sociolocial Review*, 57, October, 698-708.

Berk, R. A., Campbell, A., Klap, R. and Western, B. (1992b). A Bayesian analysis of the Colorado Springs spouse abuse experiment. *The Journal of Law and Criminology*, 83, 1, 170-200.

Bersani, C., Chen, H. J. and Denton, R. (1988). Spouse abusers and court-mandated treatment. *Crime and Justice*, 11, 43-59.

Braithwaite, J. and Daly, K. (1994). Masculinities, violence and communitarian control. In T. Newburn and E. A. Stanko (Eds.). *Just Boys Doing Business? Men, Masculinities and Crime*. London: Routledge.

Burns, N., Meredith, C. and Paquette, C. (1991). *Treatment programmes for men who batter: A Review of the evidence of their success*. Abt Associates of Canada, Ontario.

Campbell, J. C. (1992). Wife-battering: Cultural contexts versus western social sciences. In D. A. Counts, J. K. Brown and J. C. Campbell (Eds.) *Sanctions and Sanctuary: Cultural Perspectives on the Beating of Wives*. Oxford: Westview Press.

Campbell, J. C. (1999). Forced Sex and Intimate Partner Violence. *Violence Against Women*, vol. 5, 1017-1035.

Campbell, D. T. and Stanley, J. C. (1963). *Experimental and quasi-experimental designs for research*. Chicago: Rand McNally.

Carmines, E. G. and Zeller, R. A. (1979). *Reliability and Validity Assessment*. Beverly Hills, CA: Sage.

Chen, H.T., Bersani, C., Myers, S. C. and Denton, R. (1989). Evaluating the effectiveness of a court-sponsored abuser treatment programme. *Journal of Family Violence*, 4, 309-322.

Counts, D. A., Brown, J. K. and Campbell, J. C. (1992). *Sanctions and Sanctuary: Cultural Perspectives on the Beating of Wives.* San Francisco: Westview Press.

Daly, M. and Wilson, M. (1988). *Homicide.* New York, Aldine De Gruyter.

Descola, P. (1996). *The spears of twilight: Life and death in the Amazon jungle.* Translated from the French by J. Lloyd, Glasgow: Harper-Collins.

Dobash, R. E. and R. P. Dobash (1979). *Violence against wives.* New York: The Free Press.

Dobash, R. P. and Dobash, R. E. (1981). Community response to violence against wives: Charivari, abstract justice and patriarchy. *Social Problems,* 28, 563-81.

Dobash, R. P. and Dobash, R. E. (1983). The context specific approach. In D. Finklehor et al. (Eds.) *The Dark Side of Families.* Beverly Hills, CA: Sage.

Dobash, R. E. and R. P. Dobash, R. P. (1984). The nature and antecedents of violent events. *British Journal of Criminology,* 24, 269-88.

Dobash, R. E. and R. P. Dobash (1992). *Women, violence and social change.* London and New York: Routledge.

Dobash, R. E. and R. P. Dobash (1998). Violent men and violent contexts. In R. E. Dobash and R. P. Dobash (Eds.). *Rethinking Violence Against Women.* Thousand Oaks, CA: Sage.

Dobash, R. P. and Dobash, R. E. (2000a). Criminal justice programmes for men who assault their partners. In C. R. Hollin (Ed.) *Handbook of Offender Assessment and Treatment.* Chichester: John Wiley and Sons.

Dobash, R. P. and Dobash, R. E. (2000b). Evaluating criminal justice interventions for domestic violence. *Crime and Delinquency,* 46, 2, 252-270.

Dobash, R. P. and Dobash, R. E. (2004). Women's violence to men in intimate relationships: Working on a puzzle. *British Journal of Criminology,* 44,3: 324-349.

Dobash, R. P., Dobash, R. E., Cavanagh, K. and Lewis, R. (1998). Separate and intersecting realities: A comparison of men's and women's accounts of violence against women. *Violence Against Women,* 4, 382-414.

Dobash, R. P., Dobash, R. E., Cavanagh, K. and Lewis, R. (1999). A Research Evaluation of British Programmes for Violent Men. *Journal of Social Policy,* 28, 2, 205-233.

Dobash, R. E., Dobash, R. P., Cavanagh, K. and Lewis, R. (2000). *Changing Violent Men.* Thousand Oaks, CA: Sage.

Dunford, F. (2000). The San Diego experiment: An assessment of interventions for men who assault their wives. *Journal of Consulting and Clinical Psychology* 68, 3, 468-476.

Dutton, D. G. (1986). The outcome of court-mandated treatment for wife assault: A quasi-experimental evaluation. *Violence and Victims,* 1, 163-175.

Dutton, D. G. (1995). *The Domestic Assault of Women: Psychological and Criminal Justice Perspectives.* Vancouver: UBC Press.

Dutton, D. G. and Hemphill, K. (1992). Patterns of socially desirable responding among perpetrators and victims of wife assault. *Violence and Victims,* 7, 29-39.

Edleson, J. L. and Grusznski, R. J. (1988). Treating men who batter: Four years of outcome data from a domestic abuse project. *Journal of Social Service Research*, 12, 3-22.

Edleson, J. L., and Syers, M. (1991). The effects of group treatment for men who batter: An 18-month follow-up study. *Research in Social Work Practice*, 1, 227-243.

Eisikovits, Z. and Edleson, J. (1989). Intervening with men who batter: A critical review of the literature. *Social Science Review*, 37, 385-414.

Fagan, J. (1992). The social control of spouse assault. In F. Adler and W. Laufer (Eds.) *Advances in Criminological Theory*, Vol. 4, New Brunswick: Transaction.

Farrington, D. P. (1997). Evaluating a community crime prevention programme. *Evaluation*, 3, 157-173.

Ford, D. A. (1991a). The preventive impact of policies for prosecuting wife batterers. In E. Buzawa and C. Buzawa (Eds.) *Domestic Violence: The Changing Criminal Justice Response*. Westport, Conn.: Greenwood.

Ford, D. A. (1991b). Prosecution as a victim power resource: A note on empowering women in violent conjugal relationships. *Law and Society Review*, 25, 313-34.

Garner, J., J. Fagan and C. Maxwell (1995). Published findings from the spouse abuse replication project: A critical review. *Journal of Quantitative Criminology*, 11, 3-28.

Gendreau, P., F. T. Cullen and Bonta, J. (1994). Intensive rehabilitation supervision: The next generation in community corrections? *Federal Probation*, 58, 72-78.

Gondolf, E. W. (1988). The effects of batterer counselling on shelter outcome. *Journal of Interpersonal Violence*, 3, 275-289.

Gondolf, E. W. (1991). A victim-based assessment of court-mandated counseling for batterers. *Criminal Justice Review*, 16, 214-226.

Gondolf, E. W. (1997). Batterer programmes: What we know and need to know. *Journal of Interpersonal Violence*, 12, 63-74.

Gondolf, E. W. (1999). A comparison of four batterer intervention systems: Do court referral, programme length, and services matter? *Journal of Interpersonal Violence*, 14, 41-61.

Gondolf, E. W. (2001). Limitations of experimental evaluations of batterer programmes. *Trauma, Violence and Abuse*, 2, 1, 79-88.

Gondolf, E. W. (2002). *Batter Intervention Systems: Issues, Outcomes and Recommendations*. Beverly Hills, CA: Sage.

Gordon, L. (1988). *Heroes of Their Own Lives: The Politics and History of Family Violence. Boston 1880-1960*. New York: Viking.

Greenfield, L. (Ed.) (1998). Violence by Intimates. Analysis of Data on Crimes by Current or Former Spouses, Boyfriends and Girlfriends. Washington D.C.: U.S. Department of Justice.

Hart, B. (1993). Battered women and the criminal justice system. *American Behavioral Scientist*, 36, 624-638.

Hamm, M. S. and Kite, J. C. (1991). The role of offender rehabilitation in family violence policy: The batterers anonymous experiment. *Criminal Justice Review*, 16, 227-248.

Heckert, D. A. and Gondolf, E. W. (2000), Assessing Assault Self-Reports by Batterer Programme Participants and Their Partners. *Journal of Family Violence*, 15, 2: 181-196.

Heiskanen, M. and Piispa, M. (1998). Faith, hope, battering: A survey of men's violence against women in Finland. Helsinki: Statistics Finland.

Hoff, L. A. (1990). *Battered Women as Survivors*. London: Routledge.

Hosmer, D. W. and Lemeshow, S. (1989). *Applied Logistic Regression*. New York: John Wiley and Sons.

Johnson, H. (1996). *Dangerous domains: Violence against women in Canada*. Scarborough, Ontario: Nelson.

Johnson, H. and Sacco, V. F. (1995). Researching violence against women: Statistics Canada's national survey. *Canadian Journal of Criminology*, 37, 281-304.

Kelly, L. (1988). *Surviving Sexual Violence*. Cambridge: Polity.

Leibrich, J., Paulin, J. and Ransom, R. (1995). Hitting Home: Men Speak About Abuse of Women Partners. Wellington, NZ: Department of Justice and AGB McNair Associates.

Levinson, D. (1989). *Family Violence in Cross-cultural Perspectives*. Newbury Park, CA: Sage.

Lewis, R., Dobash, R. P., Dobash, R. E. and Cavanagh, K. (2000). Protection, prevention, rehabilitation or justice? Women's use of the law to challenge domestic violence. *International Review of Victimology*, 7, nos. 1, 2, 3, 179-205.

Marshall, W. L. (1999). Current status of North American assessment and treatment programmes for sexual offenders. *Journal of Interpersonal Violence*, 14, 221-239.

Masters, G. and Smith, D. (1998). Portia and persephone revisited: Thinking about feeling in criminal justice. *Theoretical Criminology*, 2, 1, 5-27.

McGuire, J. (Ed.) (1995). *What works: reducing reoffending – guidelines from research and practice*. Chichester, UK: Wiley.

Medina-Ariza, J. (2002). *Violencia Contra la Mujer en la Pareja*. Valencia: Tirant lo Blanch.

Medina-Ariza, J. and Barbaret, R. (2003). Intimate partner violence in Spain: Findings from a national survey. *Violence Against Women*, 9, 302-322.

Morran, D. M. and Wilson, M. (1994). Confronting domestic violence: an innovative criminal justice response in Scotland. In A. Duff, S. Marshall, R. E. Dobash, and R. P. Dobash (Eds.) *Penal Theory and Practice*. Fulbright Papers, Proceedings of Colloquia, Manchester: Manchester University Press.

Morran, D. and Wilson, M. (1997). *Men Who Are Violent to Women: A Groupwork Practice Manual*. Lyme Regis, Dorset: Russell House.

Mirrlees-Black, C. (1999). Domestic violence: Findings from a new British crime survey self-completion questionnaire. London: Home Office.

Pahl, J. (1985). *Private Violence and Public Policy*. London: Routledge.

Palmer, S., Brown, R. and Barrera, M. (1992). Group treatment programme for abusive husbands: Long-term evaluation. *American Journal of Orthopsychiatry*, 62, 276-83.

Pence, E. and Paymar, M. (1993). *Education Groups for Men Who Batter*. New York: Springer.

Pleck, E. (1987). *Domestic Tyranny*. Oxford: Oxford University Press.

Ptacek, J. (1988). Why do men batter their wives? In: K. Yllo and M. Bogard (Eds.) *Feminist Perspectives on Wife Abuse*. Beverly Hills: Sage.

Ribisl, K. M., M. A. Walton, C. T. Mowbray, D. A. Luke, W. S. Davidson and B. J. Bootsmiller (1996). Minimizing participant attrition in panel studies through the use of effective retention and tracking strategies: Review and recommendations. *Evaluation and Programme Planning*, 19, 1-25.

Saunders, D. G. (1996). Feminist-cognitive-behavioral and process-psychodynamic treatments for men who batter: Interaction of abuser traits and treatment models. *Violence and Victims*, 1, 393-413.

Saunders, D. G. and Hanusa, D. (1986). Cognitive-behavioral treatment for men who batter: The short-term effects of group therapy. *Journal of Family Violence*, 1, 357-372.

Sherman, L. W. (1992). *Policing Domestic Violence: Experiments and Dilemmas*. New York: Free Press.

Sherman, L. W. (1995). Domestic violence and defiance theory: Understanding why arrest can backfire. In D. Chappell and S. Egger (Eds.), *Australian Violence: Contemporary Perspectives II*. Canberra: Australian Institute of Criminology.

Sherman, L. W. and Berk, R. A. (1984). The specific deterrent effects of arrest for domestic assault. *American Sociological Review*, 49, 261-72.

Sherman, L. W. and Smith, D. A. (1992). Crime, punishment, and stake in conformity: Legal and informal control of domestic violence. *American Sociological Review*, 57, 680-90.

Sinclair, H. (1989). The MAWS Men's Programme and the Issue of Male-Role Violence Against Women. Training Manual. Marin, CA: Marin Abused Women Services.

Stark, E. (1993). Mandatory arrest of batterers. A reply to its critics. *American Behavioral Scientist*, 36, 651-680.

Stubb, J. (1997). Shame, defiance, and violence against women: A critical analysis of 'communitarian' conferencing. In S. Cook and J. Bessant (Eds.), *Women's Encounters With Violence: Australian Experiences*. Thousand Oaks, CA: Sage.

Taylor, B. G., Davis, R. C. and Maxwell, C. D. (2001). The effects of group batterer treatment programmes: A randomized experiment in Brooklyn. *Justice Quarterly*, 18, 171-201.

Tjaden, P. and Thoennes, N. (2000). Prevalence and consequences of male-to-female and female-to-male partner violence as measured by the National Violence Against Women Survey. *Violence Against Women*, 6, 142-161.

Tolman, R. M. and Bennett, L. W. (1990). A review of quantitative research on men who batter. *Journal of Interpersonal Violence*, 5, 87-118.

Wilson, M. and M. Daly (1998). Lethal and nonlethal violence against wives and the evolutionary psychology of male sexual proprietariness. In R. E. Dobash and R. P. Dobash (Eds.), *Rethinking Violence Against Women*. Thousand Oaks, CA: Sage.

Wilson, M. H. Johnson, H. and Daly, M. (1995). Lethal and non-lethal violence against wives. *Canadian Journal of Criminology*, 37, 331-362.

Chapter 11

Legislation on Family Violence and Stalking

Marijke Malsch and Wilma Smeenk

Introduction

Laws are traditionally expected to grant powers either to law enforcement officers (in criminal law) or to the parties (in civil law). These powers may be used to institute retributive measures against wrongdoing, to request some form of redress, to protect victims and the general public, or to prevent future misbehaviour. The type of law chosen (civil or criminal; a completely new law or a new version of an existing law) depends on certain cultural and institutional aspects within a country. One such aspect is the general role played by legislation and the administration of justice within a country: are most problems solved by citizens and private organisations, or does the administration of justice play an overriding part in conflict resolution within society? Do citizens generally call on the legislature to resolve problems? Is there a high number of judges per capita? What role is played by organised groups of advocates of new legislation? How repressive or tolerant is the legal culture in that country?

Most chapters included in this volume implicitly or explicitly refer to the broader societal and cultural framework, while discussing legislation on family violence. Rather than repeat this information here, we will restrict our analysis of the legislation to observable tendencies that are common in the laws and statutes of the countries discussed in this book. The question of what type of law should be chosen is particularly relevant when behaviours are criminalised for the first time. Are 'old' provisions in the law applicable, or should new ones be made? Is a civil law approach feasible, or should a criminal provision be created? Do new provisions in the law grant sufficient powers to police and prosecution?

This chapter addresses these questions by discussing both new developments in legislation related to family violence and new antistalking legislation, in the Netherlands and in other European countries. The primary reason for this comparison is that many European countries have recently drafted new stalking laws. Furthermore, the characteristics and backgrounds of both types of behaviour overlap greatly: research conducted by Tjaden and Thoennes (1998) has identified a significant link between intimate partner violence during a relationship and stalking after the relationship has ended. The backgrounds of these behaviours, the perpetrators and the victims are highly similar (see also: Malsch, 2004). Many batterers start to stalk their previous partner after their relationship has ended. In view of this strong connection between stalking (after a relationship has ended) and family violence (during a relationship), this chapter pays due attention to the legislative process related to both behaviours.

This chapter does not aim to catalogue all laws and regulations in force in these countries.[1] Instead, it formulates a number of focal points to direct the analysis. One focal point is the question whether countries have opted for the use of civil law, criminal law or a combination of both (see also: Kelly, this volume). Another focal point is the legislative evolution within some countries that has brought a new focus on process or, in other words, the criminalisation of a repetition of acts. Various countries have recently criminalised a pattern of actions instead of one single act. These developments are highlighted by examples from a number of countries.

The symbolic function of (new) legislation is also explored. This symbolic function may be contrasted with the function of providing an adequate tool to combat family violence. Symbolic function and adequate tool are not mutually exclusive, however, as will be demonstrated in a later section. Attention is also paid to immediate interventions that may be instituted in cases of family violence and stalking. The analysis provided in this chapter is based on preceding chapters in this book, additional information provided by the authors, the Council of Europe report,[2] and the literature on the function of legislation in combating certain types of behaviour.

---

1   Such a catalogue has been developed by the Council of Europe, in its report *Legislation in the Member States of the Council of Europe in the field of violence against women*, Strasbourg, 2002. Throughout this chapter, we have gratefully made use of the data provided in this report.
2   See previous footnote.

Criminal Law, Civil Law, or Both?

In many countries, family violence can be prosecuted on the basis of 'general' provisions applicable to all situations of violence against persons. Historically, criminal proceedings are not often instituted in cases of violence within a family. Family members are expected to solve their 'problems' themselves. So the state, the government and the criminal justice system need not get involved. Many chapters in this volume have highlighted past or current discussions about the roles that the law and law enforcement officers play, or should play, when confronted with a violent incident within a household.

The chapters in this book have shown that this aloof attitude is currently changing in many countries. Women's organisations, other groups within society, and surveys conducted have all highlighted the need for a more active legal system. According to Lünnemann et al. (2002, 145), a paradigm shift has taken place in various European countries. Violence within the family is no longer considered to be a private problem of no relevance to government. It is a social problem involving public interest (see also Seith, this volume; Römkens, 2001). Many countries have drafted new laws, or made their old laws more punitive towards the (alleged) perpetrators of violence within the family (Kelly, this volume). More behaviours in the domain of family violence have been criminalised, and new powers to combat violence have been created. In general, the expectations entertained of criminal law seem to have increased substantially over the years.[3] Some countries, including Belgium, Cyprus, France, Spain, Sweden and Switzerland, have either created specific 'domestic violence' offences, or changed the status of an assault in the home by making it a state offence (Kelly, this volume; Council of Europe, 2002). Some laws have specified that assaults committed in the home are more serious than assaults between strangers (Kelly, this volume). A number of countries have changed their laws on protection and/or restriction orders (Ireland, England, Wales, Sweden; Kelly, this volume). Eviction orders have been introduced in Austria and Germany. Italy,

---

3   This is not only the case in the domain of family violence, but also in other domains, such as crime committed by organisations or by groups of people. Several new provisions criminalising these behaviours have been drafted. In other domains, such as in the field of drug crimes, some decriminalisation seems to have taken place. So in various countries, the prosecution does not institute criminal proceedings if only minor quantities of drugs are involved.

Germany, Switzerland, Luxembourg and Sweden recently drafted similar laws to enable eviction orders. Hungary, the Czech Republic and the Netherlands plan to do the same. Some countries have explicitly linked criminal and civil law, by making the breach of a protection order an offence. Germany is one of these countries (Pelikan, 2004).

In light of these new legislative activities, the criminal justice system, and especially the police, must now meet stricter requirements than before regarding their handling of family violence cases. Many countries, the Netherlands included, have designed guidelines for how the police and prosecutors should deal with notifications of family violence. In principle, Dutch police officers who learn of such an incident must draw up an official report, and send it to the prosecution. The prosecution must then institute criminal proceedings in the case of a provable act. Only a few exceptions to these general rules are permitted. If the victim does not want to report such a crime officially, the police officer must draw up a report *ex officio*. Possibilities for diverting cases to social services exist, but the general emphasis is on a criminal law approach. It appears, however, that legal practice does not always comply with these strict regulations (Malsch and Smeenk, 2004).

When different countries drafted these new laws and regulations, their legislatures had to choose between a civil law approach and a criminal law approach. In civil law, it is the victim who initiates a lawuit. He or she has to submit a claim to court and present a certain amount of evidence of the partner's wrongful behaviour. The victim risks having to pay the costs of a trial if he or she loses, and has to collect the awarded claim herself if the case is 'won'. There is also a risk of secondary victimisation if the victim loses; on top of the losses, he or she may suffer from thwarted expectations (Malsch and Carrière, 1999).

If a criminal law approach is chosen, the police, the prosecution and the judge collect the evidence and decide about (proceeding with) a case. The imposition and execution of a penalty, and the collection of any damage compensation to the victim are also counted among the criminal justice system's tasks in most jurisdictions. The burden of undertaking these difficult tasks is removed from the victim. Victims generally have to testify, either before the trial or actually at the trial. This may cause secondary victimisation to vulnerable witnesses, among whom victims of family violence (Malsch, 2004). Appearing in court and being confronted with the defendant may cause the victim significant distress.

A criminal law approach would be possible if a breach of the legal order had taken place. In the past, most people did not consider cases of family violence to breach the legal order. Nowadays, such a breach is sooner judged to have taken place. The growing use of a criminal law approach in cases of family violence and related behaviours could indicate that this type of crime is now less often considered to belong to the 'private domain' (Römkens, 2001).

Some countries adhere to a predominantly criminal approach when combating family violence, whereas others rely mostly on civil law. According to Lünnemann, Belgium, France, Portugal, Spain and Italy are among the first group (Lünnemann et al., 2002, p. 13), being countries that share roots in Roman law. The legislation in these countries often allows more severe sanctions to be imposed when violence is committed within a family context (Italy, Portugal, France). Belgian law also grants wider law enforcement powers, specifically created for investigating and prosecuting family violence. Other countries, such as Austria, Germany, Ireland and the UK, have a stronger emphasis on civil law (Lünnemann et al., 2002). Still other countries occupy a position in-between.

Antistalking Legislation

The challenging question of whether to opt for civil law or for criminal law was triggered by a perceived need for antistalking legislation. Before new antistalking laws came into force, most countries enabled, and still enable, a – civil – protection or restraining order to be obtained in stalking cases. In cases of very serious stalking, which were also covered by criminal law provisions such as 'threat', 'assault', 'unlawful entry' or even 'attempted homicide', suspects could be convicted and punished for these crimes. They could be taken into preventive custody, and released from this custody under certain conditions. One such condition may bar the suspect from approaching the victim's home, or other places where he or she might stay. In the Netherlands, these conditions are designated as so-called 'criminal' restraining orders, because an investigative judge imposes them. These options are widely used, both in the Netherlands and in some other countries (Pelikan, 2004; Council of Europe, 2002). Notwithstanding these options, a predominant emphasis on a civil law resolution existed before stalking became a crime in many countries. After the United States (California) had taken the lead in drafting the first antistalking law, many

European countries followed. The direct incentives for these new laws were the killings and assaults of a number of public figures in the US, some of which were preceded by a lengthy period of stalking, in combination with wide media coverage and pressure from certain groups and individuals to create a new law.

Some countries, such as Australia, have introduced laws that describe in detail those behaviours defined as 'stalking'. High penalties (maximum penalty of 10 years' imprisonment) are associated with an infringement. Other countries, like the Netherlands and Belgium, have designed brief and qualitative provisions. The Netherlands has included less severe penalties (maximum penalty of three years' imprisonment). The Dutch legal definition of stalking, which can be characterised as highly qualitative, is phrased as follows:

> He, who unlawfully, repeatedly, wilfully intrudes upon a person's privacy with the intent to force that person to do something, to refrain from doing something or to instigate fear in that person will be punished as guilty of belaging (stalking) to a prison term with a maximum of three years or a fine of the fourth category.

In many countries, discussions have taken place about the exact formulation of the stalking law. Problems comparable with the legal phrasing of family violence have emerged: what are the boundaries of the behaviours covered by the law; are exact descriptions of separate actions needed; do certain phrasings simplify evidence collection or, on the contrary, complicate fact-finding (Sohn, 1994)? Are description of motives, *mens rea* (criminal intent or negligence) and consequences necessary? Different countries have solved these problems in different ways (Pelikan, 2004; Malsch, 2004).

Not every country has made stalking a crime. The legislature of Germany has concluded that instituting a new provision in criminal law would not be desirable: the principle of 'lex certa' (*Bestimmtheit*) would be breached because it would be too difficult to describe exactly what stalking is. On top of that, it would be too difficult to prove the crime of stalking. For these reasons, Germany only included stalking in its *Gewaltschutzgesets* ('Law to protect against violence'), thereby enabling eviction orders in stalking cases, as well as other remedies that are included in this law. So stalking, although subject to certain measures, has not been made a crime in Germany, and the imposition of a criminal sanction is not possible. To date, Austria has no antistalking law either (Pelikan, 2004).

In conclusion, the legislation of many countries has gradually moved towards a relatively more important role for criminal law, in terms of both family violence and stalking. Civil law remedies have not been neglected or removed, however. Some countries have introduced new remedies of a civil law nature, or extended the domain of existing remedies. Moreover, 'soft law', in the form of guidelines for police and prosecution, has been drafted or amended to promote a stricter enforcement of the law. The development of such legal 'instruments' has been motivated both by a changed view on the seriousness of violence perpetrated within a household and by a mix of practical motives, combined with a need to make a symbolic gesture towards victims of this type of crime. These motives are examined in more detail later in this chapter.

Emphasis on Process

Criminal codes generally contain provisions that apply to one-off situations: one action has been criminalised, and if the action is performed more than once, each action can be prosecuted as a separate crime. This situation is gradually changing as a consequence of family violence and stalking being accepted as a criminal act. A number of countries have criminalised a course of conduct, with respect to both family violence and stalking (Pelikan, 2004). For example, a new provision in the Italian Criminal Code (Article 572), identified as *Maltreatment within the family*, specifies that the violence committed must include a set of violent acts (psychological as well as physical or sexual), committed repeatedly, over an extended period of time (Baldry, this volume). The Swedish law *Gross violation of a woman's integrity*, in force since 1998, criminalises a man's repeated acts of harassment or abuse against a woman with whom he is, or has been, in a close relationship (Lindström, this volume). Spain too has included a provision in its Criminal Code that makes a crime of customary violence perpetrated within certain relationships (Pelikan, 2004). Virtually all stalking statutes, except that of Belgium (Stevens, 1999; Pelikan, 2004), refer to the repeated nature of the behaviour designated as stalking. This method of making punishable a number of incidents, instead of only one well-described event, is relatively new in criminal law.[4]

Family violence may consist of different types of behaviours, such as slapping, hitting, threatening, etcetera. Stalking, by definition, exists of various types of behaviour that are committed out of an obsession for the victim and that are repeated over time (Malsch, 2004). Included in the plethora of the most frequently exhibited stalking behaviours are: harassment by telephone, sending of letters and mail, threatening the victim, and loitering near the victim's home and workplace. Some laws specify that various types of violence may contribute to the crime of family violence, including physical, psychological and sexual violence. Italian and Spanish laws make explicit reference to the different types of violence that may be included, while the laws of other countries implicitly include other types of violence by drafting a qualitatively formulated provision. Not all laws of the countries discussed in this chapter contain explicit references to psychological acts that have been made a crime or that may contribute to either family violence or stalking.[5] It is clear, however, that actions that bring about psychological damage to the victim are a common characteristic of the types of crimes described here.

The criminalisation of a pattern of actions is in accordance with the nature of both family violence and stalking. Both crimes are generally committed within relationships or after a relationship has ended, and the background to these behaviours is heavily influenced by characteristics of the relationship.[6] In line with the crimes being embedded in relationships, both family violence and stalking are characterised by repetition.[7] Although not every incident might be severe, the combined behaviours may constitute a serious crime (see Lindström, this volume). The legislatures of various countries have acknowledged this aspect of family violence and stalking in the provisions that they have newly introduced into laws.

---

4 In Dutch law, fencing that is customarily conducted over a period of time is another example of a crime that consists of more than one action.
5 Some Latin American countries have explicitly criminalised psychological maltreatment. These countries are more innovative in this respect than many European countries. This may be due to the fact that, until recently, no legislation in this field existed (see Kelly, this volume). The difficulty of proving psychological damage may be a reason for not criminalising it.
6 Most stalking cases being processed through the criminal justice system involve stalking by ex-partners (Malsch, 2004).
7 This repetitiveness is probably related to the so-called 'cycle of violence' (Dutton and Golant, 1995). See also the final chapter of this volume.

Finding Evidence of a Pattern of Behaviours

Does the process character of these crimes lead to difficulties in proving them, or does it, on the contrary, make it easier to find evidence of family violence and stalking? Many chapters in this book have highlighted the difficulty of proving family violence, because it generally take place in the home. Some people believe that stalking victims would also be unwilling to report incidents, because reporting would lead to an invasion of their own privacy. When reporting an incident, victims are required to give the police certain, often private, information about their relationship with the stalker, and they may be reluctant to do this. Furthermore, a single witness statement is insufficient proof of the alleged crime (at least in the Netherlands). Thus, the gathering of sufficient evidence would be inhibited by the hidden nature of these crimes, making it difficult to reach a conviction, as many legal scholars and professionals expected before the antistalking law was introduced in the Netherlands.

A study of 77 stalking cases tried by District Courts in the Netherlands showed that, despite these expectations, many stalking cases were actually brought before the court and were found proven.[8] Apparently, no insurmountable thresholds existed when seeking evidence for stalking. In the analysis of the cases, it became clear that stalking behaviours materialised in so many forms that the police could easily collect pieces of evidence. Stalkers harass their victims by making phone calls that may be recorded. They send letters, which can be collected and presented to the police. They loiter near the home, as neighbours may witness. Some stalkers harass their victims at their workplace, where colleagues will witness the stalker's actions. Few acquittals have been encountered during the study of stalking cases, at least no more than for other types of crime. In conclusion, stalking appears fairly straightforward to prove, notwithstanding its 'private' character. The variety of behaviours may contribute to the finding of evidence of this crime.

Stalking, thus, leaves many easily observable traces. This is in contrast with family violence cases, where fewer directly visible traces are left. Furthermore, victims of stalking may be more willing to report to the police than victims of family violence; stalking might incite less shame in victims than if they were being abused by a batterer with whom they were still in a

---

8 Unfortunately, we do not know what proportion of *all* cases reported to the police are actually brought before court. The indications are that this proportion is small (Malsch et al., forthcoming).

relationship. A desire to continue the relationship with the perpetrator is less evident in cases of stalking than with family violence. An overview of research carried out by Jordan (2004) into intimate partner violence and the justice system suggests that stalking is reported more often to the police than other forms of violence against women.

Emphasis on Immediate Interventions

There is an increase in the number and scope of immediate interventions applicable in cases of family violence and stalking in many European countries. Newly introduced laws enable eviction orders to be issued. These orders are a clear example of an immediate intervention: in a substantial and still growing number of European countries, perpetrators of family violence may be ordered to leave the home for a certain period of time. In these countries, it is not a court that orders this type of intervention; the police are empowered to do so. The primary aim of such interventions is the immediate protection of the victim, but certain deterrent effects may be expected as well. Related measures, such as social or psychological assistance to the victim, the batterer, or both parties, may be instituted as well as the order.

Further examples of immediate interventions are arrest and preventive custody, which have recently been made possible in cases of stalking and/or (certain serious forms of) family violence in a number of countries (Council of Europe, 2002; Pelikan, 2004). This means that an intervention is possible at the first signs of violence or stalking, or shortly after, which would offer better protection to the victim. Release from preventive custody under certain conditions (the so-called 'criminal restraining orders') is a widely used intervention in many countries (Pelikan, 2004): the defendant is released from preventive custody under certain conditions, which may include an order not to come near the victim, her or his home or workplace. Psychological treatment or some other form of treatment may also be imposed as a condition for release. If such conditions are adequately met, either the prosecution may dismiss the case, or the court decision may be influenced. This procedure, too, is a method designed to bring about certain effects (among which protection, prevention or deterrence) in an early stage of the process.

Other measures that illustrate a focus on early intervention rather than a 'full' criminal proceeding cover the use of alarm systems by victims, such as AWARE (in, among other countries, Canada, the US, the UK, the Netherlands, Belgium), and the possibility of electronic tagging of the (alleged) offender (Pelikan, 2004). One advantage of these new options is the emphasis on the victim's immediate protection.

Immediate interventions are not always effective in deterring the perpetrator. An influential study by Sherman and Berk (1984) found that arrest was more effective at deterring domestic violence than separation of victim and assailant, and advice and mediation instituted by the police. Deterrence, both general and specific, became, after this study, the rationale behind the adoption of arrest as the predominant response to domestic violence (Stewart, 2001). Subsequent research has found that the impact of arrest in deterring future offending is not as clear-cut as the original findings indicated, however. Among unemployed and unmarried assailants, arrest even appeared to *increase* the rates of domestic assaults (Sherman et al., 1992). Fagan (1989) contends that criminal justice sanctions are more effective for first-time offenders but have little impact on persistent offenders.

Psychological research has identified a number of conditions necessary for punishment to be effective at changing behaviour (Stewart, 2001). The punishment must be delivered immediately after the behaviour, and every time the behaviour occurs. It must be sufficiently severe, and there must be no escape from the punishment. In comparison with a full criminal proceeding ending with a sanction imposed by a court, the direct interventions described above differ most in respect of the *speed* with which they are generally imposed. Arrest shortly after a crime has been discovered is imposed much more swiftly than a court's criminal sanction. Compared with sanctions imposed by a criminal court after a 'full' trial, arrest is generally less *severe*, however. The questions of whether the intervention occurs *every time* the behaviour takes place, and whether no *escape* is possible, can be answered in the negative for both immediate interventions and sanctions imposed by a court. Immediate interventions might, however, be applied more frequently than criminal sanctions by a court. So, from a deterrence point of view, immediate interventions have some advantages over full proceedings. However, their greatest contribution seems to lie in the domain of protecting the victim.

In introducing these immediate interventions, the character of criminal law is changing gradually from law that is primarily focused on imposing sanctions to an 'intervention type of law' and a 'protection type of law' (Groenhuijsen, 1998; uit Beijerse, 2000). With regard to the objectives of criminal law, the emphasis is shifting to protection, prevention and incapacitation instead of a primary focus on retribution. Some authors stress the positive side of such intervention possibilities. Severe and reproachful questioning of the accused by the police shortly after arrest, and possible preventive custody, may have a certain preventive effect on the accused (Groenhuijsen, 1998; uit Beijerse, 2000). These authors argue that early intervention options would therefore cause criminalisation to enhance the protection of victims.

So, new possibilities have been designed to provide immediate help. But, of course, they also have their disadvantages. Most important is the lack of certainty at such an early stage of the process as to whether the alleged perpetrator is actually guilty of the crime. Suspects may be deprived of certain liberties on the basis of statements from a single 'witness', that is, the alleged 'victim'. The measures that can be taken are sometimes invasive, although at a later point in time the suspect might be found not guilty. If a victim uses an alarm system, this invasion of the suspect's liberties is far less serious than if the suspect is arrested or issued with an eviction order. A related disadvantage is the cost of the measures, which may later be found to have been unnecessarily imposed if the suspect is not guilty.

Symbolic Function of the Law

When drafting new rules, legislators may have other motives than to design an instrument for combating certain behaviours. In the legislative process that led to the Dutch stalking law, it was contended that the proposed law was a case of *symbolic legislation* (Royakkers and van Klink, 2000). The primary aim of a symbolic law is not, or not exclusively, to develop an adequate instrument for combating certain behaviours, but to satisfy other needs. Among these other goals are: a compromise between two opposing political parties; a political party's desire to own a certain issue within the political domain, or the government's wish to appear powerful to the outside world (van Klink, 1998). Still other objectives might be: compromise between different opinions in society, satisfying certain groups in society, but also the legislator's wish to raise his or her own profile (van Klink, 1998). In all these situations, the law is not primarily focused on its contended aim, such as, for example, the sanctioning of certain behaviours; it is aimed at something else. When such other aims dominate, the law may be called 'symbolic'.

The new Dutch antistalking law does indeed present certain characteristics that point in the direction of symbolic legislation (Malsch, 2004). Certain groups, organisations and individuals in society had made explicit their wish for new legislation against stalking. Their voices were probably strong enough to convince legislators of the need for a new law. Satisfying these groups, therefore, can be considered as a driving motive for the legislature.

Furthermore, arguments for the new law were rather unclear and unsystematic, suggesting a symbolic background or motive. For example, at the time when the government decided to accept the new law, there remained a lack of clarity on what stalking exactly is, how often it takes place, by whom it is perpetrated and who the victims are. Moreover, the description of stalking behaviour in the law was not considered to be precisely defined, which also suggests ambiguity about the concept and the development of the draft (Malsch, 2004).

Symbolic law may be functional, in creating the illusion of a solution to certain problems in society. However, many conflicts or problems are so complex that no easy solution exists, and stalking might be one of these. Drafting a new law in such a situation would suggest that the problem is being addressed, although at the same time a quick and easy solution is not possible (van Klink, 1998). Many legal scholars and professionals therefore expected the law to be ineffective. The continuation of the legislative process, in spite of expectations of the law's ineffectiveness, may point to a symbolic function as well. As stated above, there was a general expectation that the law would not be applied in practice, because of difficulties in obtaining evidence of stalking.

Nevertheless, Dutch stalking cases are being processed through the criminal justice system on an unexpectedly large scale, and sufficient evidence is generally found to support a conviction in these cases (Malsch, 2004). Data on the trial of stalking cases in other countries suggest similar results concerning the use of the antistalking law (Pelikan, 2004). These findings shed a slightly different light on the law's contended symbolic character. Although a symbolic character cannot be totally equated with ineffectiveness, there is some overlap between the two aspects; a law that appears to be 'ineffective' in practice because it is not applied, runs the risk of being denounced as 'symbolic'. Motives for creating a new law that seem to suggest a symbolic law do not preclude effectiveness, however. It might even be expected that the law's new potential for combating stalking will, to a certain extent, create a demand for criminal proceedings among victims of stalking. Some victims, who reported stalking to the police after the antistalking law came into force, would not have contacted the criminal justice system without the law. Such tendencies are extremely difficult to investigate, however.

It is too early to give a definite conclusion as to the effectiveness of the new antistalking laws. Effectiveness in the sense of large numbers of cases processed through the criminal justice system, is something other than effectiveness in the sense of stopping the behaviours. In view of the offenders' backgrounds, repeated offending and inclination to breach protection orders,[9] it might be expected that a large proportion of the offenders will lapse into recidivism after having served their penalty. The longer these laws are in effect, the more we will learn about compliance with them in this broader sense. So, in the end, new legislation, in spite of its effectiveness in increasing the number of cases that come to the attention of the court, may fail to stop certain behaviours.

Not only laws can be symbolic; other types of regulations can be too. Dutch guidelines for the police and the prosecution, regulating how to treat cases of family violence, stipulate that the police must make up an official report in such cases. Only a small number of exceptions to this general rule are allowed. Police practice has shown, however, that police officers often refrain from making up an official report and sending it to the prosecution, especially in cases where the victim only wants to notify the police and does not wish to make a 'legal case' (Malsch and Smeenk, 2004). So, although such guidelines contend that they aim to promote a strict prosecution of such cases, actual practice demonstrates that law enforcement officers often do not comply with these rules. If non-compliance continues, such guidelines may eventually be labelled as 'symbolic'. To the outside world, they act as if focused on reducing a certain type of crime, but in legal practice they appear largely ineffective: law enforcement officials themselves fail to comply with the rules.

---

9   See various chapters in this book.

Conclusions

The analysis presented in this chapter has shown increasing legislative activity in European countries with regard to family violence and stalking. These activities predominantly feature in the criminal domain. Behaviours have been newly criminalised, aggravating conditions have been introduced in existing laws, new powers have been created, and new guidelines are inciting law enforcement officers to a stricter enforcement of the applicable law.

Some countries have introduced restraining orders in their civil law, or changed the regulation of these orders. The use of eviction orders has spread through a substantial number of European countries, giving expression to the principle that if a person batters another member of a household, the batterer should leave the house and not the victim. Some countries have explicitly linked criminal and civil law by treating the breach of a restraining order as a crime; other countries have refrained from doing so. The latter countries often allow for an accused person to be released from preventive custody under certain conditions, among which a so-called 'criminal restraining order', to which the suspect himself agrees. This is an example of a 'civil' element (an agreement) being introduced into criminal law.

A fairly new element in the legislations of various European countries is the introduction of a pattern of behaviours or incidents as a crime. These behaviours or incidents need not be extremely serious when regarded in isolation. Stalking is an obvious example of such a pattern of behaviours, but family violence also generally consists of a variety of actions. This new method of legislation reflects the characteristics of these two types of crimes, which share certain features and have similar backgrounds, motives and consequences for the victims. There remain certain risks, however, which led Germany to refrain from making stalking a crime. One risk is that the behaviours being criminalised are not clearly defined. The principle of 'lex certa' may be infringed if unclear criminal law provisions are designed. Other intervention possibilities, mostly of a civil law nature, do exist in German law, however, and they can be applied to combat both stalking and family violence.

This chapter has paid due attention to the transformation of criminal law into 'intervention' or 'protection law' (Groenhuijsen, 1989), evident in the relatively invasive interventions that can be instituted soon after a behaviour has been reported. Eviction orders, for example, can be imposed at a fairly early stage of the criminal process, and accused persons will experience these as highly invasive. Arrest and preventive custody are now possible in a number of countries where they were not possible before, and a number of countries offer alarm systems to victims of family violence and/or stalking.

Many elements of antistalking laws that can be applied immediately after the behaviour has been observed may be very effective *without* a formal criminal proceeding actually having to be instituted. Such immediate interventions protect the victim and may even have certain preventive effects on the suspected batterer or stalker, in which case criminal proceedings might no longer be needed. It is likely that no trial will take place in many of such cases, even when the suspect has been arrested and interrogated by the police.

Unfortunately, little is known as yet about the effects of new and old laws, or the impact of immediate interventions in cases of family violence and stalking. Where effects are known, they indicate that severe sanctions against batterers are less effective (Hanson and Wallace-Capretta, 2004). Neither arrests – as discussed above – nor restraining orders lead to the anticipated effects (Buzawa and Buzawa, 1996; Malsch et al., 2002). Treatment of batterers seems to have more positive effects (Dobash and Dobash, this volume; Hanson and Wallace-Capretta, 2004). Criminal law may serve as a condition for this treatment, presumed to make the accused more prepared to co-operate.

Research is needed to establish whether these new laws and guidelines have led to more prosecutions than in earlier times, and whether convicted persons refrain from battering or stalking their partners after having served their sanction or complied with their intervention. It would be wise to do so in a comparative setting, so that the effects of legislation could be compared between jurisdictions within Europe.

References

Buzawa, E. S., and Buzawa, C. G. (eds.) (1996). *Do arrests and restraining orders work?* Thousand Oaks: Sage.

Council of Europe (2002). *Legislation in the member States of the Council of Europe in the field of violence against women.* Strasbourg: Council of Europe.

Dobash, R. E., and Dobash, R. P. (2000). Evaluating criminal justice interventions for domestic violence. *Crime and Delinquency, 2*, 252-270.

Dobash, R. E., and Dobash, R. P. (2004). Women's violence to men in intimate relationships: working on a puzzle. *British Journal of Criminology, 3*, 324-349.

Dutton, D. G. and Golant, S. K. (1995). *The batterer: a psychological profile.* New York: Basic Books.

Fagan, J. (1989). Cessation of family violence: deterrence and dissuasion. In L. Ohlin and M. Tonry (eds.), *Family violence (Volume 11: Crime and justice: an annual review of research).* Chicago: University of Chicago Press.

Groenhuijsen, M. S. (1998), Stalking. Strafrecht als interventierecht [Stalking. Criminal law as intervention law]. *Delikt and Delinkwent, 6*, 521-526.

Hanson, R. K., and Wallace-Capreta, S. (2004). Predictors of criminal recidivism among male batterers. *Psychology, Crime and Law, 4*, 413-427.

Jordan, C. E. (2004). Intimate partner violence and the justice system. *Journal of Interpersonal Violence, 19*, 1412-1434.

Lünnemann, K. D., Tak, P. J. P. and Piechovki, J. G. (2002). *Interventie door uithuisplaatsing: de juridische mogelijkheden van uithuisplaatsing van plegers van huiselijk geweld in Oostenrijk en Duitsland* [Eviction as an intervention. The legal power to evict perpetrators of family violence in Austria and Germany]. Utrecht: Verwey-Jonker Instituut.

Malsch, M. (2004). *De Wet Belaging. Totstandkoming en toepassing* [The antistalking law. Design and enforcement]. Nijmegen: Ars Aequi Libri.

Malsch, M., and Carrière, R. (1999). Victims' wishes for compensation: the immaterial aspect. *Journal of Criminal Justice, 3*, 239-249.

Malsch, M. and Smeenk, W. (2004). Politie en relatiecriminaliteit: visies op straffen en hulpverlening [The police and domestic violence: views on punishment and assistance]. *Tijdschrift voor Veiligheid and Veiligheidszorg.*

Malsch, M. Visscher, S. M. and Blaauw, E. (2002). Stalking: de rol van de wet en van andere remedies [Stalking: the role of the law and other remedies]. In P. J. van Koppen, D. J. Hessing, H. Merckelbach and H. F. M. Crombag (Eds.), *Het recht van binnen: psychologie van het recht* (pp. 201-216). Deventer: Kluwer.

Malsch, M., Visscher, S. M. and Muijsken, J. (2004). Relatiecriminaliteit binnen politieregio Haaglanden. NSCR-rapport. Leiden: NSCR.

Pelikan, C. (2004). Ausmaß, Formen, Auwirkungen auf die Opfer un die gezetslichen Grundlagen; ein internationaler Vergeleich. Wien: Frauenförderung und Koordinierung von Frauenangelegenheiten.

Royakkers, L. M. M. and Van Klink, B. M. J. (2000). Drogredenen in het parlementaire debat. Het wetsvoorstel belaging als casus [Fallacies in the legislative process. The proposal for an antistalking law as an example]. *Nederlands Juristenblad, 7*, 315-357.

Römkens, R. (2001). Law as a Trojan horse: unintended consequences of rights-based interventions to support battered women. *Yale Journal of Law and Feminism, 13,* 265-290.

Sherman, L. W., and Berk, R. A. (1984). The specific deterrent effects of arrest for domestic assault. *American Sociological Review, 49,* 261-272.

Sherman, L. W., Schmidt, J. D., Rogan, D. P., Smith, D. A., Gartin, P. R., Cohn, E. G., Collins, D. J., and Bacich A. R. (1992). The variable effects of arrest on criminal careers: the Milwaukee Domestic Violence Experiment. *The Journal of Criminal Law and Criminology, 1,* 137-169.

Sohn, E. F. (1994). Antistalking statutes: do they actually protect victims? *Criminal Law Bulletin, 3,* pp. 203-241.

Stevens, L. (1999). Stalking strafbaar [Stalking as a crime]. *Rechtskundig Weekblad, 38,* 1377-1380.

Stewart, A. L. (2001). Can police prevent domestic violence? In D. P. Farrington, C. R. Hollin, and M. MacMurran (Eds.), *Sex and violence: the psychology of crime and risk assessment* (pp. 210-228). London: Routledge.

Tjaden, P. and Thoennes, N. (1998). *Stalking in America: findings from the National Violence against Women Survey.* National Institute of Justice Centers for Disease Control and Prevention, April.

uit Beijerse, J. (2000). De belager belaagd [Stalking the stalker]. *Nemesis, 3,* 67-69.

van Klink, B. (1998). *De wet als symbool: over wettelijke communicatie en de Wet gelijke behandeling van mannen en vrouwen bij de arbeid* [The law as a symbol: on legal communication and the Law on equal treatment of males and females in labour situations]. Deventer: Tjeenk Willink.

Chapter 12

Family Violence and Police Response: Learning from Research, Policy and Practice

Wilma Smeenk and Marijke Malsch

Introduction

The chapters in this volume have shown that interest in family violence has increased in recent decades, in the domain of research as well as that of policy and practice. The wider availability of survey findings, together with agenda setting by women's organisations and general awareness-raising campaigns, have made this problem more visible to both policy makers and the general public. Several chapters in this volume have outlined how efforts to reduce the problem effectively have intensified, and how the criminal justice system has come under increased pressure to respond appropriately to family violence incidents. The previous chapter focused on new legislation as a response to the special nature of family violence. Here, we evaluate findings and dilemmas related to the implementation of policies and laws, in the light of research findings on family violence reported in previous chapters and in the literature. This evaluation pays special attention to the police response to family violence.

Learning from Research

Research has revealed a gap between the representation of family violence in registered (police) data and the real amount of violence taking place, the so-called 'dark number'. Victims' underreporting of violent incidents to the police is well documented, while the debate still continues on how much violence victims actually do report in surveys and interviews, and therefore, what the exact size of the dark number is. While researchers agree that the dark number is large and exists around the globe, uncertainty exists as to its variability between countries, which factors influence the dark number and what relationship it has with the national context.

The chapter by Ollus and Nevala showed that family violence statistics vary by measurement instrument: asking about incidents of violence in dedicated (victim) surveys reveals higher figures than produced by general crime surveys. The explanation for this difference is that victims may hesitate to define what happened to them as a crime or to define themselves as a victim. Therefore, they are less likely to report incidents of violence in surveys that explicitly refer to such incidents as a crime, or when questions on family violence follow directly after questions on, for example, theft or burglary. For this reason, researchers need to develop instruments and questionnaires that measure family violence relatively independently of the legal definition of certain acts as crime. As an additional advantage, this would support the comparison of findings across national and legal contexts. Researchers' interest in developing such measures may, however, conflict with the interests of those providing funding for research. Criminal justice departments, for example, have an obvious interest in linking research outcomes directly to the national legal context. Another lesson from this chapter is that questions in questionnaires should refer to concrete behaviours as much as is possible, as respondents may interpret their experiences in different ways depending on their national or regional cultural background. This is a challenging task, especially where experiences of sexual violence are concerned.

When considering survey research, one should bear in mind that surveys may not reflect the full extent of violence, and may fail to address the experiences of certain groups of victims (see chapters Ollus/Nevala and Medina-Ariza/Fe-Rodriguez, this volume). Therefore, the use of other data (for example, police data and medical records), and different research designs (qualitative research and target groups) is needed to complete the picture, not only in terms of the range of violent behaviours but also in terms of the context in which violence occurs (Kelly, Römkens and Stanko, 2001).

As a result of varying definitions and survey instruments, research may lead to different findings, even within one country, on how widespread family violence is and who predominantly is affected. Such differences will not necessarily compromise research goals, as long as researchers communicate their differences and develop explanations for the differences. Discussion on the different research traditions in this field shows that such communication has not always taken place, however (Hagemann-White, 2001; Stanko, 2004; also see chapters Ollus/Nevala and Medina-Ariza/Fe-Rodriguez). Conflicting research outcomes are generally unwelcome for policy goals, on the other hand, since they inhibit clear decisions on how and where policy efforts should be directed to address the problem. But even without such policy considerations, research findings may be met with disbelief and controversy in the public domain, especially if they indicate a high prevalence of family violence.

In an attempt to provide clarity on this issue, authors Medina-Ariza and Fe-Rodriguez point out that surveys measure family violence while referring to a wide range of behaviours, including psychological violence and controlling behaviours. When the full range of these behaviours is included, prevalence of family violence is generally found to be high. Such surveys may therefore contrast with police or shelter reports of fewer, but relatively more serious cases of family violence. Using Spanish data, the chapter demonstrates that rates of partner violence should be interpreted with consideration for the frequency of violence and the co-occurrence of acts that may constitute a pattern of family violence, both physical and non-physical (see also Kelly, this volume; Dobash and Dobash, this volume).

From Incident to Pattern

An important message from the Medina-Ariza/Fe-Rodriguez chapter is that research is needed to understand whether and how isolated violent or intimidating behaviours develop into repeated or patterned forms of violence (Moore Parmley, 2004). Such research, preferably longitudinal in nature, would not only solve disputed issues in the academic world but would also better inform policy makers, so that the needs of victims of family violence may be better served. Theoretical concepts have been developed to interpret the supposedly longitudinal nature of this type of violence. To explain the relationship dynamics in partner violence, authors have used the concept of the 'cycle of violence'[1] to describe a situation of escalation and de-escalation recurring over time (Dutton and Golant, 1995; Walker, 1979). References to 'hostage-taking' can also be found, describing a process of adaptation and anticipation for the purpose of self-protection that children and adults go through in (extremely) unsafe situations of violence and abuse (Freud, 1942). While these more psychological notions focus on processes that keep people in violent situations, other explanations have focused on barriers that prevent them from leaving the violent situation. Such barriers arise from structural inequalities between men and women at a societal level, finding expression in dependencies within families and male-female relationships, as well as in societal attitudes discouraging third parties from interfering in family problems (Dobash and Dobash, 1994).

References to the cycle of violence are fairly common in the policy and legal domain. Few empirical studies, however, have investigated the 'cycle of violence' concept through a longitudinal design, mostly because of a lack of adequate data. Police data are limited in value because they are based on the registration of separate incidents, although police reports may contain references to earlier incidents or a risk of escalation, which are worth investigating in retrospect (Stanko, 2004). While potentially rich in context, such references depend strongly on accounts by individual police officers. Qualitative accounts by victims, offenders and professionals working with victims of violence have, however, contributed much to the concept being accepted as a heuristic device that helps explain the dynamics of partner violence.

Cultural Differences in Experiences of Family Violence

In a time of global migration, cultural differences exist not only between countries but increasingly also within a country. The chapter by Condon describes victim experiences of family violence by women from different cultural backgrounds, and at the same time alerts us to the complexities involved in trying to capture such experiences through surveys. The findings for France show that French migrant women report higher rates of violence than French native-born women. The former are also more exposed to social contexts fertile for family violence: bad neighbourhoods,

---

1　In criminology, the 'cycle of violence' concept has also been used to study the long-term consequences of childhood victimisation, and the transmission of violence between generations (Spatz Widom, 1995).

financial stress and insecurity, social isolation, and dependency. For second-generation immigrants (women born in France with parents of foreign extraction), elevated rates of violence are reported for younger women and women who have left their partners. Condon offers the explanation that younger women tolerate family violence to a lesser extent and are more likely to leave their violent partners, which is reflected in their increased tendency to report experiences of violence in the survey.

The relative scarcity of literature on migrant experiences of family violence shows how difficult it is to grasp cross-cultural differences in experiences of family violence, let alone develop an appropriate response to potentially culture-specific experiences. American research suggests that lower levels of trust in the legal system and fear of or experiences with stigmatisation may lead minority women to report to the police in even smaller numbers (Rasche, 1995). The debate is still ongoing as to whether and to what degree the same factors also affect survey outcomes. It is clear, however, that this subject warrants continued attention (Stanko, 2004).

Disclosure

Several authors have drawn attention to the fact that while at one point in time, victims may not be willing to report incidents of family violence to the police, they may be willing to do so in the future (Kelly, Chatzifotiou – this volume). As such, the dark number in family violence also has its own dynamic in time. As incidents keep recurring, victims may develop an awareness that the violence will not stop, but will only get worse, or will escalate in another way to include the children or other members of the family. At this point, they may call the police or report the violence. On the other hand, the chapter by Seith, while discussing pro-active policies, raises the point that matters may become worse with the passage of time: victims may lose their sense of autonomy and become less rather than more inclined to report incidents to the police. While professionals working in the field (including the police) know that both outcomes occur, little is known about when the dynamics of this process gear towards calls for (police) intervention and when isolation is the result. The chapter by Chatzifotiou on Greece, however, makes clear that societal attitudes that belittle family violence as a minor and private problem hamper the development of awareness in victims that they need and deserve help from outside.

We consider 'disclosure' to be a theoretical concept that is potentially fruitful in research into the dark number and its dynamics over time. Disclosure in family violence refers to victims revealing the violence to third parties. As a more general term, disclosure covers not only calling or reporting to the police asking for assistance, but also telling a friend about the violence, contacting a helpline or a shelter as a victim of family violence, or telling one's general practitioner the real reason for one's injuries. Important for research purposes is that disclosure may also refer to the reporting of violence in surveys, by filling in a questionnaire or by telling an interviewer about violent incidents. For example, Condon's notion of changes in the acceptance of violence among younger generations of French migrant women leading to higher reported rates of violence in surveys, also has bearing on the concept of disclosure.

By considering victims' reporting to the police within the more general concept of disclosure, researchers may, furthermore, draw upon insights from related fields. They can explore changes in the extent to which family violence remains hidden from the police, medical care providers, and support or intervention agencies (see chapter Seith – this volume). For example, research asking general practitioners about their experiences with family violence among patients shows results similar to those found in police research, when it comes to hesitance to intervene or invade privacy, professional task conception and professional competence to deal with this type of violence (Mol, 2002; Richardson et al., 2002; Rodriguez, Quiroga and Bauer, 1996).

Conclusion

The existence of a large 'dark number' is a prominent feature of family violence that has obvious relevance to the (criminal justice) response to family violence. Incidents do not come to the attention to the police, or fail to end up in police registrations. Another important feature is the repeated and patterned nature of family violence, drawing attention to the factors influencing the co-occurrence of violent behaviours and the escalation and de-escalation of violence over time. Finally, the dynamic character of the dark number draws attention to differences in disclosure by (groups of) victims, and to processes contributing to victims' disclosure or reporting of violence at a certain point in time.

Trends in the Criminal Justice Response to Family Violence

Various chapters in this volume have documented recent efforts by policy makers to combat family violence. These efforts are visible in policies and protocols that aim to promote the implementation of existing legislation, in new legislation, and in measures outside the criminal justice system. A number of trends can be discerned that reflect the law makers' and policy makers' intention to respond to the special nature of family violence. The Swedish law 'Gross violation of a woman's integrity', for example, allows consideration of a combination of incidents that have occurred within a certain time period. This new law signals recognition of the repeated nature of the violence and a departure from traditional 'incident-based' laws. Similarly, the new Italian law on maltreatment in the family aims to cover patterns of violence, including psychological violence, rather than separate incidents.

Several other chapters have documented the increased possibilities for restraining orders, eviction orders, immediate interventions and victim-protection systems, all of which serve to prevent violence from happening or escalating, and specifically refer to the increased likelihood of future violent acts by a known offender (see Kelly and Malsch and Smeenk, this volume).

Another development is that police organisations or individual police officers are informed and trained to better respond to reported incidents of family violence or early signs of potentially violent escalations. The Swedish chapter shows that the training of police officers will help them to implement new legislation and register incidents according to new provisions.

The notion of repetition is furthermore reflected in specialisation, in the form of designated police officers, prosecutors, or special domestic violence courts. Such specialisation aims to prevent the loss of information on earlier or related incidents and thereby enhance evidence building, as demonstrated by the Italian experience (Baldry, this volume). It furthermore protects victims from having to recount earlier incidents of violence when they come into the police station.

Information exchange is increasingly promoted between the police and extra-legal professionals and organisations that work with victims of family violence. Besides the police and women's organisations, information exchange is occurring between professionals in the medical field, schools, social workers, community organisations, and housing associations.

Privacy considerations may form a hindrance to such information exchange, however (Seith, this volume).

The growing recognition that family violence is 'not a crime like any other' (Kelly, this volume) is furthermore reflected in the development of abuser programmes that may be imposed instead of or in addition to the traditional prison sentences. The chapter by Dobash and Dobash in this volume has documented the increase in the development of these programmes. In an evaluation of one programme, they show that offenders' controlling behaviours, attitudes and beliefs are indeed associated with the (continuation of) violent behaviour, and may be reduced by completing such a programme.

Finally, awareness-raising campaigns among the general public have reflected a wider recognition that an attitude that condones family violence contributes to both the origination and continuation of family violence.

Policy Meets Practice: Lessons from Implementation

Laws and regulations in practice may work out differently than intended. In her review of recent legislative developments, Kelly signals how existing laws that might cover family violence were in practice applied less stringently when violence in the home was concerned, as compared to stranger violence. Seith argues that, after all the effort put into research and the formulation of policies, the implementation of these policies is now critical in the response to family violence. In the previous chapter, implementation considerations turned out to play their part in the preparation of new laws.

The various country chapters in this volume report on the implementation of existing as well as new laws and instruments to combat family violence. The chapter on Sweden shows that the implementation of its new law is only partly successful. The first results from evaluation research indicate that judges pass slightly longer prison sentences with reference to the new law. However, these court decisions concerned relatively serious offences that would have been tried under existing law as well. The intention of the Swedish legislator to treat less serious forms of violence more seriously when considered in the context of families and relationships is, in practice, not followed. The preventive effect of restraining orders seems to be limited as well. The Swedish police do not give information to all victims and the prosecution issues orders only when a violent incident has already taken place, or when previously convicted offenders are involved. While more restraining orders are issued, women report that they do not feel any safer because little happens when orders are breached, and investigations are ended because evidence is lacking.

In the same vein, Baldry's chapter on the Italian experience conveys the twin message of both increased efforts to deal with family violence through policy and legislation initiatives, and at the same time the existence of concrete obstacles at the level of the police and judiciary. While it is too early to draw conclusions on the implementation of the new Italian law on family violence, the author makes clear that evidence gathering poses a clear obstacle. The fact that violence takes place in the privacy of the home obstructs testimony by witnesses that would make a strong case in court. The author's observation that many Italians still consider family violence as a private rather than a public problem does not help matters and works against the prosecution of offenders.

The chapter on Greece illustrates how victims' appeal to the legal system regularly meets the response by police officers that victims should go back to a violent husband and 'sort things out'. While police officers showed more understanding and willingness to help, in recent interviews with the author, they are still reluctant to intervene because they feel inadequately equipped to address the problem.

These findings are in accordance with research indicating that the criminal justice system is more strongly geared towards 'public' violence, committed by strangers outside the home, than towards violence in the private sphere (for an overview, see Jordan, 2004). Existing criminal law is built upon 'cases' and incidents, which often denies the process nature of events that is typical of family violence incidents where offender and victims are so closely related (Malsch and Smeenk, this volume). Apparently, providing an adequate criminal justice response to family violence is a challenging task, even if measures are designed to meet the special nature of family violence. Below, we will examine in more detail the role of police task performance, and thereby pay attention to the discretional powers of the police.

The Role of the Police

The police represent the first point of entry into the criminal justice system when victims of violence call for help or report an incident. The fact that so few victims of family violence report the violence to the police, and the negative experiences of those who do, have drawn attention to the role of the police as 'gatekeeper' to the legal system (Seith, this volume).[2] Such a role is possible because in most of the countries considered here, the police have considerable discretionary powers that may discourage a strict prosecution of family violence incidents. Police discretion is most clearly evident in the decision to make a formal report, the decision to call in suspects and witnesses for questioning, and ultimately in the decision to send the case to the prosecution.

Among the motives for victims failing to report violent incidents are negative expectations of what the police can do and negative experiences with the police in the past. Victims who turn to the police to report a violent incident find that the police either fail to act at all, or that they, on the other hand, provide a strictly criminal justice response that does not meet their needs (see chapters by Seith, Chatzifotiou, Baldry, Lindström). However, some authors criticise the police for taking on the role of mediator between conflicting parties (see Seith, Baldry, this volume).

From the perspective of the police, problems arise when victims of family violence first report an incident but later want to withdraw their formal report, even if, legally, this is not possible. Also, victims may no longer cooperate in the prosecution of the incident (see Lindström, this volume). Dutch police officers report uncertainty about victim cooperation as a reason for them hesitating to invest a great deal of time in making a formal report that runs the risk of being withdrawn in a later phase. Lack of victim cooperation is taken as a sign that victims do not know what they want or are at least ambiguous about the prosecution of the offender (Flight and Terstappen, 2001). It is increasingly recognised, by the police too, that victims might withdraw a formal report or stop cooperating in the investigation because they fear retaliation or escalation, or are otherwise concerned about their own well-being and safety and that of their children. In this respect, police training on the background and dynamics of family violence has increased police officers' sensitivity to the dependencies involved.

Interestingly, the police themselves also show ambiguity towards a strictly criminal justice response to family violence. In the Netherlands, police officers consider their role in the response to family violence primarily to be one of assistance rather than repression (Malsch and

---

2   Countries may differ in terms of the task division between police and the prosecution, and who may start the prosecution of a case.

Smeenk, 2004). The police may be reluctant to respond repressively because they fear for the safety of the victim(s): they know that considerable time will pass before an offender will appear before the court, and an escalation may take place in the meantime. Also, they doubt whether a prison sentence will affect the offender's beliefs and attitudes regarding their use of violence towards their partners (Flight and Terstappen, 2001; Malsch and Smeenk, 2004; see also Dobash and Dobash, this volume). For police work generally, research has distinguished a service-oriented style among police officers, advocating the use of discretion to help solve social problems (as distinguished from a legalistic style, opposing discretion because it interferes with the duty to enforce the law equitably, Wortley, 2003).

Notwithstanding an inclination towards a non-legal approach, the police as an organisation are embedded in the criminal justice system. A prominent role for evidence and procedures for evidence gathering are associated with this. The average police report shows that police officers hold this criminal justice model in their heads and act in accordance with it when they register and handle incidents. As family violence typically takes place behind closed doors, evidence gathering is more difficult and this obviously reduces the likelihood of prosecution. Moreover, in their work the police are strongly dependent on the other parties in the criminal justice system. They find themselves confronted with professionals like prosecutors, judges and lawyers whose primary task is to follow the criminal justice model. If before, the outside world considered the police to be hesitant in acknowledging family violence as a problem they should deal with, now the prosecution and judiciary meet similar criticism (Gilchrist and Blissett, 2002). While the police in the Netherlands and abroad have in recent years spent much effort on training and information exchange (Flight and Terstappen, 2001; Metropolitan Police London, 2001), this cannot be said of prosecutors and judges. So, even if the police are willing to take a case to the prosecution, they may be reluctant to do so because they do not expect that evidence will support the allegations in later phases.

In a similar vein, the fact that the police organisation is embedded in the criminal justice system poses a disincentive to respond to recent calls for pro-active intervention. The emphasis on future behaviours in pro-active measures conflicts with a criminal justice response that traditionally leans heavily on past behaviours, with a prominent role for evidence of the facts that have taken place.

The negative experiences of victims have led some to argue that the criminal justice system is by definition unfit to address victims' needs (Ferraro and Pope, 1993; Römkens, 2001). In this volume, Kelly disagrees, arguing that expected or experienced lack of cooperation by victims at an earlier point in time is not a justification for the police to deny victims a strictly criminal justice response when they need it.

The message that comes across from victim experiences is that the match between victims' needs and the police response is crucial for victims' trust in the legal system and thereby directly related to the dark number in family violence. This match depends strongly on victims' awareness regarding their right to be protected from violence, and this awareness may change over time. The notion of the development of victim awareness suggests that police officers should be able to adjust their response to the (developing) need of the victim. Individual police officers seem increasingly willing to do this but it is questionable whether the police organisation and the criminal justice system can provide police officers with such flexibility. A strictly criminal justice response, or pro-active intervention before the violence escalates, remains problematic given the structure of the criminal justice system.

Conclusion

Characteristic of family violence is that it takes place in private homes and that incidents recur over an extended period of time. The longitudinal nature of family violence has important implications for legal interventions, which are traditionally geared towards one-off incidents of violence that take place in public. This chapter discussed how the intention of reacting to the patterned nature of family violence and preventing future violent episodes is at odds with the traditional criminal justice response, and that intention and actual response conflict when implemented. Also, it was argued that, for a number of reasons, this conflict is most visible at the level of the police organisation. Because this is where victims of family violence turn when they call for legal intervention, victims run the risk of their expectations being thwarted. If victim experiences result in loss of trust in the legal system, the dark number in family violence will remain high or even increase. As such, we integrated findings from earlier chapters regarding the way that characteristics of family violence interact with (implementation of) the policy response to this type of violence in a particular legal framework.

In this volume we set out to learn from experiences of the police response to family violence in other national and legal contexts. At this point, we express the hope that the experiences documented in this volume will inspire others to address comparative questions in future research undertakings (also see Gondolf 2004, special issues *Violence Against Women* 2001, 2004). For example, the development and implementation of the International Violence Against Women Survey offers an opportunity to examine whether and how the extent of police-reported violence varies between countries. Relationships with attitudes among the general public may be examined to further explore such differences.[3] To investigate police priorities at street level, a comparative scenario study may be applied. Also, differences in the use of police discretion may tie in with country-specific task divisions between police and prosecution in bringing cases to court. Disclosure of violence to third parties may be a further topic for comparative research, as countries may differ in the division of tasks between legal and non-legal organisations involved in the response to family violence (police, women's organisations, medical care, social work). Finally, the migration processes in present-day Europe call for a study of commonalities in family violence experiences within the context of migration.

All in all, there may be good reasons to be critical of a purely legal approach to the problem (also see Stanko 2003, p. 4). The call for an 'integrated' response, popular among researchers and policy makers alike, seems a logical next step. Such an approach promises a combination of responses that accords with victims' needs and allows parties involved to address a variety of problems associated with the violence or related problem behaviours, such as alcohol or drug abuse. However, integrated responses at the level of policy do not guarantee an integrated response at the level of practice. The chapter by Seith shows that victims of family violence may ask for assistance or legal intervention through a variety of 'entry points' but there is less coordination and information exchange among the agencies than considered desirable from a so-called multi-agency perspective. This chapter highlighted how police discretion is affected by structural and organisational factors and attitudes. In a multi-

---

3   Melich (1999) reports an EU-wide implemented opinion poll, asking the general public about their attitudes towards domestic violence.

agency setting, such factors are multiplied, as each organisation brings its own view, structure, and culture on what constitutes the problem, what causes it, and what is the best way to deal with it (Hester, 2004).

Training programmes should pay attention to such differences, for example by offering joint training programmes for the various professional groups involved (Kelly, this volume). Such programmes should pay attention to the differing motives and needs of victims of family violence when they call the police or make a formal report. The research reported in this volume shows that such motives and needs may change over time, and may require different combinations of legal support and assistance. Future research is needed, however, to assess the development of victims' needs over time so that an adequate response is possible. When trained to signal these needs adequately, the police may actually use their discretionary powers to provide flexibility in their response, and a combination of legal and assistance interventions that meets the needs of victims. In order to realise such 'informed implementation', good working relationships between the police and other professional groups are called for. Such 'informed implementation' has the potential to prevent continuation or escalation of the violence and is more likely to influence victims' trust in the legal system in a positive sense.

References

Dobash, R. E. and Dobash, R. P. (1994). *Women, violence and social change*. London: Routledge.

Dutton, D. G. and Golant, S. K. (1995). *The batterer: a psychological profile*. New York: Basic Books.

Ferraro, K. J. and Pope, L. (1993). Irreconcilable differences: Battered women, police, and the law. In N. Zoe Hilton (Ed.), *Legal responses to wife assault. Current trends and evaluation* (pp. 96-123). Newbury Park, CA: Sage.

Flight, S. and Terstappen, I. (2001). Leven Tussen Hoop en Vrees. Huiselijk geweld in Zuid-Holland-Zuid [Living between hope and fear. Domestic violence in police region South-Holland-South]. Alblasserwaard-Vijfheerenlanden: Intomart Beleidsonderzoek.

Freud, A. (1942). *The ego and the mechanisms of defense*. New York: International Universities Press.

Gilchrist, E. and Blissett, J. (2002). Magistrates' Attitudes to Domestic Violence and Sentencing Options. *The Howard Journal, 41*(4), 348-363.

Gondolf, E. The need for intervention studies. *Violence Against Women, 10,8*, 855-859.

Hagemann-White, C. (2001). European Research on the Prevalence of Violence Against Women. *Violence Against Women, 7* (Special issue: European perspectives on violence against women), 732-759.

Hester, M. (2004). Future trends and developments. Violence against women in Europe and East Asia. *Violence Against Women, 10*(12), 1431-1448.

Jordan, C. E. (2004). Intimate partner violence and the justice system. An examination of the interface. *Journal of Interpersonal Violence, 19*(12), 1412-1434.

Kelly, L. Römkens, R., and Stanko, B. (2001). Guest editors' introduction. *Violence Against Women, 7* (Special issue: European perspectives on violence against women), 727-731.

Malsch, M. and Smeenk, W. (2004). Politie en huiselijk geweld: visies op straf en hulpverlening [The police and domestic violence: views on punishment and assistance]. *Tijdschrift voor Veiligheid en veiligheidszorg, 3*, 18-31.

Melich, A. (1999). *Eurobarometer 51.0: The Elderly and Domestic Violence, March-May 1999*. Brussels, Belgium: INRA (Europe), 1999 [producer]. Ann Arbor, MI: ICPSR/Cologne, Germany: Zentralarchiv fur Empirische Sozialforschung, 2001 [distributor]. Codebook: PUB-053(51.0). ICPSRNO# 2864.

Metropolitan Police London. (2001). *Enough is enough. Domestic Violence Strategy*. [Available: http://www.met.police.uk/enoughisenough/strategy.htm.]

Mol, S. S. L. (2002). *Trauma, life events and PTSD. A challenge for patients and family doctors* (PhD Thesis). Maastricht, The Netherlands: Maastricht University.

Moore Parmley, A. M. (2004). Violence against Women Research post VAWA. Where have we been, where are we going? *Violence Against Women, 10*(12), 1417-1430.

Rasche, C. E. (1995). Minority women and domestic violence: the unique dilemmas of battered women of color. In B. R. Price and N. J. Sokoloff (Eds.), *The criminal justice system and women: Offenders, victims, and workers* (2 ed., pp. 246-261). New York: McGraw-Hill.

Richardson, J., Coid, J., Petruckevitch, A., Shan Chung, W., Moorey, S. and Feder, G. (2002). Identifying domestic violence: cross sectional study in primary care. *British Medical Journal, 324*, 1-6.

Rodriguez, M. A., Quiroga, S. S. and Bauer, H. M. (1996). Breaking the silence. Battered women's perspectives on medical care. *Archives of Family Medicine, 5*(3), 153-158.

Römkens, R. (2001). Law as a Trojan Horse: Unintended Consequences of Rights-based Interventions to Support Battered Women. *Yale Journal of Law and Feminism, 13*(2), 265-290.

Spatz Widom, C. (1995). The cycle of violence. In D. Chappel and S. J. Egger (Eds.), *Australian violence: contemporary perspectives II* (pp. 253-270). Canberra: Australian Institute of Criminology.

Stanko, B. (2004). A tribute to 10 years of knowledge. *Violence Against Women, 10*(12), 1395-1400.

Walker, L. E. (1979). *The battered woman*. New York: Harper and Row.

Wortley, R. K. (2003). Measuring police attitudes toward discretion. *Criminal Justice and Behavior, 30*(5), 538-558.

Index